also by bobby hall

Supermarket

THIS BRIGHT FUTURE

a memoir by

BOBBY HALL

SIMON & SCHUSTER PAPERBACKS
New York · London Toronto Sydney New Delhi

Simon & Schuster Paperbacks
An Imprint of Simon & Schuster, Inc.
1230 Avenue of the Americas
New York, NY 10020

First Simon & Schuster trade paperback edition September 2022

SIMON & SCHUSTER PAPERBACKS and colophon are registered
trademarks of Simon & Schuster, Inc.

For information about special discounts for bulk purchases,
please contact Simon & Schuster Special Sales at 1-866-506-1949
or business@simonandschuster.com.

The Simon & Schuster Speakers Bureau can bring authors to
your live event. For more information or to book an event,
contact the Simon & Schuster Speakers Bureau at 1-866-248-3049
or visit our website at www.simonspeakers.com.

Interior design by Lewelin Polanco

Manufactured in the United States of America

10 9 8 7 6 5 4 3 2 1

Library of Congress Cataloging-in-Publication Data is available.

ISBN 978-1-9821-5824-8
ISBN 978-1-9821-5825-5 (pbk)
ISBN 978-1-9821-5826-2 (ebook)

For Brittney and Little Bobby

CONTENTS

I saw a kid with no smile on his face today.

Where is my place in this bright future, I heard him say.

—*Manfred Mann's Earth Band,*
"Lies (Through The 80s)"

THIS
BRIGHT
FUTURE

PROLOGUE
THE GOOD MEMORIES

My first memory is of me looking out a window, waiting. It's one of those super-early memories, the ones that are so distant and far away that they're barely memories at all. More like a bunch of hazy, half-remembered images all jumbled up. But I can clearly recall standing at this window in a nice suburban townhouse. I'm three years old, maybe, living with a family, a black father and a white mother and a girl and two boys. The other kids are older than I am, almost teenagers. Sometimes the two boys pick me up and swing me around by my ankles, and the girl teaches me how to put on my socks.

"But which one's the right one and which one's the left one?" I ask.

"They don't have a right and a left," she says.

"But the shoes have a right and a left, so which sock goes where?"

"It doesn't work like that," she says. "They're socks."

The mom and dad are good parents. They make dinner every night. The house is nice and clean. They're strict, too. One night I want to watch *The Simpsons*, and the mother won't let me. She says it isn't a cartoon for kids, and I don't understand why there's a cartoon that isn't for kids.

But even though they're good parents, I know they're not my parents. The woman making me dinner and washing my clothes, she's not my mom, and I know she's not my mom because I want my mom. Which is less of a conscious thought and more like this primal feeling that's inside me all the time: *I want my mom.* Even though I have my own room with my own toys in it, I know I'm not supposed to be here. Which is why I'm at this window. I stand here every afternoon, looking out at the sidewalk that leads to the street, waiting for the woman who left me here to come back.

I don't know how long this goes on. It feels like months, a year, maybe. Then one day: She appears. This petite white woman with dark brown hair, walking up the driveway like an angel. My heart jumps. She comes inside and plays with me in the playroom, and she's cool. I've got this wooden block that's shaped like a cigar at the end, and I'm holding it up, going, "Look at me! I can smoke this cigar!" It makes her laugh, and making her laugh feels so good. We play for a while, and then the mother of the house comes in and says it's time. The angel who's come to see me gets up, says goodbye, and leaves. It's only a visit. She doesn't take me with her. Then the next day I'm back at the window, waiting and wanting her to come back again.

From there the record skips. Clearer memories start to form. They're still scattered fragments, but they begin to tell a story. In these memories, I'm living with my mom. She's not the woman who comes to visit anymore; she's actually my mom. I'm four now, and we're living in a little apartment in Germantown, a small town northwest of Washington, D.C., in Maryland.

When I reach back to the Germantown years, the first memories that come up are the good ones, the ones where my mom is supercreative and artistic and fun. She's this bundle of energy bursting with ideas and working on little projects. She paints murals all over our apartment. One of them is a beautiful trail of bubbles on the ceiling and on the walls. If you follow the bubbles from the front door to the master bedroom, you find a giant fish, like the Jesus fish but with all this intricate detail in turquoise and purple, which I love.

My mom writes stories for me, too, about a character who's based on me, Little Bobby. There's one where Little Bobby has this watch that lets him go on adventures in time. He can go back and see the dinosaurs or go visit the Wild West. But no matter where he is in time, Little Bobby has to come home every hour to check in with his mother, so she knows he's safe.

One year she sets up an Easter-egg hunt for me. She wakes me up on Easter morning and takes me down to the creek that runs between our complex and the next one across the way and I run around all excited, picking up these plastic Easter eggs with grape and strawberry jelly beans in them.

Probably the most fun we have is when *The Fresh Prince of Bel-Air* comes on. Every time the theme music starts, we jump on the bed and sing, "In West Philadelphia born and raised, on the playground is where I spent most of my days." We do that, and I laugh and laugh.

I don't have too many memories of my dad being around. One of the few memories of him that's a good one is Halloween. My mom never lets me celebrate Halloween. "It's the devil's night," she says. But then one year my dad's around, and she gives in and lets him take me to Target to get a costume. We get to the Halloween aisle and I look up and I'm in kid heaven. It's like they've got every cartoon character and superhero on the planet. My dad points down the aisle and says, "You can be whatever you want!" I can't believe it, because we never have money for stuff like this.

"Listen here," he says, "I'm gonna be a ninja. Maybe we should go as ninjas together."

"No way," I say. "I'm gonna be Superman."

So I'm Superman, and for the next couple of years I wear the shit out of that costume because it's the only costume I have. I put it on and run around outside. I go and jump on top of the big green power transformer behind our apartment building and stand there for like twenty minutes at a time, securing the neighborhood, my skinny five-year-old wrists and calves sticking out of this worn-out, skintight Superman outfit made for a toddler.

The thing about the good memories, though, is that when I reach back for them, there aren't many to choose from. There's the fish bubbles and the Little Bobby stories and the *Fresh Prince,* and after that it falls off pretty quick. And it sounds strange to say, but the good memories are the ones that make me sad. It makes me sad that the most precious memories of my childhood are the ones that the average person would throw away. Most kids probably don't remember the exact flavor of jelly bean they got in their Easter egg, because those kids got to do Easter-egg hunts every year, so it was no big deal. But for me it was the one time when I was four. Still, even though the good memories hurt, I cherish them and hold on to them because they're the only ones that I have.

The bad memories outweigh the good, by far, but they don't hurt as much anymore. I've dealt with them. I understand them. In a lot of those memories, I'm by myself. Most mornings I wake up and go out to the living room and I'm on my own, empty cans of Coors Light littering the coffee table, ashtrays piled high, the apartment reeking of cigarettes. The fun, creative mom who's up all night painting murals and writing stories, I won't see her until she wakes up at ten or eleven, sometimes noon. If we have milk, I make myself a bowl of cereal and watch TV, then putter around in my pajamas and play with the few toys I have.

Sometimes when my mom's asleep, I get bored and want someone to play with, so I leave. I have a few memories of doing that, like the time I wander out looking for the kid who lives across the hall and I get locked out and I start banging on the door, but my mom doesn't come and I start crying and I'm out there for what feels like forever, banging and crying, and eventually I have to go to the bathroom, so I shit in my underwear.

Eventually my mom comes to the door and lets me in. She isn't worried that I left the apartment, only pissed that I woke her up. She goes right back to bed, doesn't even help me with the dirty underwear. I have to take it off in the bathroom and clean up myself.

It's always like that. In this other memory I'm at the breakfast table eating a ham sandwich for lunch. It goes down wrong and I start to choke and my mom's not around. I can't breathe and I'm choking and I'm alone and I'm terrified. Finally I cough it up, spewing chunks of ham sandwich everywhere. I run to my mom in the next room, crying, afraid. But she doesn't hug me and tell me everything's okay. She scolds me for making a mess. Then she drags me back to the table and yells at me to clean it up.

I have so many memories of moments like that, moments of whiplash anger, moments of my mom doing things that, even as a kid, I know moms aren't supposed to do. But even more than the huge pile of bad memories or the handful of good memories, what I remember most is the screaming. Every day, from the time I'm a tiny little toddler, she screams. She's on the phone all afternoon, screaming and cursing at somebody from Medicaid or the welfare office. Then she's up in the apartment in the middle of the night, screaming and cursing at the nobody who isn't there. The sound of it is like a screeching demon being born from the pits of hell, and it just goes on for hours.

PART I
SIR ROBERT

Okay, BITCH! I got another one of your FUCKIN' numbers! I've already got seven! No, this ain't the number, call the other number! You call the other fuckin' number and you gotta wait for another fuckin' number! Then call fuckin' Baltimore! Then find out what state you're in. Then call THAT fuckin' number! And then find out they didn't take the fuckin' Medicare!"

My mom was on the phone again.

"Now, cunt Mary motherfuckers of the planet, YOU do this shit! All this shit! Every fuckin' time for TWENTY YEARS I have called these motherfuckers it's like this! Don't know what the fuck you're talkin' about!"

I was around fifteen years old, just getting into hip-hop and recording everything I could all the time, songs off the radio, stuff off the TV, my friends goofing around. So one day I decided to record one of her phone calls.

"Fuck it! I'm a psychopathic, cocksuckin' fuckin' sinner! Jesus, if you're going to do something to me, then DO IT! I can't fuckin' take it!"

What you can't hear on the page is that she's screeching so loud the neighbors can hear it in the next apartment, and what you can't see is that she's frantically pacing back and forth, chain-smoking, slamming her fists on the kitchen counter, and throwing shit at the wall, like a child having a tantrum because she's been put on hold for the millionth time.

"Yeah, you stupid cunt, it's correct! Fuckin' bastards! Fuckin' swine! Fuckin' motherfucker! Are you gonna fuck with me or help me?!"

It was like this every day, and this was mild.

"Fuckin' bitch! Fuckin' knows how to fuckin' tell me how to fuckin' CALM DOWN! She can't even fuckin' see the name of the fuckin' benefits!"

She was calling some government agency about her medication, whichever pill she was taking that month to balance her brain. Zoloft, maybe. I can't remember them all. One day it was her medication, the next day it was welfare or food stamps.

"All I want to know is if these GODDAMN people pay for this FUCKIN' medicine! Because what am I supposed to fuckin' do?! Go back to the fuckin' doctor here? This medicine they don't pay for. I don't know . . . write me out another one! Okay, here, go to the pharmacy. Oh, they don't pay for this. Okay, let me go back to the doctor again! Here, hmmm, let's see . . . take this medicine!"

She was a sick person, and she was in pain, so she was lashing out at the people who were trying to help her. Which is pretty much the story of her life.

"Thanks! That's all the FUCK I wanted to know! Why couldn't I get somebody a fuckin' half hour ago to say that! We're dropping like flies 'cause we fuckin' want to kill ourselves so they get a POPULA-TION CONTROL!"

Whenever I tell my story and I get to the stuff about my mom, part of me feels like a liar and a fraud, like I must be exaggerating this stuff to make myself sound tougher, because if I tell it this way, I've got one of the craziest American come-up stories in history. Then I go back and listen to this tape, and I remember: "Oh. Right. It was actually more fucked up than what I usually tell people."

Still, as strange and fucked up as my life may have been because of her, her life was actually way worse than mine.

✕⎯✕

My mom was born in 1961 in Washington, D.C. Back then, before all the husbands, before she was Terry Lee Bell or Terry Lee Stone or Terry Lee Bransford, she was Terry Lee Miller. But all the rotating last names didn't matter so much because my whole life everyone just called her Terry Lee.

By the time I was born, my mother was estranged from her family, so I don't know a whole lot about them. From what I understand, they were well-off. Not super-wealthy or anything, but they owned a house and a car and things like that. My grandfather, I don't have any memories of him at all, not even what his name was. I know my grandmother's name, but only because I found it once on the back of an old photograph. I don't have many pictures of me as a child, a dozen maybe, but there's this one Polaroid of me as a ten-month-old baby, and on the bottom it says, "Nov. 27, 1990 Bobby's first cucumber at his Grand-mas Judie."

So that was her name: Judie.

My mom told me her heritage was German and English, which to look at her was true, I guess. She had green eyes and pale skin with freckles and brown hair that she always wore short, never past her shoulders. I never saw my mom as ugly, but I wouldn't say she was particularly attractive. Her teeth were all crooked and filled with

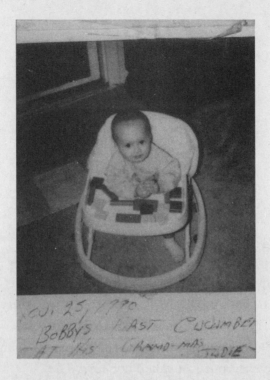

gaps and she was insecure about them. We'd be watching *Seinfeld* in the apartment, and whenever she laughed she'd cover her mouth, even with nobody else there.

I only know two stories about my mom growing up. The first one she always used to tell was how when she was five she got this brand-new Schwinn bicycle, the one with the banana seat. She loved it so much and she used to ride around her neighborhood and it was on one of those rides that she was sexually assaulted for the first time. A man in the neighborhood exposed himself to her and made her touch his penis. She went and told her mom, but her mom reacted like too many people do when it comes to sexual abuse. She tried to minimize it, bury it. She told my mom that the man was just playing a game and not to worry and let's all get back to pretending everything is normal and perfect. Which fucked my mom up, obviously, as it would.

The other story my mom told me was how when she was fourteen she brought home a boy she wanted to date. His name was Duncan, and he was black. "Duncan was so beautiful and sweet and kind," she used to say, but then her parents completely flipped out on her. "We don't mix with those people," they said, and they made her break up with him. Something about that incident had a huge impact on her, though I'm not entirely sure why. For the rest of her life, she was attracted to black men. She had all of her children with black men, and I only ever saw her with one man who wasn't black, her second husband, Kenny. At the same time, deep down, because of her upbringing, part of her was every bit as racist as her parents.

The Duncan story and the bicycle penis-touching story are the only ones I know. She never told me anything else; it was like she didn't have a childhood. Everything else I know about her starts when she was seventeen, when she ran away from home and fell into drugs and prostitution. I don't know if she ran away because her parents were abusive or if that's when her issues with mental illness started to come up. All I know is that my mom never fit in, with her family, or with anyone, anywhere.

The impression I have is that when she ran away she was a stoner pothead, hanging out with the white guys listening to AC/DC and the brothers listening to Run-DMC. I imagine her life being like that movie *Detroit Rock City*, a bunch of burnouts having a good time trying to scam their way into a KISS concert. But things turned dark pretty fast.

She never talked much about her prostitution years. The subject would only come up every now and then, typically out of anger, as a weapon she could wield against me. I'd be watching cartoons and bouncing off the walls, being a typical kid, and she'd flip the fuck out and start screaming at me, and I'd be like, "But *Mom*. I'm just having fun."

"Fun?" she'd scream. "You want to have fun?! You should just be grateful that you have a fuckin' place to sleep and live and eat, because I sure fuckin' didn't. You don't even fuckin' know. When I was a kid, I didn't have anywhere to go. I had to walk the fuckin' streets at three a.m. getting picked up by truckers who raped me and threw me out and left me for dead on the highway!"

In another story she told me, she was in an apartment with these two guys and one of them put a butcher knife on the stove until it was red-hot and then he held her down and sodomized her and said if she made a noise he'd stab her with it.

"He *sodomized* me," she said, red-faced and screaming, as usual. "That means he stuck his *dick* in my *ass*."

She told me that when I was maybe about ten.

Then there was the one she told me about why she was mostly deaf in her left ear. It was permanently damaged from when some man had been beating on her.

Once she started in with these stories, she'd get so wrapped up in her own pain that she'd start lashing out, like she did with the people on the phone. Since I was the only person there, she'd be lashing out at me. "*You* don't know what this world is," and "*You're* gonna feel real pain one day," and "I *hope* you feel pain!" and "You *deserve* to feel pain!" She'd be screaming this shit at me, and I'd be thinking to myself, "Bitch, I'm just trying to watch *SpongeBob*."

At some point in those years my mom married her first husband, Eugene Bell, a guy she met at a party. Eugene played guitar and buckets on the street. Black guy. Dark skin. They had three kids together before getting divorced. There's Amber, who's the oldest, seven years older than me; then Geanie, who's five years older; and then my brother Jesse, who's only two years older than me. When Jesse was five, Eugene took him and climbed up a tree with him so he could videotape a woman undressing in her apartment. He did this *with* his kid—that's the kind of guy Eugene was.

Even though he got caught doing that shit, he still had primary custody. Which is crazy, but it probably says a lot about my mom. So my siblings sort of lived with us sometimes, but mostly they didn't. I have no memories of us sharing a home and being a family. The only real memory I have is them throwing me a birthday party when I turned four. It was weird because I didn't know what a birthday was, since no one had never celebrated my birthday before. I woke up and walked out to the living room and in this beautiful morning light there were balloons everywhere and cut-up pieces of construction paper all over the floor like confetti. I went and woke up my brother and sisters and said, "I don't know what's going on. I think a clown broke into the house or something."

"Dude," they said, "it's your birthday!"

"My what?"

"Your *birthday*!"

And that was the last time I saw them. Not too long after that Eugene threw them on a Greyhound bus and took them to California and by my fifth birthday they were gone, which I know for a fact because now that I knew what a birthday was I woke up and ran out of my bedroom yelling, "It's my birthday, Mom!" But I didn't get shit. No balloons, no cake. Nothing.

From then on, it was like I was an only child. We never had any family besides me and my mom. What's crazy is that I felt that way even though my mom's parents still lived a few miles away. I've got the picture of me eating cucumbers at Judie's house, so I have to assume my mom and her parents tried to reestablish their relationship, but it didn't work out. The only real memory I have of my grandmother is calling her and asking if I could come spend the weekend, and her giving me a bunch of excuses why I couldn't.

"Can I come and stay with you?"

"I don't think we can right now."

"What about the guest room?"

"Well, it's being worked on."

"What about the couch?"

"Oh, you don't want to sleep on the couch."

"What about the floor? I'll sleep on the floor."

I kept trying, and she kept saying no. Part of me, thinking back to the story about Duncan and why my mom ran away, wants to believe that the rift between my mom and her family was because I was black, because they were racist. And that had to have been part of it; racism never makes anything any easier. But ultimately I think the reason my mother's family wasn't in our life was because of my mother. Some people are so toxic you have no choice but to cut them off, and my mom was that person. Because of the cucumber photo, I have to believe that my grandparents at least tried to help me and eventually gave up because they were like, "We can't fuck with this bitch. She's crazy." Which is why it was always just me and Terry Lee, and everything I know about her family and her life is from her screaming at me during *SpongeBob*.

But as fucked up as my mom's stories are, I absolutely believe that they're true. You'd think that someone like her wouldn't be the most reliable narrator of her own life, that her stories must be delusional or detached from reality. But whenever she talked, she talked like someone who'd been scarred, who'd relived those stories a million times in her head. The details were always the same, too, like they were burned into her memory. That shit's real, for sure.

Then there's my dad.

ᎤᏃ

The hard thing about my dad's story is that it's impossible to know what's true and what's not because he's a fuckin' liar. All I can do is piece together the half-true stories he's already told me because he isn't in my life right now. Maybe he will be again someday, but recently I had to stop talking to him because he asked me for eight hundred grand so he could buy a house and turn it into a studio for his band.

We're working on boundaries.

Robert Bryson Hall was born somewhere in Pennsylvania. That much I know is true. I also know he had two brothers. His brother Michael was a cool dude; I got to meet him and know him a bit. There was another brother, too, but I forget his name. He died. It might have been drugs. I have an aunt on that side, too. She sent me a letter a couple of years ago, but I've never spoken to her. I think her name is Robin or Roberta or something like that.

Both of my dad's parents were alcoholics. I never met them because they both died long before I was born. My grandfather, as the story goes, went out on Christmas Eve and got shitfaced drunk and as he was coming up the front steps he slipped on the ice, fell back, hit his head on a rock, knocked himself out, and froze to death in the snow. They found him on Christmas morning. Crazy.

My grandmother had a serious drinking problem, too. What my dad told me about her was that she drank herself into some insane state and had to go to the hospital and practically went into a coma. When she came to the doctors told her, "If you drink again, you'll die." Not long after that, she was at a Christmas party—which is weird, because of how her husband went—and she got drunk and fell asleep in a chair and never woke up.

My dad has told me those stories a few times and the details always add up and there's no reason why my dad would lie about how his parents died, but I still can't be sure since he's told me so many stories where the details don't add up at all. For most of my life, pretty much everything that came out of my dad's mouth was bullshit. He's a slick motherfucker, for sure, the definition of a hustler—a smooth, silver-tongued dude who can talk his way into or out of just about anything. With the exception of fatherhood. He denied that I was his when I was born, but then he got a paternity test, which I had no idea about until a couple of years ago when my dad, who's now a recovering crack addict in his sixties, found out that he'd knocked up a twenty-three-year-old heroin addict even though he got a vasectomy after he'd had me.

"Can you believe this shit?" he said. "I got a vasectomy and I'm still having another kid."

"What the fuck?" I said. "When did you get a vasectomy?"

"After I had your ass."

"Damn. Well, how do you know it's yours?"

"Because I got a paternity test."

That gave me this feeling I couldn't shake, so a couple of months later I called my dad and said, "So, wait . . . did you get a paternity test with me?"

"Fuck yeah!" he said. "You *know* I did!"

So that was special. I don't know if the test was something my parents did together, but the safer bet is that the motherfucker snuck me off somewhere and got a paternity test on his own—you know, just to be sure—and it came back positive. But he didn't need a test to tell him that. He's 100 percent my dad. We're both skinny and lanky, both with the same hunched-over posture that we need to work on. The only difference is that while I look mixed, he's definitely a black guy.

At some point my dad moved to D.C. with huge ambitions as a musician. He played congas and percussion and sang all over the Chocolate City Go-Go scene. He played with Chuck Brown. He played in E.U. What he wanted more than anything was to be Smokey Robinson. He'd introduce himself that way, too. "Hi, my name's Smokey." So everyone called him Smokey, which I find hilarious 'cause he's a crackhead who named himself Smokey. And when it wasn't Smokey Robinson, it was Prince. I think I heard my dad cover "Purple Rain" about a million times.

My dad was a legit musician, though. He had real talent. But he was also an addict. My whole life I've met people who did gigs with him, and they've all got stories. After the show, he'd go to the promoter and get the money and then run out on his bandmates. Like, he'd do that to his own people. Did he think he was never going to

With my dad.

see them again? But that's an addict's mentality. He couldn't help himself, or he didn't want to help himself.

The few times my dad came around, he'd always be playing the big shot, talking about his new band, his gigs, the deals he was working on. If you were a kid and didn't know any better, you'd buy it because the dude had swag. It was the '90s, so he had the do-rag with the waves back, rockin' a jumpsuit. It'd be that or he'd have on a brand-new suit. He wore a lot of suits. Everything was about appearances with my dad. One time he rolled up with a car phone, and I was like, "Yo, this is *crazy*. You have a *phone* in your *car*." He'd always be snapping his fingers and saying, "Let's go! Let's go! Let's go!" Like big things were happening and we needed to get moving, like he's the guy and he's killin' it. But he wasn't really. If you looked closer, you'd see that the Acura he was driving was ten years old, the cell phone didn't actually have any minutes on it, the suit he probably stole it to get it, and whatever big scheme he was talking up was just him trying to finagle money to go buy crack cocaine.

What's fucked up, and what frustrates me, is that because my dad lived in a swirl of lies about who he was and where he came from, I have no connection to my past. To me, the stories about my dad's parents dying are just some crazy stories; I don't have any feeling of loss when I hear them. The tragedy isn't losing my grandparents. The tragedy is never having them. The tragedy is not being able to remember their names or what they did or where they were from, and not even being sure that the few things I do know about them are true. It's the same thing on my mother's side. I have a picture of me eating cucumbers at their house, but that's about it.

As a rapper, as Logic, I know exactly where I come from. I know where I sit on the family tree. I know that before there was Logic there was Wu-Tang Clan and Nas and the Roots, and before those guys there was Big Daddy Kane and KRS-One, and from there it goes all the way back to Grandmaster Flash and the Sugarhill Gang and DJ Kool Herc. I know who Logic's ancestors are, but when it comes to my own life I don't know shit about shit. I only know a bunch of half-told stories from drunken and drug-induced states that, especially on my dad's side, may or may not have actually happened. Most of the time I'm like, "Fuck. Who knows what's real and what's not?" I have no lineage, no heritage. I have no people. In the grand scheme, I know that I come from slaves and their masters, and that's all I know.

The one thing about my background that I do know, that I kind of wish I didn't know, is the story of the night I was conceived. Most people know the story of when they were born, what hospital it was at, how their mom went into labor, how the delivery went. I have no idea about any of that, but trying to reconnect with my dad a while back, I asked him how he and my mom met and I got more information than I was looking for.

There was this woman named Ruth that my mom knew. They'd do drugs together and then get clean together and then slip and do drugs together again. Ruth lived in this apartment at the end of West Deer Park in Gaithersburg and every year on December 23 she celebrated Christmas Eve Eve. Whenever we'd see her around that time, we'd go to her apartment and I'd get a present on Christmas Eve Eve. It was in Ruth's apartment, my dad said, that he met my mom for the first time.

"I met your mom when I was smoking crack with that bitch Ruth," he told me. "I came over one night, and me and your mom were kinda hangin' and feelin' each other, and three days later I fucked her on the floor and made you."

Okay. Thanks for that image, Dad.

They didn't get married. It would have been nice to know they at least tried, but it never would have worked anyway. With two addicts it rarely does. Regardless, marriage or no marriage, nine months later, on January 22, 1990, I was born. When the time came to fill out the birth certificate, my parents started out naming me after my dad: Robert Bryson Hall II. Then, at the last minute, my mother took the form and added "Sir" to the front of my name, so it became Sir Robert Bryson Hall II.

To this day, my dad insists that the "Sir" was his idea. "Because you're royalty," he says. But as we know: The dude's a fuckin' liar. The "Sir" was my mom's idea. She's the only motherfucker eccentric enough to come up with that shit, which she says she did because of our English bloodline or whatever.

Growing up, I hated the name. Every year I had problems on the first day of school, because the administration had my first name listed as "Sirrobert" in the computer. The teachers would always, *always*, try to say it with some kind of fucked-up French or European accent, thinking they were being sensitive to my cultural heritage or some shit, and I'd have to tell them it was a computer error. The only teacher who ever got it correct was this hard-ass U.S. history teacher I had one year. Everyone else got it wrong.

It'd come up again and again for the rest of the school year. My name would get called over the PA system because I was getting sent to the principal's office or because my mom was picking me up early and the entire school would hear and all the kids would laugh. I'd get jokes for days and I'd be totally embarrassed. Today I'm glad I have the name. I'm glad my mother gave me something so unique and so special. Over the years I've grown to understand you can't fit in and stand out at the same time, but back then all I wanted was to fit in. Thankfully, other than those mix-ups with "Sirrobert" at school, everyone just called me Bobby, and Bobby fits in everywhere.

The only person who called me anything other than Bobby was my mom. From her I'd get all three, actually. If it was a regular day and we were headed out to run errands, it'd be Bobby. Like, "C'mon, Bobby, let's go to the store." If she was being stern or serious because I'd misbehaved, I'd get a very short, terse "Robert!" But when she was losing her shit, then it was always Sir Robert. She'd be off her meds and on the warpath and she'd scream, *"Sir Robert!"*

I'd hear that name and I'd tense up and I'd think, "Oh, shit. Here we go."

ᄊᅑᄀᅑ ᅐ

Because my mom slept till noon and because I didn't learn my lesson after I got locked out and had to shit in my underwear, I still wandered out of the apartment sometimes whenever I got bored and wanted someone to play with. So one day I decided I wanted to visit this kid I knew who lived up the street. I got dressed and went out to the main road and walked the half a mile or so to his apartment complex and when I got there I walked up the stairs to the unit where he lived. I knocked on his door and waited for a bit and no one was home, so I turned around and headed back down the stairs, where I met these two women coming up.

"Hi," I said. "Do you have any kids that I can play with?"

"What?"

"Do you have any kids that I can play with?"

They started looking around, a little confused. "Uh, do you . . . live here?"

"No."

"Where do you live?"

"Up the street."

"What's your name?"

"Bobby."

"Bobby, how old are you?"

"Four."

"Bobby, why don't you come with us."

They took me back to their apartment, gave me a snack, and got on the phone. "We're going to call someone," they said.

"Okay. Who?"

"The police."

"Okay. Do they have any kids I can play with?"

A few minutes later a cop showed up, this big, scary-looking white dude who wasn't nice to me at all. He put me in his car and started driving up the street, telling me to point out where I lived, which I did. He pulled up in front of our unit, parked, took me up to our apartment, and started banging on the door. It took a few minutes, but my mom came out, and he went off on her. "You've got a fuckin' four-year-old kid running around the fuckin' neighborhood all by himself? The fuck is wrong with you?"

And on and on. She held it together while he was there, apologizing and saying, "Yes, Officer" and "It won't happen again, Officer." He let her off with a warning and the second he was gone she turned and ripped into me. "What the *fuck* did you do? What the *fuck* are you thinking? Bringing the fuckin' cops home? Go to your fuckin' room." And I burst into tears.

Even with a cop reading her the riot act, nothing really changed, because my mom was my mom. Even when she was awake, she rarely left the house. She didn't go outside unless it was to run some errand, and even then she'd just go, do whatever it was, and come right back. If I wanted to do anything, I had to do it by myself, which was how I learned to ride a bike. We had this old black-and-orange kids' bike that we got somewhere. I wanted to learn how to ride it, but she couldn't teach me because she wouldn't come outside. So I had to take it out to the parking lot on my own and figure out how to ride from watching the older kids do it. I spent days teaching myself. I'd get on and fall down, get on and fall down, get on and fall down, and eventually I learned how to do it, but I ended up with scrapes and scratches all over my legs and my knees from trying.

Because my mom didn't go anywhere, our world was small. We'd go to the grocery store or the drugstore, to her therapist's office or A.A. meetings, or church. Other than that our world didn't extend much beyond the apartment complex in Germantown where we lived, which was called Farmingdale and had L-shaped blocks of cookie-cutter apartment units all branching like spokes off this rotary in the middle. There was a little hill behind our apartment that to me was like Mount Everest, and down the other side of it was the creek where I'd had my Easter-egg hunt that one time.

One of the only times my mom took me out to do a thing that normal families do was this trip we went on to the National Zoo in Washington, D.C. When we got off the train at the Metro station the platform was packed, all these people jostling and rushing past. One thing I knew from going to the store with my mom was that she didn't wait for me. She walked fast and it was on me to keep up. We stepped off the train into this sea of people, and she took off. I was yelling after her, "Mom! Wait!" But she kept walking, stopping only to bark "Keep up!" over her shoulder as I got lost in the crowd and was running around and looking for her and crying and freaking out. After what felt like forever I found her and I ran to her and I grabbed on to her, but she didn't turn and clutch me and hold me tight and say, "My son! I lost you! I was so worried!" None of that. She snapped at me, "I *told* you to keep up! *Don't* do it again!"

I have no idea if we actually made it to the zoo because I can't remember any pandas or anything like that, and you'd think that I would.

My dad took me down to D.C. once, too, only instead of taking me to the zoo, he left me in a car for five hours while he went into some crackhouse to smoke crack. Which to this day he swears never happened, but I know that it happened because it's such a fucked-up memory how could I forget? He picked me up in his mid-to-late-eighties piece-of-shit Acura. Some woman was in the front with him, I was in the back, and he drove us in from Maryland and parked on the side of this fucked-up street somewhere in Southeast D.C. It was like something straight out of a movie, with crackheads-in-the-alley type shit. My dad and this woman got out of the car and they left me there and he walked with his Bill Cosby walk up to this house and disappeared inside and I waited and waited for them to come out and eventually I just fell asleep.

For the most part, my dad just wasn't around. We're talking maybe two, three times he was in the house for whatever reason, dropping by to spend some time pretending to be a dad, which on a good day meant making a big deal about spoiling me, but him spoiling me was him buying something cheap that he probably got out of some clearance bin somewhere, like the time he brought me this stuffed bear that sucked because its fur was all prickly and itchy but I loved it and slept with it anyway because it was one of the only things he ever gave me.

I went and stayed with my dad a handful of times that I can remember, like the time I went over and as soon as I got there he just took me and dropped me off with these old people who didn't have TV and left me with them for two or three days. Which I didn't understand at the time, but obviously it was to go off and do drugs. When I did stay over with him, I wouldn't call what he did parenting. He and his girlfriend would stay up watching late-night Skinemax movies or that show *Real Sex* on HBO, where they went around interviewing people who are into sex dolls or whatever. My dad used to love that, and they'd let me lie there and watch it with them. At the time I thought, "Oh, my dad's cool." But, like, no, he's not. A child shouldn't be watching interviews about sex dolls. I did that a few times and then his house got raided by the police and I didn't see him for a while.

For a long time I thought my dad was a great dad because my mom was the bad guy and he was the cool dude who bought me candy.

But other than spoiling me with shit from the dollar store, my dad's only other parenting mode was to show up and crack the whip and play the disciplinarian, which was a joke because he was the one who needed the discipline because he needed to stop smoking fuckin' crack cocaine and be a real father. Luckily, since he was only around those two or three times, I have memories of him hitting me only two or three times.

The first time I was out on the grass outside our unit, and me and the other kids were playing Jackpot. My whole childhood my mom used to make me come inside and check in every hour—even in high school she made me do this—and so this kid was about to pass the ball to me and I looked at my watch and I realized, "Oh, fuck, it's 6:03, I'm three minutes late." But I stayed in the game and the kid yelled, "Jackpot!" and I was like, "Yo, this is it!" I started running and running and running and it was one of those runs where you're running straight ahead but you're looking backward over your shoulder like you're looking for a Hail Mary pass into the end zone and I went to put my hands up into the air to grab the ball and as I turned to look back in front of me I suddenly saw my dad and he was running toward me with one hand behind his back and then out of nowhere he whipped out this giant fuckin' belt and started whoopin' my ass in front of everybody, hollerin', "*Boy!* You were supposed to come in at six o'clock!" and all this other shit.

I got so hot about it. In my mind I was thinking, "Really? You're gonna embarrass me in front of the whole neighborhood and you're not even my pops? Like, you are, but you're not. You don't deserve to do this. You haven't earned the right to do this. You think you can go smoke crack, get clean for six days, come to my fuckin' house, and then decide that because my mom's a fuckin' moron and thinks that I need male discipline you're going to whoop me? Fuck that."

This other time I was hanging out with my dad at his apartment with his roommate; he always had a roommate because he couldn't make his own rent since all his money went to the gold chains and the bracelets and the watch and the car and the fresh suit and obviously the crack. I was at his place and I was playing Ninja Turtles and I had these ninja throwing stars that weren't real ninja throwing stars—I think they were the plastic ninja stars from that time he took me out in a ninja Halloween costume. So I was throwing these ninja stars around, and my dad had this lamp with one of those black-light bulbs, because this was the '90s, when you'd put the black-light on when you were trying to fuck a bitch, and I threw one of these ninja stars and it shattered the black-light bulb.

My dad stormed in from the kitchen, yelling, "What the fuck?! What was that?!" I was like the dog in the corner, going, "I don't know! It wasn't me!" and the dude stormed over and he started whaling on me. In that moment I can clearly remember thinking, "Fuck this guy." I went from loving this guy to "I can't fuck with you." Because I didn't feel there was anything disciplinary about it. He wasn't a real dad. He was just a dude who was beating on me.

I didn't have parents. I mean, I had them, but I didn't. Between my mom never leaving the house and my dad never being at the house, I was mostly left to raise myself, whether it was teaching myself how to ride a bike or knowing I should probably duck down and hide in the backseat of the piece-of-shit sedan parked outside of the crackhouse. I was like an orphan with parents, if that makes any sense. The only mother figure I had was fucked up and crazy, and there was no father figure at all. That shit didn't exist.

The closest there ever was was Tony.

Tony Bransford was a guy my mom met at a party while she was still with her first husband, Eugene. Tony was actually friends with Eugene and once Eugene left she and Tony were on and off. They finally got together later on after she had me with my dad, and with my dad mostly out of the picture Tony was around for most of my life while I was growing up. The only time Tony wasn't around was when he was in prison.

Tony was a handsome dude. He was mixed, part black and part French, but he looked more black for sure. He was built like a bodybuilder and bald as a motherfucker on top, but with a horseshoe of long hair around the sides, which was why he wore bandanas everywhere he went. Cowboy boots, too, which worked on him because he was rugged like a cowboy. He had these hands. Big fuckin' hands, dry and calloused, the cuticles on his thumbs always ripped up and red from working construction. He was a welder. He worked at the waste management company sometimes, doing trash-man shit, but he was mostly a welder. My mom would take me to see him working on construction sites, six stories high in the sky, sitting up there with a twelve-pack of Coors and Bud Light, having a good time welding steel beams together. So cool.

Insane alcoholic, though. He would drink until he shat blood. I was only four, five years years old, going into the bathroom and seeing a bunch of blood in the toilet, and the dude would be flushing it down like there was nothing weird about it at all. But that's alcoholism. Tony had definitely done hard-core drugs; there's no doubt he'd smoked crack in his day. But like my mom, he was an aging addict, late thirties, mid-forties, which meant he didn't want to work that hard to get high anymore. When you get to that point, your drug of choice is alcohol. It's cheap and easy to get and you numb yourself and you're good. The crazy thing about Tony was he could open his throat, so he could cock his head back and pour a can of beer down, the whole thing disappearing in one gulp.

More than anything, Tony was just crazy. He had a reputation. He was famous. All the cops and the corrections officers in Montgomery County knew Tony Bransford. We'd see the police walking through the mall, and they'd be like, "Tony! What are you up to, man?" Whenever the cops got called on Tony—like when my mom called the cops on Tony—they'd show up like it was old times. "Oh! Tony's back at it!" I wouldn't go so far as to call Tony a criminal, but he definitely committed crimes. I saw this dude bloody, coming home with his hands and his face all busted up. Drunk and disorderly. Fistfights. Fuckin' dudes up.

Still, everybody will tell you that Tony was a good guy. He was an alcoholic with an anger management problem, for sure. But he was never out to hurt people. All the fighting was usually because somebody insulted him or mouthed off about a woman he knew. That's when he'd get into it and start throwing punches and the cops would come and he'd run from the cops, racing away on his Harley and shooting back at the officers chasing him down. Tony wasn't packing some little revolver, either. This motherfucker had Desert Eagles. Which, if you've never seen a Desert Eagle, it's a fucking hand cannon, a giant silver weapon of death. Line three guys up and it'll blow all of their heads off with a single shot. Tony would be racing down the street, firing off this fucking hand cannon at all the cops chasing him.

One time it took eight cops to take him down. They were chasing him and he was on his bike, going off into ditches and into the woods and speeding and getting away and he hit a ramp and wiped out and broke his leg and the cops caught him and took him to the hospital. The dude was handcuffed to a gurney and still got caught trying to wheel himself out of the hospital with his one good leg. Still, all the cops loved him because when he wasn't drunk off his ass and shooting at them he was a cool dude.

Even as a five-year-old I knew Tony was a good man despite his faults. He was down-to-earth, the sweetest guy. One time my mom told Tony she wanted him to whoop my ass. I'd gotten into big trouble. There was this mixed kid named Ian who lived in the apartment complex right next to ours. Ian was sweet and innocent, but there were these two older kids who ran around those apartments all the time, too. White kids, a brother and sister. They were these two badass little fuckers who never wore shoes; I always thought they were weird.

Anyway, one day me and Ian and these two weirdos were out running around. It wasn't the first time I'd hung out with them, but it was the first time they'd brought cigarettes. It wasn't hard for kids to get cigarettes in those days because so many parents worked and we were running around unsupervised half the time, like the kid next door to me who used to sneak out his dad's *Playboy*s and show them to everybody. Which is how I saw my first titties and my first bush when I was five. Which is definitely too young to see them, and for some people being exposed to pornography that young fucks them up and it was certainly weird but I don't think it fucked me up or anything because I just saw a hot, naked woman and it was cool.

So there we were, me and Ian and these two white kids with no shoes on all huddled in the bushes, and these two fuckers were pushing cigarettes on me and Ian. "Here," they kept saying, "smoke this. Smoke this."

Ian was scared. He didn't want to do it. He wised up and said, "I'm going home."

I didn't want to do it, either. But I stayed. They handed a cigarette to me, and I took a puff. It was so gross. I thought I was going to throw up. Then they said, "No, no. You gotta inhale it. You gotta inhale it."

"What do you mean?" I said. "What are you talking about?"

"You know. Inhale it. Suck the air in."

So I took the cigarette and I inhaled and I started coughing up a lung and right at that moment Ian's mom came out and caught us because Ian must have told on us. So Ian's mom went and told my mom and Tony and they sat me down in the living room and did the whole "We're so disappointed in you" routine. Which I actually have to give my mom credit for. It was one of the few times in my life she didn't flip out and go crazy on me for misbehaving. It was the closest thing to a Cory Matthews, *Boy Meets World*, father-mother sit-down I ever had. But that's as far as her reasonableness went. When it came time for the punishment, she decided that I needed "male discipline," which meant I needed an ass-whooping and Tony needed to be the one to do it.

Tony got up and walked me down the hall and into the back bedroom and closed the door behind us. I was so scared I was in tears, almost. It was bad enough when my mom beat me, and she was just this skinny white lady. Tony was this jacked-up monster of a dude with fuckin' cinder blocks for hands. But once the door closed, I looked up at him and he wasn't angry. He sat me down on the bed, took a seat next to me, and said, "Listen, when I was a boy like you, my dad used to beat me up. He'd punch me in the face, make me bleed. He'd beat my sisters and my brothers, too. So I promised myself that I would never touch a child. So I'm not gonna whoop you. Okay?" And he was so sweet, so reassuring in the way he said it, like he could see the fear in my eyes and he wanted me to know I didn't have anything to be afraid of. I looked up at him, like, "Wow." I'd never had an adult show that much kindness to me. I could barely comprehend it.

"But," he said, "you gotta help me make your mom think I'm

taking care of this. So what we're gonna do is we're going to *pretend* that I'm whooping your ass in here."

I smiled. "Okay," I said. "You got it."

Then Tony got up and he started smacking his hands together, like he was giving me the worst spanking of my life, and I started yelling, "Ow! Ooof! Oh, Tony, stop!" I was going so over the top, I should have gotten an Oscar for my performance that day. Then he and I had a good laugh. I was having so much fun with it that even after he left the room, I was still going, "Ow! Tony, Stop!" and he had to run back in and say, "Dude, shut up! It's over! I can't be in the other room and still in here whooping your ass at the same time!"

It was literally one of the kindest things anyone had ever done for me. Tony and my mom were addicts, and addiction is a selfish disease. It destroys the addict's ability to recognize the needs and the feelings of other people. But Tony wasn't selfish. He had an empathy that my mom and my dad completely lacked.

Tony could be a monster for sure. Boy, could he yell. He had this deep, raspy voice, and I'd hear him screaming at my mom in the next room, going, "I *told* you, woman!" They would fight like crazy late at night when they'd both been drinking, like the night I was alone in my room when I was around five and it was late and my mom and some friends were out in the living room and Tony was there and Tony's sister, Danielle, was there and out of nowhere I heard this massive fight break out. Voices yelling, shit breaking. I peeked out to the living room and saw these two cops. They had my mom by the arms and they were dragging her out the front door and down the front steps and she was kicking and screaming and there was blood streaming down her legs and ankles from all the kicking and being dragged along the hard concrete.

I have no idea why it happened or what came after it or when my mom came back, but even that didn't make me scared of Tony because I knew how kind and gentle he was. We just had this connection. It was better with Tony because he was a good presence and it was nice to be with someone and not get hit or anything.

My only problem with Tony was that he would disappear. Sometimes for a few days or weeks, sometimes for months. I eventually sorted out that any time Tony wasn't there it was because he was in jail. He'd get picked up for drunk and disorderly and spend a few days in lockup. Or maybe assault. In which case he'd be gone for three to six. Some of my earliest memories are going with my mom to visit him at the Montgomery County Detention Center, which everyone called Seven Locks because it's on Seven Locks Road. Since we never had a car, it took four different buses to get there, and we'd be waiting for the fuckin' bus out in the freezing winter or the blazing summer for half an hour, waiting for a transfer. I hated making that trip, but I was old enough for my mom to explain to me what prison was and why Tony was there and why we had to take this long-ass trip that took up our whole Saturday to go see him.

"Why do we have to go here?"

"Do you remember when the police came?"

"Yeah."

"Well, this is where you go when the police come get you."

"Like when you do something wrong."

"Yes. Tony did something wrong, and so he has to come here, so don't do what Tony did."

"Don't do what we do" was something I heard a lot, like when my mom, with a cigarette hanging out of her mouth, would tell Tony to whoop my ass for smoking.

When we got to Seven Locks, we'd go through security. The guards would be checking her, feeling her up. They didn't ever check the kids, though. The first time we went, my mom tried to hide something on me that she wanted to give him, but he was on the other side of the plate glass, so she couldn't pass him anything anyway.

We'd take a seat at the plate-glass partition in the dingy visiting room. I'd be in her lap, or in a second chair if there was one. Then

Tony would show up. He and my mom would each pick up a phone and talk. I'd get on and say hi, which was nice. Hearing his voice was something I missed, but not enough to take four buses and sit in a sad beige room all day; it's hard to make a five-year-old interested in somebody who's on the other side of a plate-glass window. Mostly it was the two of them talking and me playing with the one toy I'd brought that I got at Goodwill.

Sometime during kindergarten or first grade, Tony went away and we didn't visit him and he didn't come back. He was just gone. The next thing I remember we were living somewhere else, in a different apartment complex, the one that was over Mount Everest and across the creek, and I don't know why. I don't know if it was because we didn't have money now that Tony was gone or if the neighbors got tired of the noise and the fighting and the cops being called. All I knew was my mom said we couldn't go back to Farmingdale and she was friends with the superintendent of this other apartment complex and she'd made a deal with him to let us camp out in one of the vacant units while she figured out where we'd go next. It felt like we were there for a month or so, maybe longer. The sink and the toilet worked, but there was no electricity and we didn't have any furniture, just a mattress on the floor that my mother had brought over from our old place.

The apartment with nothing in it is one of my good memories. One of my best, actually. Because in spite of the screaming and the anger and the hurtful things that I didn't yet understand, I still had that primal feeling inside me of loving my mom and wanting to be with my mom, and in that empty apartment I got to be with her. Every morning I woke up and I wasn't alone. She was right beside me, her warm body curled up next to mine on this mattress on the floor. During the day, we'd play and goof around, running through the different empty rooms. At night, with no electricity it would get dark fast, but my mom had candles because she always had candles because she loved candles, and as the sun went down she'd light them up one by one and they'd fill the room with a soft, gentle glow.

She had a flashlight, too, and one night she taught me how to do shadow puppets. We had this two-liter of Coca-Cola and she was letting me drink Coke straight out of the two-liter, which was pretty much the greatest thing that had ever happened. Then she took the flashlight and she shone it against the wall and she showed me how to shape my hand to make all sorts of cool animal shadows in the light and together we huddled on our mattress on the floor and we made these puppies and bunnies dance across the empty wall of this empty room in this empty apartment.

And it was really, really beautiful.

ㅊㄸㄲㄸㅎ

My mom loved to watch old movies, all those black-and-white classics from the forties and fifties. So many nights she'd pop a tape in the VCR and put me on the couch to watch with her. We watched *Singin' in the Rain* with Gene Kelly, *The King and I* with Yul Brynner. We watched the one about Helen Keller, *The Miracle Worker*, with Anne Bancroft and Patty Duke. We watched the Elvis movies and the Rat Pack movies with Sinatra and Sammy and Dean. Sinatra wasn't the best actor, but Gene Kelly was great. I especially remember *To Sir, with Love* with Sidney Poitier. That one was cool because it actually had a black guy in it. All the other movies were great and I loved them, but I was always watching them a little skeptical, like, "Yo, where are all the black dudes at?"

We must have watched hundreds of those old black-and-white movies. Even the ones that weren't in black and white, I saw them in black and white because for a long time we only had a black-and-white TV. I hated that TV so goddamn much. I mean, at least we had TV, and that was cool, but any time I wanted to watch it I had to pull this button out to turn it on and then click it like *click, click, click, click, click* to change the channel and all we had were the channels we could get on the antenna and every time there was an explosion or if the commercials were too bright the TV would zap off. Then I'd

have to get up from the couch, push that button in, count to twenty—
one . . . two . . . three . . . four . . .—then unplug it and turn it back on.
I remember watching *Speed* with Keanu Reeves and Sandra Bullock
for the first time and I was all excited and Sandra Bullock was diving
on the floor and Keanu was like, *"The bomb is gonna blow, man!"*
and then: *Zap!* Nothing. There was also that time in *Independence
Day* when the White House blew up. Everybody else got to see that
shit and I didn't because I had to get up, hold the button, wait twenty
seconds, and by the time I turned it back on, the scene was over.

Most of the old movies we watched we got on tape from the library, because we almost never had cable. We watched them on pi-
rated cable every now and then, with that illegal black box you could
hook up to the set. But the only time we ever had legit cable, like that
you pay for, was when Kenny was living with us.

Kenny was my mom's second husband. Kenneth Stone. White
dude. The only white dude I ever saw her with as a long-term thing.
I don't know how they met, but for sure it was through the program.
My mom's Alcoholics Anonymous meetings were a chore for me.
Every week I got dragged to a place I didn't want to go where a
bunch of people sat around and told boring stories about how their
lives sucked. But for her and a lot of other people it was a social place
as well, like a bar for people who can't go to bars anymore. New people were always coming in and out, young people coming for the first
time, usually mandated to be there by the court, so everybody was
hanging out and dating and fucking each other, which probably was
how Kenny entered the picture.

There were a lot of different boyfriends. It wasn't like a revolving
door of men all the time. It would go up and down and it would all
depend on my mom's mood, like, "What's she feeling right now?"
Sometimes for months there'd be no men at all. Then maybe she'd be
bringing home some bad-ass white boy 'cause she was in a Chili Peppers grunge mood. Or maybe she'd been listening to lots of Funkade-
lic and she was feeling the brothers that week. It was always random.

Sometimes she'd bring home guys she'd met at the bus stop. She was in her late thirties, early forties, bringing home nineteen-, twenty-year-old dudes off the street. There were nights I'd be asleep in my room and I'd have school the next day and she'd come in and shake me awake at like one in the morning, going, "Robert! Robert! Wake up! I want to introduce you to this nice man, this kind soul I met at the bus stop tonight."

I'd sit up all bleary and half-awake, and this dude with dead eyes would be staring at me, like, "Heeeeeeeey, little man. What's up?"

They'd leave me in bed and go off to her room or the living room. Sometimes I'd lie in bed, terrified, not knowing what was going to happen. Other times I'd roll over and go back to sleep, too exhausted to care. The next morning I'd wake up feeling like I'd dreamed the whole thing and I'd go to the kitchen to get some cereal and all the cereal would be gone and I'd be like, "What the *fuck*?" Then I'd walk into the other room and the dead-eyed dude from the night before would be sitting there, finishing off my sugar flakes. That happened once, maybe twice a year or so, her bringing in guys off the street. Mostly it was guys from the program and for a while it was just Kenny and they actually got married.

I want to say I was at the wedding—and I most certainly was at their wedding—but they would have gotten married at City Hall and we were down at City Hall paying fines and dealing with legal shit so often that all the trips blur together. I know Kenny was there when we moved out of the empty apartment in Germantown because my mom was still with Tony the night the cops dragged her down the concrete steps. Then Tony was gone and there was this other guy, this lean, skinny black dude with a strong face and they were having sex for a while when Tony was in jail. Then Kenny showed up and we left Farmingdale and then we were in the empty apartment with the shadow puppets and then we left there and went to stay with these friends of Kenny's who lived in the Middlebrook trailer park. They let us live in their trailer for a couple of months until we got back on our feet. This family had two kids, a brother and sister who were always kissing each other. I know they were young and just experimenting, but it was still weird. This trailer park had all these sewers and tunnels and shit down below it and I was small enough to slip through the bars and run around in there like the Ninja Turtles. Eventually we left and moved to the West Deer Park apartments in Gaithersburg, where it was me and Kenny and my mom all sharing a bedroom in the apartment of this friend of theirs named Cindy.

Cindy was this crazy-ass bitch who might have been into witchcraft. At least that's what my mom used to whisper to me about Cindy, because Cindy wore lots of black and lots of leather. But my mom wore lots of black and lots of leather, too, and she was super into Jesus, so who knows. Cindy didn't work. Most of my mom's friends didn't work. Everyone was on some kind of government assistance. Cindy was on disability because her leg was fucked up and she walked with a limp and her arm was always curled up under her bosom and she had a brace around her wrist. It was like she'd had a stroke or something, which was weird 'cause she was so young, like around thirty. But she might have just been that way.

Cindy was cool, I guess. I never paid much attention to her because I was busy lying on the floor watching *Speed Racer* all day. But Cindy had this pit bull named Chance, and I quickly learned to pay attention to Chance. One night Cindy and Kenny and my mom were sitting around getting shitfaced because they all knew each other from the program. My mom was sitting next to me on this couch playing with Chance and talking to him in this playful baby-talk voice, going, "Who's a good boy? Who's a good boy?" And out of nowhere Chance fucking lunged at her and sank his teeth into her cheek. He was ripping and tearing and wouldn't let go and my mom was freaking out and blood was everywhere and I jumped onto the back of the couch with my back against the wall, screaming my head off, and the whole time Cindy was crying and losing her shit. But only about the dog. "Oh no! Please don't put my dog down! I don't want my Chance to be put down!" Which I thought was fucked up, since my mom had just had her face almost ripped off. An ambulance came and I had to get in the back to ride to the hospital, where I watched my mom get her face stitched up. It was quite horrific. Luckily we didn't have to deal with Chance much after that. Cindy moved away and we moved into the vacant unit across the hall, which was #203. Then it was only me and my mom and Kenny.

Kenny was younger than my mom, in his late twenties. He was kind of in a band but not really. Mostly he worked construction, painting houses and building decks in people's yards and stuff like that. When Kenny was around, we had things like cable and groceries all the way to the end of the month. The first year he was with us for Christmas was the only year I ever had Christmas. Like, for real. That was my *only* Christmas. Every year I'd see the kids in my neighborhood getting presents, and not just the families with money. Even the broke-ass kids on welfare would still be getting Xboxes and shit and I'd be begging my mom, "Please? Can't I get something?" But she always said no. She'd try to make it about religion. "It's Jesus' birthday, goddammit!" But really it was about us not having money. Every year she'd bake a cake that said, "Happy Birthday, Jesus," and that was all we got, which I always thought was fucked up. But the year Kenny was there I got real presents. I even got LEGOs and I never got LEGOs because LEGOs were so expensive. That year was crazy. It was almost as if my mother had married into money, but really she just married into a dude with a job and van.

Kenny was cool and I liked him. He had weird friends, though. There was this one dude. Tattoo artist. Big fat guy. Not super-fat, but more sort of mid-fat. Dude was mentally fucked up, too. One time he gave my mom a feather tattoo on her thumb and she let him pierce my ear with an ice cube and a needle and I got this fake diamond stud put in. I was six. I thought it was awesome and I wore it all the time until my dad stole it to pay for crack. It was this one night when I was staying with him and his girlfriend Donna. It was getting close to bedtime and my dad told me to go take a bath and I did and when I got out of the shower he'd come into the bathroom and he was standing there with a towel, going, "Here, lemme help you dry off." Which I remember feeling weird about because I was definitely old enough to shower and dry off by myself. But he got a towel and started drying me off. It wasn't sexual in any way. He wasn't helping me dry off my dick or my ass or my legs or my feet or my waist or my stomach, just my shoulders and my hair. But he was rubbing my head, really getting in there, saying, "You gotta get it nice and dry, boy!" Then, all of a sudden, I heard this clattering sound. *Plink-ta-tink-tink-tink*.

"What was that?" I said. "Was that my earring?" I reached for my ear to feel it and it was gone. "What happened?"

"Oh, I don't know," my dad said. "I don't know what happened to it. Let's look for it."

I got down on my knees to look for it, and he got down on his knees to look, too. But he was only pretending to look for it. Because he knew it wasn't there. Because he'd already scooped it up. Think about how sick that is. This earring was probably cubic zirconia worth maybe ten dollars. He's a grown fucking man. He's my *father*, and to pay for his drugs he stole the only valuable thing I own, literally off my naked body, and then put on a show of getting down on his hands and knees to look for it. He put more effort into convincing me that he didn't steal it than he put into the sloppy way he stole it.

The same mid-fat weirdo who pierced my ear also tried to kidnap me once. Bohrer Park is Gaithersburg's main city park. It sits right behind my old apartment complex and it's got these big open fields and trails and a playground and a lake and a swimming pool. One afternoon there was this big fair going on near the lake and we went over there and I was with a bunch of other kids in the bounce house and the mid-fat tattoo-artist guy was in the bounce house with us and we were all jumping on him and it was weird because no adult should be in a bounce house with kids.

After the fair we were walking back to the apartment and my

mom and Kenny were walking ahead of us and we got separated. I started yelling for them but they couldn't hear me so this guy walked me back home. When we got there, the door was locked because for whatever reason my mom and Kenny hadn't made it home yet. Instead of waiting, this guy said, "Hey, man. Let's just take a ride." So I got in his car and he drove me around. He took me to a toy store and bought me an RC car, all this shit. At one point on the drive he turned to me and said, "If I black out while I'm driving, you put the car in neutral." Which doesn't even make any sense.

We drove around for what felt like hours. Then he took me to his sister's house and she went off on him. "What the fuck is wrong with you? Why'd you take some random kid from his parents and buy him a remote-controlled car?" It turned out my mom and Kenny had been frantically trying to find me but this was before cell phones so it was just me and this dude driving around.

Given all the random, fucked-up, and frankly unhealthy people who came in and out of my life when I was a kid, one thing that surprises me is that I wasn't sexually abused or assaulted. And when I say I wasn't sexually abused, what I mean is I'm like 99.9 percent sure I wasn't sexually abused. Sometimes I sit and I rack my brain: *Was* I sexually abused? Because when you think about the odds, it would totally make sense if I had been, and there were more than a few of what you might call near-misses.

The first one was Kenny's father-in-law from his first marriage, this black guy, older guy, nice dude. One time my mom and Kenny dropped me off to stay with this guy and his wife and they were sweet and they also had a hot tub and the guy asked me if I wanted to go in it. I told him I didn't have any swimming trunks. "You can go in naked," he said. "Or wear your underwear." So I did. Wear my underwear, that is. Naked would have been weird. Eventually his wife came home and was like, "Uh . . . this is really strange that you're in the hot tub with this kid in his underwear . . ." But that was it. There was no touching or anything like that.

Then there was this other guy who took me to my first baseball game to see the Orioles in Baltimore. It was this Christian family that we met at church. The dad wasn't weird at all. He was actually super-cool, but he was so cool that it made me uncomfortable because my mom's issues with men had wormed their way into my head and I didn't feel comfortable around men I didn't know.

My mom, literally, when I was a child, sat me down and told me, "If a man ever tries to rape you, as he's entering you, you scream out at the top of your lungs that you have AIDS." That was verbatim how she said it, too: "As he's entering you." And again, I was like seven and she was telling me this shit and I wanted to say, "Yo, what is AIDS? What is 'entering'? What are you *talking* about?! I just want to go play with my toys. Can I please go play with my toys?"

And that's exactly what it was with this dad and the baseball game. I was in the car with him and he was all "We're going to see the Orioles!" and he was so hyped and excited and loud that it scared me. He was just a dude being a dude about sports, but it freaked me out because I wasn't used to being around unfamiliar men.

So those were the near-misses, or what felt like near-misses. Maybe there's something buried deep in the vault and I've blocked it out because it was so traumatic, but I've been over it and over it and I don't think there is. I'd be totally honest about it if it had happened, but I'm pretty sure it didn't except maybe if you count that one time when I was nine and my dad's girlfriend Donna kissed me with tongue in the laundry room of their apartment.

Donna and my dad were together for like fifteen years. I don't think they ever got married. I want to say she was a bartender because one time when I was around four or five my dad took me to meet her at a bar—like that scene in the movie *Big Daddy* where Adam Sandler takes the kid to the bar and he's using the kid to hit on this cocktail waitress. It was like that, except I was sure she was the bartender because she was behind the bar.

Donna was super-cool except that she was a chain-smoker and a hard-core drug addict and alcoholic. She loved ginger ale, too, but let's not hold that against her. When she was younger, I think, she'd been a looker. But the years had been rough. She was skinny, white, and middle-aged. But like a *hard* middle-aged. Skin like a deflated football, like someone had taken a chicken neck and stretched it into a horse saddle. She was always wearing a fucked-up dress and smeared lipstick. Gross-colored lipstick, too. You know that department-store lipstick that's not red but it's not pink but it's not purple but it's kind of all three? Like that. The easiest way to describe Donna would be to say she looked like the Cryptkeeper from *Tales from the Crypt* but with a Van Halen hairstyle. And I'm not even joking.

At the time my dad was living in a room he'd rented in the basement of a house across the street from a church parking lot where I used to skateboard all the time. I was in the laundry room with Donna and I was eating Skittles and I don't remember how exactly it happened but she was definitely drunk and she walked over to me and she took some of my Skittles and she put them in her mouth and she said, "Hey, come here." So I walked over to her and she leaned down and she passed the Skittles from her mouth to my mouth, which then turned into her tongue-kissing me. It was more than one Skittle, so I could really taste the rainbow—and the cigarettes and the ginger ale and the lipstick, all of it at the same time.

I look back as an adult and obviously it was wrong and creepy and weird. But I won't lie, as a kid I was like, *"Awesome!"* Which is that weird double standard we live with where if any man does anything it's abuse, but if it's some hot lady teacher it's somehow not as bad, even though it is. But anyway, the kiss was all that happened. It wasn't like she grabbed my little balls or anything. So maybe that counts as sexual abuse. Except that it doesn't. Unless maybe it does.

Either way, Donna was probably the closest I ever came, and not any of Kenny's weirdo friends. I liked Kenny and it was fun with him having money and a van and all, but then the drinking got worse and things got strange and his friends got even stranger. A couple of them were Satanists or something. Like, actual Satanists. They said or did some wild shit to my mom and freaked her out. I remember one of them yelling, "Bitch, I'll kill you," or some shit, and then out of nowhere Kenny and his friends weren't around anymore because Kenny had cheated on my mom with some woman from the program, and that was that. One day he was gone and me and my mom were alone in #203 and there was no more van and no more Christmas and no more cable and we were back to getting tapes from the library and doing the *click, click, click* to try to get a decent channel on the television.

✗ﾅ☒☒◌̄◌̄☒

When we moved into the West Deer Park apartment, my mom didn't paint any big murals of fish or anything like that. Instead of murals, what we had in this place were shutters and mirrors. My mom used to hang up all these old window shutters that she'd salvage from dumpsters and paint them in different colors, usually black or white, which was how she dressed, too, in all white or in all black. It was almost like when she was feeling okay she'd wear the lighter color, and when she wasn't she was in the darkness. Very weird.

Then there were the mirrors. Fucking mirrors everywhere. Every room had at least one mirror, if not several. Big mirrors, little mirrors, mirrors from yard sales in decorative frames. In the living room she put up these huge plate-glass dance-studio mirrors, maybe six-by-four, one-sided, no frames, all three of them lined up against the wall. You'd think somebody who didn't like herself that much wouldn't want to look at herself that much, but she was obsessed with mirrors. You'd stand in the middle of the apartment and look around and see all these different images of yourself reflected and refracted from weird angles all over the room. It was like living inside a kaleidoscope.

I was probably around seven, eight years old when I first started hearing words like "schizophrenic." That was the big one. That and "bipolar." I'd hear my mom screaming them all the time. It was always bipolar this and schizophrenic that. *"I went to the fuckin' doctor, and this bitch told me that I'm fuckin' schizophrenic!"* I'm sure I heard those words way before that, too, but seven, eight years old is when you start to get a grip on everyday life and understand the world of grown-ups a bit, so that's the first time they registered.

We were always in and out of therapists' offices, and it was always a different therapist's office. Like, *always*. She preferred women doctors. There were a few men here and there, but mostly women. After the sexual assault and abuse she'd suffered, the last thing she wanted to do was take advice from something with a penis, which I totally get. But even the women doctors never lasted long. My mom would go for a month or so. It'd be two hours to catch three different buses to go to the appointment and I'd have to tag along and then wait those two hours and then wait for another hour in the waiting room and all the furniture would be brown and old and the floors would have these old nasty rugs. It smelled like old white people everywhere we went.

I'm pretty sure the only reason my mom put up with any of it was that she wanted medication. The caseworkers and doctors and therapists were just the obstacle to her getting the medication. We spent a lot of time in pharmacies, too, usually the CVS in the back of the supermarket. I'd be running around, goofing off, waiting for the pharmacist to fill her Zoloft and her Ambien and the muscle relaxers she took for her slipped disc and her sciatica. I was always playing with the blood pressure machine, sitting on that little bench and sticking my arm in the cuff. So much fun. I think every kid in America has probably fucked around with sticking their arm in that machine. But then inevitably the therapist, man or woman, would say something my mom didn't like—or, more likely, a truth that she didn't want to hear, like maybe you should stop drinking and sleeping with strange men from the bus stop. She'd come storming out of their office, screaming,

"Fucking asshole motherfucker!" Then she wouldn't see anyone and she'd white-knuckle it until the prescriptions started to run out, and then it'd be off to find someone else.

For self-medicating, my mom's drug of choice was Coors Light. She and Tony drank it like water. It was never hard liquor, just the cheapest beer she could find. I'd wake up in the mornings and there'd be empties littered across the living room and ashtrays piled up with stubbed-out Marlboro 100's. Poor people always smoke 100's because it's a longer cigarette and you can put it out halfway through and get two smokes out of it. My mom did that for as long as I can remember. From the time I was a baby our apartment always reeked of stale beer and smoke, like a pool hall.

She'd go through stretches of sobriety whenever she was rededicating herself to Christ or whatever, but it never lasted long, a few months maybe, and even when she was off the booze her body was still a cesspool of whatever her doctor was giving her, which, when she started drinking again, would leave her slurring and sloppy and stumbling around. She was always covered with a million bruises. She'd look at them and be like, "I don't know. I must be anemic or something." But the truth is she was constantly banging into shit, getting into arguments, beating on random guys she'd just picked up and brought home, putting her fists through shit, fucking everything up, crying, crashing, sobbing, passing out naked on the couch with my friends seeing her goods, and yelling and wheezing and coughing from all the cigarettes. It was pretty much every night. Imagine a Picasso OD'ing on the kitchen floor. That was my mom. And for a kid, to see this powerful person who's supposed to protect you, to see them all fucked up, it's kind of scary.

Inevitably the binges would be followed by withdrawals, especially when the doctors would cancel her prescriptions for being noncompliant. My mother used to sweat buckets when she'd sleep. I never understood it at the time but now I realize, "Oh, she was going through withdrawal." Still, every now and then she'd be all right.

Every now and then she would take her pills in the right amount and dial back on the booze just enough and the chemicals in her brain would be leveled out and she'd be okay for a day or two, but that never lasted because she'd quit taking the meds she'd been so desperate to get by going to all these doctors in the first place. She'd be like, "I don't like these pills. They're making me think different," and I'd think, "Well, yeah. That's kind of the point."

That these doctors never had the nicest waiting rooms had a lot to do with the fact that they were never the best doctors, just whoever would take her Medicare. I doubt many of them were genuinely interested in treating her. Most of them were just trying to manage her. That's the way it is with all of these programs for poor people, whether it's food stamps or welfare or HOC. We can't let those people die, but we can't help them, either. Or we don't want to help them, so let's put them off to the side and give them the bare minimum it takes to survive and not cause riots and burn everything down. I don't know that my mom wanted to be in therapy, but for people like her, in order to get access to the health programs and the welfare programs, the treatment is mandatory. You're under court order. The system is checking in on you.

When you grow up poor, one of the first words you learn is "recertify," which is a big-ass word for a six-year-old. You know how people say, "You had one job"? When you're poor that's your one job: You gotta recertify. Every six months you have to go down and recertify with the welfare office, with disability, with Medicaid, with EBT, which is food stamps, and with HOC, which is the Housing Opportunities Commission, the office that determines how much of your rent should be subsidized by vouchers and how much you have to pay yourself out of your welfare check.

As with the trips to the therapists, I was always getting dragged to these dull beige government offices. We'd sit and wait for our caseworker and everyone's miserable and everyone's angry, either because they're poor and they've been waiting there all day or because they work there and they've had to deal with belligerent poor people all day. A lot of the caseworkers reminded me of cops. They probably started out wanting to help people but after twenty years dealing with people like my mom it burned them out and they stopped giving a fuck.

Most of our trips to recertify would end in screaming matches, with my mom crying and wailing at the caseworker, "I'm going to be out on the street with my son!" I'd be sitting there, barely six years old, daydreaming about cartoons and hearing this and thinking, "We're going to be out on the street? What?!" Invariably she'd end up cursing everyone out and storming out of the building, grabbing my arm and saying, "C'MON, SIR ROBERT!" Which was a phrase I probably heard more than any other in my life. "C'MON, SIR ROBERT! C'MON, SIR ROBERT! C'MON, SIR ROBERT!" Then we'd storm out and I'd be scared we were about to be evicted and I wouldn't know what the fuck was going on.

Everything about being on public assistance is a double-edged sword. On the one hand, it's a dead end, a trap, which is why they call it trap music: "We in a trap." Because you're trapped selling drugs or you're involved in criminal activity or whatever. Welfare's the same thing. It's a place you can't get out of, because the system isn't really put in place to help people with problems. It's put in place to manage people with problems so they don't become a problem for the people who don't have any problems. It's like, "Here's enough food to eat, but barely. Here's an apartment that's only got a few rats in it. Here's enough money to stop you from going and breaking into somebody else's house that's nicer than your house." It's a low-key form of social control. They give you just enough money so you have to choose between paying the electricity bill and buying crack cocaine in the hope that it'll force you to choose the electricity bill.

At the same time, for somebody like my mother, that kind of management was what she needed. They could for sure make the system less frustrating and less dehumanizing, but she needed it because she wasn't capable of having the healthy relationships with friends and family that you need to help you through hard times, and she certainly wasn't capable of holding down a job.

The few times she tried to work, it ended in disaster. One time she worked at the supermarket for like three weeks, but then she couldn't do it anymore. This other time she got hired at the Chick-fil-A when that was new and poppin'. I actually went there once and saw her in her uniform and thought it was cool. Here was this woman that I had only ever seen sleeping until noon, and here she was getting up and going to work and shit. It made me proud. But it lasted for like two seconds and that was it. She couldn't handle the stress, couldn't bear being told what to do, which is what having a shit job is, having that shitty manager who wants to have power over you like a bully because his life sucks, too. My mom couldn't handle it. The system, on the other hand, gave her a routine that even she could manage: Live crazy. Recertify. Live crazy. Recertify. Live crazy. Occasionally she would clean houses for money on the side, but that was rare. So mostly we stayed poor, living in our subsidized apartment on West Deer Park with the shutters and the mirrors all over the walls.

The big mirrors in the living room were for dancing. She'd use them like a dance studio because she loved to dance, and she really could dance. She used to talk all the time about how, growing up, she wanted to be a dancer and how, when she and my dad were dating in the '90s, they would go to the club and tear it up. "We'd fuckin' make a circle," she'd say, "and we'd force motherfuckers to get out of our way. We would clear the floor and kill it and have a great time."

When I was about seven Janet Jackson had this video in heavy rotation on MTV, "Together Again," the one where she's in Africa doing some crazy dance and there's elephants and cheetahs and shit. My mom recorded it on the VCR and for the next few days she got in this zone where she watched it over and over, obsessively rewinding it again and again and again and again to learn the beats and learn the dance. Then she cleared the living room floor and got in front of those big mirrors and, bam, she fuckin' *nailed* it, and this was some forty-year-old white lady pulling off what only these super-fit twentysomething dancers on MTV could do.

My mom also loved to sing. She would do this thing where she would put a hand over one ear, like she was on a headset, and she'd go and stand next to this ghetto boom box we had, put her ear to the speaker, and sing along. That was where I saw her different moods come out because she would get in these zones. One night it would be nothing but Sinatra and "Fly Me to the Moon." The next night it'd be Nirvana cranked up with her screaming "Rape Me" at the top of her lungs. Then the next night it'd be gospel hymns and Joel Osteen worship music and nothing but "Praise Jesus, thank you, Lord!" Then a week of Run-DMC and then back to screaming "Rape Me" again. The DJ was whatever the chemicals in her brain were telling her to do at any particular moment.

When she was up, she was up, and the singing and dancing would go on late into the night. If it wasn't music she'd be reading the Bible, listening to sermons on the radio, painting and drawing dream catchers or bird feathers or different animals. She was always writing, too, scribbling away in this crazy beautiful cursive handwriting she had. She'd have a big jar of pens and pencils beside her, writing, writing, writing, writing, writing. Sometimes it was in notebooks, but more often on loose sheets of printer paper, filling pages and pages and pages that would pile up in her room. I never knew what it was she was writing. Poetry and stories. Psalms and scriptures, maybe.

She was obsessed with dictionaries. We had a million dictionaries in the house. We had regular dictionaries, rhyming dictionaries, small dictionaries, those big fucking reference dictionaries that are eight inches thick and sit on their own podium at the library. We had encyclopedias, too, almanacs and reference books about the Amazon and the Antarctic and the jungle. All of them were bound with leather, which my mom used to do herself. She'd take old leather jackets and leather purses she bought at the consignment store and she'd cut the leather into sheets and use a hot-glue gun to paste them over the cloth covers of the books and we'd have rows and rows of these tomes lined up on shelves that she made out of two-by-fours and cinder blocks.

We lived in that apartment for ten years. It's where most of my childhood memories are from, though there was nothing memorable about the place itself. Every apartment in a low-end apartment complex looks exactly like every other apartment in every other low-end apartment complex. You walk in the front door and you're literally in a box, an off-white, beige box. You have your living room box and your dining area box. Then off the living room is a sliding glass door that leads to a cement balcony, which is like an open-air box, and off the dining area is the kitchen box. Down the middle is a hallway and you walk back and it takes you to a bedroom box and then the bathroom box, and then a master bedroom box and off of that is another box and that's the walk-in closet.

My room moved around a bit because my mom liked to move her room around. She'd settle in one room and then one day up and decide she wanted another room, for no real reason. Usually I was in the regular, smaller bedroom, but there was a time when we set up the dining room as my room and there was even a stretch when I was in the master bedroom because she wanted to put her bedroom in the living room. Wherever my room was, I never had much in it. I only ever had a few toys that I'd collected over the years.

I never had many toys, but we always had pets. We had maybe a pet a year, but my mom would never take care of them and we for sure couldn't pay to take them to any vet, so they'd always get fucked up and then she'd just throw them away. We had this beagle that shit the size of human turds and then that motherfucker was gone. We had a gerbil that died.

We had a little shih tzu named Lincoln. Piece of shit, that dog. He would always bite you and he was annoying. My mom clipped his nails once and she didn't know that dogs have nerve endings inside their nails and she was just cutting them all the way off and he was crying and yelping and bleeding and she was like, "What?! I don't understand it! Why is he freaking out?" and she just kept doing it.

Mostly it was cats, though. All around West Deer Park you had all these people who didn't get their cats fixed, so they were always having litters and giving cats away, so you'd take a cat. Then you'd end up with this feral cat and it'd attack you and scratch you and my mom would always get fed up and toss them out. She'd literally grab them by the scruff of the neck, carry them howling and meowing down three flights of stairs, and throw them out into the parking lot and then I'd come home that evening, going, "Mittens?" But Mittens was long gone and that kind of didn't suck for Mittens because he probably ate better out of garbage cans than he ever did at our house.

When you're poor, you mark the time of the month by how much food is in the fridge. Since my mom was never awake in the mornings, breakfast was cereal. Occasionally there was oatmeal, but that was

With my mom and one of our many cats.

rare and what kid actually likes oatmeal? So it was always cereal and it was always the off brand. It was never Froot Loops, always Hood Loops. Lunch was sandwiches. That was easy. Ham, cheese, mayo, bread—done. Dinner was the one real meal I could kind of count on because my mom would at least be up by then, so she'd be hungry and we'd eat. Beginning of the month would be chicken, and she made this breaded chicken that was dope. We'd have that with Kraft mac & cheese or mashed potatoes, maybe green beans or peas. Then by the end of the month it'd be powdered milk and that goopy sweet corn that comes in a can.

For the last couple days of the month, the question was always, would we make it to the first? Sometimes we would and sometimes we wouldn't. The way welfare and food stamps are doled out, you ought to be able to make it. So the fact that sometimes we did makes you ask, "Okay, what happened in the months that we didn't?" And the answer is drugs and cigarettes and alcohol. That's where the money was going. She'd sell the food stamps for cigarettes or trade them for cash that she'd blow and we wouldn't have enough to eat and we'd get to the end of the month and she'd wake up and look in the cabinets and say, "Go to your friend's house for dinner and try to bring me back something."

My friend Mike, his mom worked at Dunkin' Donuts, and sometimes he'd bring us the leftover day-old donuts and that would be dinner. As a kid, at first you're like, "Fuck yeah, man! Donuts! For dinner! This is the shit!" Then the next night it'd still be donuts, and you'd still be like, "Awesome!" But by the third or fourth night, you're staring down at the plate, going, "Shit . . . donuts? Again?"

Since I had no older brothers or cousins for hand-me-downs, my clothes always came from Goodwill. We'd get vouchers for a certain number of pants and shirts per month. So that was what we would do. The only thing I ever got new were shoes, because kids' shoes are hard to come by at Goodwill. So every year I'd get a new pair of shoes and I loved them and I'd immediately want to show them off and I'd run out the door and go play in the dirt and then they wouldn't be new anymore and I wouldn't care.

For a long time I thought my mom was the way she was because we were poor. "If only Mom had money, she would be all right. If we had money, she wouldn't be angry all the time and yelling or screaming or upset." Which is how a kid thinks. I remember being in kindergarten and my mom was having one of those episodes where she was up in the middle of the night screaming at the walls about being broke and not having any money. She screamed about money all the time, about how we didn't have any money, how badly we needed money. That night I could hear her through the walls, so I took some sheets of construction paper and a pair of scissors and I cut out a bunch of rectangles and drew dollar signs on them and I took them to her. "Here you go, Mom. Here's money," I said, hoping it would stop the screaming, but it didn't.

The absolute worst part of us being poor was being poor in the suburbs, because being poor in the suburbs means not having a car in the suburbs. It's fucking brutal. All those stories old people tell about the Great Depression, "In my day, we had to walk five miles to go to the store for groceries . . ." That was me. In the 1990s. We walked everywhere. A half-day bus pass was $1.25 and an all-day pass was $2.50. Two measly dollars and fifty fucking cents, and most days we didn't have it. The rule we had was if something was more than ten miles away, we'd suck it up and pay for the bus. Anything closer than that, we'd walk. An hour to get to a friend's house for dinner? We'd walk. Two hours to get to a doctor's appointment? We'd walk. Freezing in my shitty coat in the dead of winter? Sweating my balls off in the swampy summer heat? Didn't matter. We'd walk.

The worst was going to the grocery store, because we had to haul all the food back. From my street, we'd walk all the way past the Exxon to the Food Lion and then back. It was treacherous, walking alongside this major road with no sidewalks at ten years old, barely weighing sixty pounds, carrying two massive gallon jugs of milk with the handles of the plastic bags digging into my hands and leaving these deep red creases in my palms. Then we'd get home and my mom would start in about all the problems with her back from all the walking, shouting, *"I've got a slipped disc!"* and *"My fucking sciatica!"* and who knows what else and who knows if it was real or if it was bullshit to get on disability. I do know she had calluses on her feet like a fuckin' horse, though, because I remember her making me file her calluses down, which if you've ever been to a fancy Italian restaurant and had them do that thing where they come by and shave Parmesan cheese on your pasta, that's what filing your mother's calluses down is like.

The thing that gets me is it didn't have to be as bad as it was. Part of the reason we were as poor as we were was because my mother's illness came with a deep streak of stubbornness and pride. She used to say, "I'm so proud I won't ask anybody to pass the salt." So she wouldn't ask for help even when we needed it. At Christmas, she wouldn't go to the Toys for Tots drive or any of those things. She can say it was about pride, but what it was really about was her fear of being judged and rejected by people.

"Hey, can you pass the salt?"

"Fuck you, bitch! Get your own salt."

"Oh, shit, I was scared that was going to happen."

So we suffered through it alone.

It wasn't all bad. I was going through some old papers recently, and I found a note she wrote me, basically an apology. "Dearest Bobby," it read. "I love you so very much! I'm sorry of my anger. You did wonderful today Bobby and I am very proud of "you." Love, Momma." And it was all decorated with hearts and smiley faces and a Jesus fish. So there were times when she was self-aware and lucid enough to write an apology like that, and during those lucid moments things could be okay.

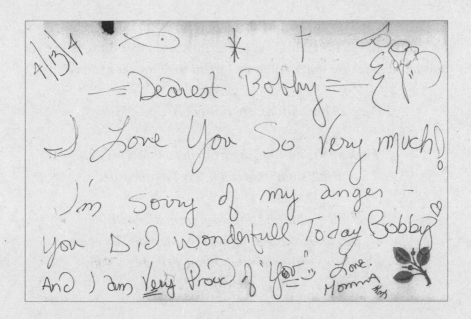

I know for a fact that I wouldn't be the rapper I am without her. She was the one who taught me how to memorize. One year in elementary school we did this living wax museum where the kids all had to dress up as some historical figure and read a short biography about who the person was. "I'm Thomas Edison, and I invented the light-bulb . . ." That sort of thing. I was Shakespeare, and when I showed my mom the bio I was supposed to read, she said, "You're not going to read it. You're going to memorize it." And she drilled into me the way to memorize, which is to commit one line to memory, then do that line plus the next line, then do those two lines plus the third line:

"My name is William Shakespeare."

*"My name is William Shakespeare. I was
born in Stratford-upon-Avon."*

*"My name is William Shakespeare. I was born in
Stratford-upon-Avon. I wrote* Romeo and Juliet.*"*

And on and on all the way through until eventually you've memorized the whole thing. It's one of the most valuable things she ever taught me, because that's still how I memorize my raps today.

"Fuck all the bullshit, dig from deep down inside."

"Fuck all the bullshit, dig from deep down inside.
I wrote this sittin' shotgun in my favorite ride."

"Fuck all the bullshit, dig deep from down inside.
I wrote this sittin' shotgun in my favorite ride. Reflecting
on memories from my childhood, bringing a baby
in this world, I hope my child good."

She taught me a lot about language, too. She was always making me look shit up. Any time I had a question, I could never get an answer out of her. All I got was "Look it up." She'd use a word like "equivocate" or "inexplicable" and I'd ask what it meant and she'd send me to the dictionaries and say, "Look it up." I hated it then, but I totally respect her for it now because it taught me to teach myself, to seek out the answers for anything I'm curious about.

My mom did have good qualities. When the chemicals in her brain were somewhat leveled, she'd help me with an after-school project or we'd go on a walk together and she'd surprise me by having a picnic in a basket. She was funny, too. The personality that comes out in my music, the comedic timing, making funny songs and shit like that, I know I got that from her.

Those windows of normalcy did happen, but they were rare and they'd last for maybe fifteen minutes, maybe an afternoon, tops. It was like on a cloudy day when the sun breaks through for a second and it feels amazing and you bask in it but then just as quickly another cloud comes along and it's windy and gray again. That's what the good moments with my mom were like. They were these glimpses into the person she might have been if the illness hadn't taken hold of her.

If spending hours listening to a woman scream at doctors on the telephone qualifies a ten-year-old boy to render a mental-health diagnosis, I'd say my mom was definitely bipolar, of that much I'm sure. But whether she was actually a borderline personality or schizophrenic or whatever, I have no idea. All I know for sure is my mom was the crazy woman screaming in the middle of the supermarket. She was a broken person. She screamed, she cried, she laughed, she slept till two in the afternoon. She had issues.

It's sad to reflect on now, this woman with all this talent and who she might have been but for all the abuse she suffered and the problems she had. It was sad to see her dance these amazing dances but then collapse because her back was seizing up or she was hacking and wheezing and about to pass out because of her COPD, the chronic obstructive pulmonary disease she had from all the chain-smoking and the drugs and everything else.

Because as traumatic as it was for me to live with her, I can only imagine what it's like for her to live with herself. Because we all have brains that are a little fucked up. We all have demons. We all have those dark, intrusive thoughts that pop into our heads, the voices that say scary, fucked-up things. We hear ourselves, and we're like, "How the hell did that thought even come into my head?" But someone who's sick the way my mother was sick is held captive by those voices, by this other side of themselves. Eventually they succumb, and those dark, disturbing voices become the only ones they can hear.

⌐ꟼꟼⴹᛠꟼⴺᒧᒧⴹ

When I was about seven, my mom sat me down one day being totally matter-of-fact and not hysterical at all and she said, "Bobby, I've been thinking about it, and I think we need to move to an Indian reservation."

She'd been getting way into Native American stuff for the past month. She'd always been mildly obsessed with it, wearing moccasins and painting dream catchers and shit, but now she was going overboard with it, going down to the library and checking out tons of books and videos about the history and culture of Indigenous People and painting pictures of them and talking about them and writing about them nonstop. Then out of the blue she hit me with this shit about moving to a reservation. "But you have to understand," she said as I just stared at her, "to get there we're going to have to get on an old canoe with paddles like the Indians did, and when we paddle upriver and wash ashore they may attack us with bow and arrows."

"Why?"

"To establish their dominance."

"But . . . why?"

"Because we will be perceived as the white man."

"Okaaaaaay . . ."

I kept nodding along, agreeing with her because she was the grown-up and I didn't know any better. But even then, even to a seven-year-old, moving to an Indian reservation didn't make a whole lot of sense. I mostly sat there, utterly confused, like, "All right, dawg. But I'm just trying to go ride my bike, so . . ."

Obviously, looking back, it was completely delusional. We were too poor to take a train into Washington, D.C., let alone buy a canoe and paddle to some reservation in Montana. Not to mention the fact that Native Americans live in houses and have electricity and casinos and they don't attack white people with bows and arrows anymore. But my mom wouldn't know that because she was literally watching the History Channel and coming up with these crazy ideas and, low-key, those History Channel shows always have white people structuring the narrative, so they never show Native Americans being regular people living in regular houses doing regular shit, just tepees and canoes and whatever, and that's what my mom believed because she was ignorant.

The Native American thing was just one of my mom's obsessive phases. She was always cycling through different ones, trying them on like outfits in a department-store changing room. It followed a pattern. She'd hook into something and then she'd start dragging me down to the library, where she'd check out literally every book or video they had on the subject. She'd dive into it furiously for a few weeks and then drop it like it never happened. Then she'd be on to the next thing. One month it was Native Americans, the next it'd be sewing—"We're going to make all of our own clothes!"—then that would be over, too.

I was never there for the inception of these things. I'd wake up from a nap or come in from playing with friends and find her surrounded by stacks of books, immersed in whatever the new thing was she was using to try to fix her brokenness. It would come out of nowhere, never announced or planned, and then just as abruptly it would be abandoned. It's what a lot of broken people do. They have no coherent drive or sense of self, so they're always searching for a way to make the world make sense.

One time my mom started whooping me with a belt every single night whether I'd been bad or not. She'd read somewhere that it was a good way to manage your children's aggression and keep them in line, so she started doing it every night at a set time. I'd be in my room in my tighty-whities playing with Hot Wheels and not misbehaving or anything and she'd come in with this thick-ass fuckin' belt and say, "You know what time it is." If I was bad, I got a whoopin'. If I was good, I got a whoopin'. It didn't matter. That went on for a month. Then, out of nowhere, it stopped as abruptly as it'd started because she'd read some other thing and was on to something else, which more often than not was the Bible. Through all the ups and downs of all her different phases, the one constant was religion. She always came back to it. It controlled her life, and so for a long time it controlled my life, too.

We had so many Bibles in our house. I think we had all the Bibles. We probably had more Bibles than we did dictionaries, and we had dictionaries like a motherfucker. There was the King James Bible, the New American Bible, and she made me sit and read that fuckin' book with her every fuckin' day—every single day, for as long as I can remember, pretty much from the minute I slid out the canal. Sometimes it'd be like a ceremony, with a bunch of candles and hymns and shit. Other times we'd just sit and read. And it was never for twenty minutes. Bible reading with my mom usually went on for forty-five minutes to an hour in the morning, then maybe another two hours at night. When she was going full tilt, there were times it went on for six hours straight—six fucking hours of "Abraham begat so-and-so who begat so-and-so who begat so-and-so," which was then followed by an hour of singing.

My mom dragging us to church was as fucked up as her reading the Bible. We were always going to church, but we never belonged to any one church. My mom changed up her churches and denominations the way she'd switch up her musical genres. It was whatever she was feeling, and week to week it was different. We went to white church, black church, Spanish church, Catholic church. We did Sunday church, Friday church, Thursday church. We did them all. One week we'd go to the laid-back, take-it-easy hippie church, then the next week we'd hit the rabid evangelical monster megachurch where the sermons were nothing but "Homosexuals shall not enter the kingdom of heaven, and pretty much everyone else is going to hell, too."

The church where I got baptized was one of those crazy Pentecostal speaking-in-tongues megachurches. That was bullshit. I was around ten, eleven years old with some fuckin' weirdo dunkin' me underwater. We had no connection to this place, but it was where my mom decided I needed to be baptized just because. Everybody there was white as shit, running around in the aisles, spouting gibberish. *"Habba-sabba-babba-babahbasa-habahaba!"* I had to wear this spongy robe and I was completely naked underneath it and the creepy pastor dude was touching me and taking my shoulders and leading me into the water and saying, "Accept the Lord!" and there were all these white people surrounding me like I was some goat they were about to sacrifice, going, *"Yesssss! Accccept the Looooord!"* They were putting their hands on me and spouting gibberish and my mom was right in there spouting gibberish with them and I wanted it to be over so I was like, "Sure. I accept the Lord. Let's do this." But it turned out that I couldn't actually be baptized until I had the Holy Spirit in me and if I wasn't speaking gibberish like they were, that meant I didn't have the Holy Spirit in me, so I started jibber-jabbering the same way everyone else was jibber-jabbering, *"Shoulda-boughta-Honda!"* And the moment I did, everyone started cheering and smiling. "Yeah, he's got it! He's got it!" But I was looking around like, "Yo, I ain't got shit. I'm just fuckin' with y'all." Then the creepy pastor guy dunked me in the water and

I came back up and that was that and we went to that church a few more times and then we never went back.

There were times when we wouldn't go to church at all, like for a year maybe, and then just as randomly we'd be back going to church all the time. It's funny, but I think the times my mom let go of religion were the times when she was actually happier, because she'd let herself do more than read the Bible and go to church. When my mom was with Kenny, that was kind of the best time, because that was when she let herself be more secular; I remember way more Chili Peppers and Nirvana from that era. Something about having a man taking care of the family allowed her this sense of freedom.

It was when she fell away from religion that we'd jump on a bus and go to the countryside and go for a walk and have a picnic, or meet up with some families she and Kenny knew from the program and I'd play with some random kids I didn't know while our parents hung out and drank and had a good time. But then inevitably she'd start to feel like she was losing her bearings and she'd go back to religion. She'd strip away anything that was indulgent or social or fun and drag us right back to the hard-core white-people-with-pursed-lips, everybody's-going-to-hell church. It was masochistic. The more of a sinner she felt she was, the more she used religion to punish herself. Not that it changed anything. She was still unwell, still an addict, still smoked like a fucking chimney. But instead of pounding beers and shots with friends, it would be wine and prescription medication and reading the Bible.

The hardest I ever saw her come down on herself was when I woke up one morning and I went to get some cereal and she was on her knees, crying and wailing and praying in the living room.

"Come here," she said, calling me over. "Say a prayer for your brother."

"My brother? What are you talking about?"

She kept wailing and praying and eventually I realized she was holding a funeral service for the fetuses she'd aborted. And not just abortions but miscarriages, too. I also got the sense that she was angry with her own mother because she'd gotten pregnant while she was a teenager living at home and her mom had made her get an abortion and that was why my mom had run away.

Whatever had happened with these pregnancies, she'd decided to hold this memorial service where she prayed for the fetuses and gave them proper names so that she could mourn them. I'd just happened to wake up and walk into the middle of it. It went on for the rest of the day, this long, totally insane, drawn-out thing. She was calling out the names of the fetuses, crying and wailing and rocking and moaning like a black woman in Compton who just witnessed her son getting gunned down in a drive-by, only it was my mom by herself in the living room in the middle of the afternoon.

I stayed for a bit, but most of the time it was like she couldn't even see me; it was like I wasn't there. I wanted to scream at her, "Yo, why are you doing this to me? I'm a kid. And not only am I a kid, but I'm *your* kid. I'm *alive*! And you're over there wailing about some kids who were never born but you won't do shit for me?!" But I knew better than to say anything, so I went back to my room and played with my action figures.

I also knew better than to ask her why she was doing it. Like any kid, I had legitimate questions about religious stuff that didn't seem to make any sense, like: "Why is Jesus always white?" or "The native people who live in the Amazon and have never heard of Jesus, why do they go to hell, too?" But any time I asked her anything like that, she'd just snap. *"Shut the fuck up! Don't ask me that!"* That was her blanket response to everything. She didn't want to hear any questions because she didn't want to admit that she didn't know the answers, and the reason she didn't know the answers was because she'd never asked the questions herself. To her the Bible was just a set of instructions to be followed blindly.

After everything my mother put me through with religion, it's shocking I didn't turn into a Satanist out of pure spite. I have friends and people I work with who are very religious, very spiritual, and I totally respect that. If it makes you happy and it can center you, then cool. I've kept an open mind about it, too. I still believe in a God and Higher Power, and maybe Christianity really is the way. Or maybe it's Islam. Maybe it's Buddhism. Maybe science has a lot of the answers, too. Who knows? But that open-mindedness, that curiosity, is exactly what my mother couldn't abide because she was clutching on to religion for certainty and stability.

My mom wasn't *actually* Christian. She didn't believe in Christ's teachings of love and kindness and turning the other cheek. She would get off the phone after one of her screaming fits with the welfare office and say things like, "I'd have killed and murdered a whole bunch of people if it wasn't for religion. If I wouldn't go to hell, there'd be some dead motherfuckers in this world."

Faith is never the most logical thing, but my mother's faith was straight-up *illogical*. I'd get frustrated about my homework or stub my toe or something, and I'd say, "Jesus!" and she'd spin on me and she'd scream, *"Don't take the Lord's name in vain, goddammit!"* Which pretty much sums up everything there is to say about my mom and religion.

When you're a kid you always get pissed off at your parents because you want something you can't have and you say, "Can I have it?" and your parent says, "No," and you say, "Why?" and your parent says, "Because I said so." Eventually you grow up and mature and realize the reason the answer was always "Because I said so" is because parents have to make rules that kids don't understand because parents understand the world in a way that a kid does not.

That's not true when your mom is mentally ill. My mom's rules didn't make any sense. She would wake up every morning and say the sky was blue, and for months and months the sky would be blue. Then she'd wake up one morning and say the sky was green, and when I asked her why, the answer was always "Because I fuckin' said so." When I was really young I never questioned any of it. But as I got older, turning six, seven, eight, I began to see plain as day that my understanding of reality was correct and hers was not. But I could never say anything. I could not have a rational conversation with her about anything. "What if Jesus doesn't exist, though? What if the Big Bang really did happen? Why do Adam and Eve have belly buttons? What if science is real?" If I ever asked her any question that included the word "why," fuckin' forget it. It would always end up with *"I hope you feel pain!"* and *"Don't ever talk to me again!"* and *"Get the fuck out of my house!"*

Words were my mom's weapon of choice. It could turn physical, too. If I asked a question she didn't like or if I was jumping off the walls, I'd get my ass whooped. But the physical abuse was random and the most it happened was maybe once a week or so. It was nothing compared to the psychological abuse. Or the racism.

The racism I experienced growing up was weird. It wasn't outside in, it was inside out. My introduction to racism wasn't the Klan burning crosses on our lawn. It was my mom talking shit about the black people in her life. When she was angry at the supermarket cashier, she'd scream, "That dumb, fat black bitch!" And I'd be like, "What does 'black' have to do with it?" But she'd inject race wherever she could, even with her son.

When she was really pissed she called me a nigger. *"You little nigger!"* She did it my whole life. The first few years I heard it, I didn't understand what she was saying; I didn't know what the word meant. But she knew, and she used it. And we're not talking about some white lady thinking she can get away with "nigg-*a*." This was the real shit. That hard "r" was always right there, and it would come out of nowhere. We'd get in an argument about some shit and I'd be pushing back, going, "This doesn't make any sense. Nothing you're saying makes sense. Why? How come?" And she'd just shoot back, *"Shut up, you fuckin' nigger!"*

My mom was like a walking Internet comments section. When she'd come at someone, she'd reach for whatever weapon would cut the deepest. If you were fat, she'd call you fat. If you were ugly, she'd call you ugly. If you were black, she'd call you a nigger. She wasn't walking around being racist all day, but she knew that the racism was there, like a weapon she could reach for whenever she needed it.

With the understanding of mental health that I have now, I can look back and know that somewhere inside my mom was the person she would have been and could have been if not for the abuse and the trauma and mental injury she suffered. I can look back and know that my mother wasn't a bad person. She was a broken person being shouted down by the demons inside her head. She was a little girl trapped alone in the dark with monsters, and she spent her entire life lashing out at the world because she was scared and in pain and she legit did not know if the sky was green or the sky was blue, which left her terrified all the time, which was why she'd cling to anything that told her what color the sky was, whether it was the Bible or some book that told her to hit her kid every night or to go live on some Indian reservation somewhere. And if I so much as questioned that, if I challenged whatever rules she was living by that week, even though I was just an innocent kid asking innocent questions, what I was really doing was questioning whatever tenuous, white-knuckle grasp she thought she had on reality. In her fucked-up mind, *I* was the one threatening *her*, and she would lash out in anger and fear to try to destroy me.

So I learned very early on to just not ask anything. Keep your head down. Don't poke the bear. Don't make a sound. Literally. The walls and the floors in our apartment were paper-thin. There was no privacy. You could hear everything your neighbor was doing, everything the person in the next room was doing. At first I never cared. I'd clomp around and drag my feet and make noise, and my mom hated it. If I walked hard in her house, I'd never hear the end of it. *"You don't EVER walk on the heels of your feet in my house!"* And if I said so much as a word in protest it was: *"Because I fuckin' said so!"* and *"Get the fuck out of my house!"* and *"You little nigger!"* and sometimes the back of her hand.

So I learned how to walk like a ninja, or a kitty cat. I'm not kidding. I spent my entire childhood tiptoeing around the apartment for fear of making a sound that might set my mom off, and that's how it was with everything. It was like I was always walking on eggshells, only the eggshells were made out of broken glass.

Later on in life I developed some issues with anxiety.

But we'll get to that.

ﾒﾑ石ﾉﾑﾜﾁ

After Kenny moved out, for a long time it was me and my mom except for this stretch of time when my dad and Donna the Cryptkeeper came to live with us and I had to share a room with them and it was annoying because Donna would sleep all the time and she never slept with bottoms on and whenever she'd lie down I'd see her pubes like a tarantula. But then I caught my dad smoking crack in the bathroom and my mom kicked them out and it was just the two of us again.

So much of my childhood was lonely. There were the Kenny years and the Tony years, but other than that my mom and I spent so much time alone. The people who were there were always in and out, coming and going. I have so many memories of being with random people that I can't place, people who were in our lives for a second and then they were gone. Often these people were complete strangers, by which I mean random people off the street. Since my mom couldn't form relationships with normal, healthy people, the only people in our lives were other broken people, which is a thing you see all the time with broken people: trying to fix those who are more broken than they are, as if by doing so they will somehow fix themselves. My mom was always trying to help other people pick up the broken pieces of their lives and glue them together because she couldn't do it for herself. One time she brought home this one kid and she was like, "Hey, meet this nice young man I found sleeping at the bus station." He was young and wore glasses and played video games all day and he was kind of a weirdo. He stayed with us for a few weeks. I'd wake up every morning and get out of the house as quickly as possible. "Okay, I'm gonna go play outside with my niggas! Bye!"

Then there was the time she brought home a whole family. They reminded me of the Manson family. Like, these people were straight off Spahn Ranch, these weird drifter-hippie types with this dark, menacing edge. There were six of them, the baby, the father, the mother, and a couple of friends. They lived in our living room for at least a month, maybe two, and it was fucking weird. Then, a few days after they finally left, I saw them on the local five o'clock news: The couple was going to jail because they'd killed their baby. It was probably by neglect or it got smothered or some other gnarly shit, but at the time it freaked me out because in my little-kid brain it was like these people were murderers who might have killed us.

If the people passing through weren't complete strangers, they were her new "friends." She met most of them through the program. There'd be A.A. and N.A. meetings at St. Martin's or Shady Grove. Thursday nights over here. Friday nights over there. I started going with her from the time I was four, maybe five. We'd go and we'd be in some dingy basement and there'd be a podium and people would get up and do the routine.

"Hi, I'm Steve, and I'm an addict and an alcoholic. I'm two and half weeks clean."

"Hi, Steve."

They'd tell their stories and everyone would clap and they'd get their seven-day chip or their two-year chip or whatever. All the kids would be at the back, scarfing down donuts and listening to the grown-ups tell these crazy stories about stealing money from their families. Every now and then some kid would get too rowdy while the addicts were trying to speak, and you'd hear somebody's mom shushing them from the front of the room. "SIMON! SHHHHHH!" For some reason it was always the white kid that was being weird. Thursday nights the meetings would be followed by a dance, which was like being in a cheesy '90s nightclub doing the Macarena but without any drugs or alcohol.

I wouldn't necessarily call A.A. "treatment." It's more like something to do for people who are fucked up. It's a social thing, a community, a place to belong. But you get a bunch of addicts together and it either goes good or it goes bad, and once you were outside the meetings it could go pretty bad. I'd see somebody up at the podium talking about how hard they were fighting to get sober and then the next week they'd be getting drunk in our living room with my mom. And even though the rules are that nobody's supposed to be dating, everybody's fuckin' everybody for sure.

That was our world. My mom would meet someone and we'd hang out with them for a bit and they'd become "friends." In some cases we'd even go and stay with them, sometimes for weeks, because that's how addicts are. They cling to each other. But then inevitably there would be the falling-out. It happened a million times for a million reasons, but it would typically end with my mom arguing and screaming and yelling and then shaking me awake at two in the morning with "We're gettin' the fuck out of here!" Then we'd go storming out, walking or hitchhiking for four miles back to West Deer Park in the middle of the night.

It happened even when relationships were going well, because my mother was so quick to end them, which was a power thing. She'd blow it up so she could feel like she was the one leaving to avoid being the one who got left. My mom was the type who, if you tried to help her, she'd get mad at you and call you thirty-five times in a row and when you didn't answer she'd leave you screaming voicemails that went on for five minutes until the voicemail machine cut her off midsentence. Then she'd call back and scream for another five minutes. She did that to everyone in her life. I know. I've heard the voicemails. People used to play them for me.

A lot of the moving around from church to church to church was because my mom would meet somebody new through the program. They'd invite us to their church and we'd go and they'd be nice people but then they'd say something my mom didn't like or my mom would freak out and either we'd be asked to leave or my mom would storm out, muttering, "They think they're too good for us," or some shit like that.

We never stayed at any of these churches long enough to form any real relationships or community, which is half the reason for going to a church in the first place. Even with all the churchgoing we did, I don't remember a single person from any of the churches except for that one dude who took me to a baseball game who I thought was a child molester but who was just really into baseball.

Some of these families, we'd never see them again. Others we'd cycle through again and again, and those relationships were the closest my mom came to having real friends. They were an odd crew. There was Cindy, the witch we lived with for a while at West Deer Park. There was Ruth, the woman who celebrated Christmas Eve Eve and owner of the floor where my parents smoked crack and fucked and made me. Then there was Carol Ellen, who was probably my mom's best friend.

Carol Ellen was a big woman, like Jabba the Hutt big. She was married to this super-cool guy named Alex. He was some kind of Middle Eastern dude who worked in construction doing big jobs, like restoring the Washington Monument. To me, they were rich, like filthy rich. Every time we went to their house, everything was nice as shit. They had two or three cars and a dog and basement and TVs and VHS tapes and video games and Jordans and their kitchen was full of sodas and Cheetos.

Carol Ellen and my mom genuinely cared for each other, but they would fight over everything. We'd be hanging out and everything would be fine and then out of nowhere they'd both be screaming "Motherfucker this" and "Goddamn that" and "Fuck you, you fat bitch!" and "Fuck you, you crazy bitch!" Then we'd be storming out Carol Ellen's door at three in the morning.

It was because of Carol Ellen that we were Catholic for three weeks. She and my mom were both super-religious and one day they were talking, and the next thing I knew my mom popped up and said, "We're Catholic now." All of a sudden I was going to Mass and kneeling and eating the Body of Christ and thinking, "Huh. This is weird." But then my mom and Carol Ellen had another one of their fights and on a dime my mom said, "We're not Catholic anymore." So we weren't Catholic anymore. But it had nothing to do with God or theology; it was because my mom didn't want to see Carol Ellen again.

Of course, we did see Carol Ellen again. After a few months or maybe a year we cycled back and they were best friends again and it was like nothing happened, because of course they would never acknowledge or deal with what happened, even though the only way to move past something is to face it. But nobody in the program ever

At Carol Ellen's for Christmas.

did that. Like, nobody. Everybody was always angry and yelling and screaming or passive-aggressively biting their tongue until it all blew up again, which is a dynamic you see in poor families, especially poor families struggling with addiction.

If you have real money and status and success and a happy family and a spouse who loves you, it's easy to let the little shit slide. If somebody makes a comment or the cashier at the Food Lion is rude to you, you can say, "Whatever," and let it roll off your back because you've got more important shit to deal with and you've got a sense of dignity and self-respect and self-esteem from plenty of other places and nobody can take that away from you. It's when you don't have that, when you're fighting for every last scrap of dignity and respect you can get, that all this petty, meaningless bullshit becomes life or death. *"In this house, we call the TV controller the remote!" "Well, I call it the clicker!"* Which will then turn into not speaking for three months. When you're an addict, there are no goals, no hobbies, no enjoyment of life. Which is why those people are angry. They have nothing else in their life. They get addicted to the anger and the dysfunction because it's the only emotion they get to have.

Which is why I say I'm not sure you could even call my mom's relationships actual friendships, even though she and Carol Ellen have known each other for going on forty years now. It's more like Carol Ellen was someone my mother clung to because she didn't have anyone else to cling to, and for whatever reason Carol Ellen kept bringing my mother back into her life. Most people my mom would run off in a matter of weeks or months. The main reason was because of her animosity and envy toward them, especially women who didn't have to work and had a man who provided for them and had kids who rode bikes and did all the normal shit. She resented those moms because she wanted to be them, but she felt like she wasn't good enough for them and that she was being judged by them, which she probably was. So all these people would come and go and fade in and fade out and at the end of the day it was always just me and her and then one day the doorbell rang. I went and opened the door and it was my two older sisters, Amber and Geanie, ready to move back in.

It had been at least four years since I'd seen them, four years of them being nothing more than a phone call at Christmas. But some things had transpired, apparently. Amber and Geanie had been getting tired of Eugene's bullshit. To hear them tell it, they'd basically been left to fend for themselves because Eugene would take off, leaving the two of them and Jesse alone in this shack of a house they were renting, not knowing how to get food or what to do. Then Jesse accidentally set the garage on fire and the landlord's car was inside and it exploded, so then they got kicked out and Jesse and Eugene were living in Eugene's car and Amber and Geanie were out in the streets on their own, so they jumped on a Greyhound and came all the way back to Maryland to live with my mom. Jesse hadn't come with them. He'd stayed in California and then moved in with an aunt for a while before ending up in foster care.

My siblings were a total abstraction to me. My mom used to sit around cursing Eugene, going, "He stole my kids. He stole my kids." But

Amber.

it was like it didn't compute for me that I was anything other than an only child. Now Amber and Geanie had shown up out of nowhere and I went from being trapped alone with my mom to having actual siblings in this weird, dysfunctional, almost kind of family. But I had no concept of them as my sisters at all, so much so that I can remember thinking, "Oh my God, these girls are *so* pretty." I was acting all shy and awkward around them the same way you would with a cute girl at school. Which is weird, a kid having a crush on his sisters because they're cute and he doesn't realize they're his sisters. But that came and went and eventually I figured it out. "Oh, they're my *sisters*. Right. Got it."

Amber was cute but she had buckteeth because she sucked her thumb when she was a baby and still does to this day, even as a woman in her late thirties. Super-light skin, but also obviously black. Super-skinny with black hair, big beautiful lips, strong nose, brown eyes. Super-ghetto, too. If you look up "ghetto" in the dictionary, you'll find Amber. That black woman comin' around the corner shouting, "Hell, nah, nigga! You better come get this pussy, nigga! You betta take care of yo kids out here, nigga!" That's Amber.

She's a beautiful person, though, very sweet, a beautiful soul. If you knew her, you'd see that the kind person on the inside shone a little brighter than the rough and tough person on the outside. If she'd had decent parents, who knows what kind of life she might have had. But she lost everything the minute she came out of a vagina like my mom's into the arms of a father like Eugene. When Amber came home from California, she was in high school and she would still sit on the couch with *Go, Dog. Go!,* trying to learn how to read. She'd have to sound out the words, like, "The . . . little . . . dog . . . went . . . to . . ." And I'd be like, "Holy *shit*." I couldn't believe it. For everything my mom did to me, at least I learned how to read. Eugene wasn't even sending the girls to school.

Geanie was, and still is, different from Amber. Where Amber was more serious, Geanie liked to cut up and crack jokes. She had an attitude, too. She was down to fight and she saved me from an

Geanie with her daughters,
Daisjha and Brianna.

ass-whoopin' at least once by getting up in this kid's face, like, "You wanna fight my brother, you gotta fight me, motherfucker." I saw that and I was like, "Oh, okay. This is what it's like having an older sister. Cool." Geanie looks mixed but has olive skin that tans brown in the summertime. Curvier than Amber but still in shape.

I thought it was super-cool having Amber and Geanie home, but they took off almost as soon as they showed up. When they first knocked at our door my mom was all overjoyed. "My babies! I have my babies back!" But Amber and Geanie weren't babies anymore. They were moody, rebellious teenagers. They were young, assertive, independent black women who cussed and back-talked and yelled even louder than my mom did, and my mom couldn't handle it. She had to have everything exactly her way, and Amber and Geanie weren't going to go along with that.

Maybe a couple of weeks after they got home I heard Nas blasting out of their room, "I remember the first time, girl, you and me;

F-U-C-K-I-N-G," and my mom was banging on their door, completely losing her shit. "What is this music? Is this music about *sex*?!" Meanwhile, last month on the Terry Lee Show, she'd been screaming "*Rape Me!*" into a boom box.

Amber and Geanie would also just refuse to go to school. They were in and out, skipping and hanging out with friends whenever they wanted, and this one morning my mom was yelling at Geanie, who was trying to stay in bed and sleep. Geanie kept shouting, "Fuck you, bitch! I'm not going to school! I don't give a fuck!" So my mom stormed off to the kitchen and got a bucket full of ice water and came back and dumped it all over her. Then, when Geanie still refused to get up, my mom called the cops on her for being truant. Which, let's be honest, is not how you raise a child. You don't call the cops on your own kid for not wanting to go to school. I mean, who does that?

So there was always some bullshit drama going on, and a few months after they moved in they moved right back out and went to live with Eugene's mother, Grandma Etta Jane, who lived up in Stewart Town. Amber and Geanie never lasted long at Grandma Etta Jane's, either. They were too all over the place and they ended up butting heads with her, same as with our mom. They'd get pissed off at her and then they'd come back home and then either my mom would kick them out or they'd get pissed off and leave on their own and they'd go back to Etta Jane's. Then she'd kick them out and Amber would come home and Geanie would go stay at a boyfriend's but then that would get fucked up and then Geanie would come home but then Amber would leave and then she'd come back and then they'd both leave and then they'd both be back again and sometimes I'd go with them and that was the first time I ever heard somebody getting shot.

Stewart Town was the hood. You didn't fuck around in Stewart Town. But one night Geanie lied to her grandmother and said she was taking me over to a girlfriend's house but then really she took me to this fucked-up drug house and nobody was around but there were all these drugs and guns and shit. Then she left me there while she was running around and getting drunk with these dudes out in the neighborhood. I was in this bedroom and it was very cramped and there was a window and I remember crying myself to sleep because I was alone and I didn't want to be alone.

Then all of a sudden I jolted awake to the sound of gunshots and screaming. I freaked out and I ran downstairs and there were cop cars everywhere and a body on the ground and I was frantically looking through the people gathered in the streets and I saw Geanie and she saw me and she ran over and grabbed me and said, "Thank God!" Then Etta Jane came running through the crowd and found us and she wasn't having any of Geanie's bullshit. She was like, "What the hell y'all doin' out in the streets?!" and then she dragged us back home.

Once we got home, she made us go upstairs and lie in bed and watch cartoons and I remember Geanie being so salty with me, like it was my fault that we got into trouble or some shit, because if she hadn't had to leave me alone in the drug house then she wouldn't have gotten caught doing anything and she could have stayed out having fun. Me, I was just happy to be with an adult who could protect me. Plus I was stoked because *Looney Tunes* was on and I was like, "Yo, I got Wile E. Coyote right now," which made me feel safe and happy.

So Geanie and Amber weren't exactly what you'd call role models, but they did teach me something important: They taught me that it was possible to stand up to our mom. Until they showed up, no matter how crazy or abusive my mom got, I never questioned her, never stood up to her, never complained. Because I didn't know what she was doing was wrong. She was my mom. She'd built my world. She'd built my reality.

When Amber and Geanie first moved in and started causing all kinds of trouble, I used to tattle on them all the time. They called me Mom's Snitch, Mom's Informant, because I thought we all had to live according to Mom's crazy rules. I'd seen so many people butt heads with my mom as they came in and out of our lives. But seeing her own kids do it, that was different. I saw these two teenage girls asserting themselves and defying her and back-talking her and getting away with it, and slowly, gradually, it opened my eyes a bit. "Oh. Maybe Mom isn't always right." The lives Amber and Geanie were living maybe didn't represent the healthiest choices, but they showed me at least that there was another way to live. They were the first crack in the prison wall that allowed me to see the daylight outside.

ꙮꙮꙮꙮꙮꙮ

I never got a bucket of ice water dumped on me for refusing to go to school, in part because I was so well trained that I never talked back or questioned my mom about anything, but also because I genuinely loved going to school.

My first school, Summit Hall Elementary, was right across West Deer Park from our apartment. It was exactly the kind of school you'd want your kid to go to. Super-cute. Little classrooms with walls covered in colors and shapes and kids' arts and crafts projects. I was the poor kid with the weird mom, but when you're that young, you can make friends with pretty much anybody and you don't notice who's poor or who's got a fucked-up home. You might notice who's got Super Nintendo and who doesn't, but when you're at their house, you're so happy to be playing Super Nintendo that you don't think about it that much. School was the one place I got to go and be like everybody else. I was also different from my mom in that I genuinely liked people. I hated being alone all the time. I was so hungry for normal relationships with normal people that I couldn't wait to run into my classroom every morning.

But as I moved up through the grades, my love of school started to wane because so many of the teachers and administrators started treating me like I was a rotten apple. And sure, I was a cutup and a class clown and I was fidgety during story time, but A) I was bored and I wasn't being challenged, and B) I had a bony ass because we didn't have enough food to eat. If you have a bony ass and it's time to sit crisscross applesauce—which is what they say now because you can't say "Indian-style" anymore—then you're going to be fidgeting and getting up and lying down and moving around because it's un-comfortable to sit crisscross applesauce when you have a bony ass because you're not getting enough food. I didn't have any problems other than we could have used some more food stamps, but instead of getting me more food stamps the school decided I was a problem that needed to be fixed.

There were a few teachers who knew that I was underprivileged, so they were extra patient and went the extra mile. But the truth is that most of them didn't give a shit. They all thought I was fucked up even though I wasn't. I'll grant that, statistically, they probably weren't wrong to think of me the way they did. Odds are that a fucked-up situation like mine is likely to produce a fucked-up kid. But I was the exception, and they couldn't see me as an exception.

In fourth grade, the school started making me see a therapist. We found one, but it wasn't ever really about what was the best for me so much as who took the insurance. I started seeing this one ther-apist named Mary and this was at the height of the ADHD craze and this therapist Mary said I had ADHD but then maybe I didn't have ADHD and then maybe I did. So she convinced my mom to put me on Ritalin or whatever's the cheapest generic form of whatever Ritalin is. So for a while I was on Ritalin and what I remember most about being on Ritalin is that everything . . . slowed . . . down . . . and . . . became . . . really . . . really . . . really . . . boring. It was like the world of all the things I enjoyed became dull so I could focus on other shit, like math. I'd be in school absorbing all this information and it was like I was present but I wasn't. Things I used to love and care about, I didn't give a fuck about anymore. If anything, it almost made me feel depressed. And then my mother had a falling-out with that therapist, so I wasn't on Ritalin anymore.

After the Ritalin failed to fix me, they had people start coming into the classroom to monitor me and see how I behaved, and of course the diagnosis was "He's constantly moving and fidgety and jittery" and all this other shit. So then there was this big meeting with the principal and my teacher and my counselor and they brought in my mom because they feared there was "an issue at home."

Which, obviously, there was.

Everyone at the school knew that my mom was nuts. She could hold it together long enough for when the cops came by or when social services visited the house to do an inspection or whatever, but at school, with her picking me up and dropping me off every day and having to regularly interact with humans, there was no hiding it. And when she went into this meeting, she lost it. She started rambling and screaming about how she'd been raped and she'd been sodomized and telling all the fucked-up stories she used to tell me, and all these school administrators sat there with their jaws on the table like, "Holy shit."

After the meeting the administrators made me take this aptitude test that measures how fucked up you are. Whatever the standard is for "fucked up," apparently I met it. They said that I needed to be taken out of Summit Hall and sent to a school for the emotionally disturbed. I put up a fight about it. I kicked and screamed and said, "I don't want to go!" My mom didn't want me to go, either. She fought back. But the ultimatum was "If he doesn't go to this other school, then we're going call social services and they're going to take him away." We had no say in the matter. We never did. No poor person does.

So they took me out of Summit Hall and now I was the kid who had to ride the short bus. Instead of a five-minute walk across the street to school, I was on this route where it literally took the driver three hours to drive around and pick up the fucked-up kids from all over the county so they could corral us and dump us off at a central location.

I hated it immediately. The school itself, Shady Grove, was just a regular school with one classroom of special-ed kids on campus. So all the "normal" kids had their homerooms together and I was stuck in this special-ed class. Back at Summit Hall I'd been the kid with the weird mom and all the kids were cool with it and I fit in with no problem. In the special-ed classroom, everybody was the poor kid with the weird mom. Now I was the normal one by comparison. Most of the kids had severe issues. There were extremely slow kids. There were autistic kids. There were a bunch of violent hood kids with anger management issues who always wanted to fight and argue and start some shit, like this one black kid who would always sniff his upper lip and was a fuckin' bully and an asshole.

If you acted out, you had to go into this room called ASC. I can't remember what the "A" stood for but I'm pretty sure the "SC" was solitary confinement. It was a padded detainment room where there was one lonely window and all the walls were covered with those blue vinyl mats they have in gym class. The teacher and the aides would be in there like asshole cops, pinning the kids' arms and stepping on their backs to hold them down because they were going crazy and having tantrums. The kids would be crying and screaming, "You're hurting me!" and they'd have to stay there for like thirty or forty minutes until the teacher said they could come out again. It was fuckin' gnarly.

I had to go to the padded room a few times, usually for dumb shit like being a clown or sassing the teacher or the time I got into an argument over snacks. But these other kids were going into the ASC all the time because they were just violent. I got bullied and picked on constantly, kids pushing me and messing with me. I wanted to fight back but I knew I couldn't. I knew if I fought or incited or participated in violence in any way, I would further prove their point that this was where I belonged. So I didn't. I allowed myself to be bullied, and I took it and took it and it fuckin' sucked and I fuckin' hated it.

I'd sit there in class and think to myself, over and over, "I don't belong here." But then I did the same thing at home, too. I'd be up in the middle of the night, listening to my mom scream, thinking, "I don't belong here." I'd be walking home from the store two miles in the snow carrying thirty pounds of groceries, thinking, "I don't belong here." Everywhere I was, I never belonged, but I felt it especially in that special-ed class because at lunch and recess we'd go and be with all the regular kids and I'd play with them and I got on fine and I knew that was where I belonged. I even met this cute girl named Sarah and I would sit with her every day at lunch and we were fifth-grade boyfriend and girlfriend.

But it also sucked outside the special-ed class because so many of the normal kids liked to bully and beat up on the special-ed kids. I remember getting pinned up by this one asshole in gym class. He was a fuckin' jockstrap and he grabbed me by my neck and shirt and pinned me against the lockers in front of all the girls and held me up and made me feel powerless, and I know he only did it because he was jealous that I was talking to all the girls and they liked me better than him even though I was one of the special-ed kids and he fuckin' hated that.

The whole thing was fucked up. One of the worst experiences in my life. The kids were so mean and it fucked me up so much to the point where I couldn't stand it anymore and eventually my mom decided to take me out and homeschool me. She found a desk for me to sit in and this ghetto chalkboard that she nailed to the wall and she even made me this fake badge for a fake school. She took my picture with a disposable camera and she cut it into a square, like an ID photo, and then she laminated it onto this card that made me look like I was enrolled at some academy that didn't actually exist.

The badge looked legit, so one day I put on a nice collared shirt and some khakis and I clipped the card to my breast pocket and got a clear plastic bucket and went over to the nicer neighborhood right behind my neighborhood in the back of Summit Hall Elementary. I knocked on people's doors and said, "Hello, my name is Bobby, and I'm here for the Poor People of America Fund. Would you like to donate a dollar or more to the cause of blah blah blah or whatever?" And all these rich white people, they didn't even give a fuck. They were like, "Yeah, whatever. Here's a dollar. Just get the fuck out of here."

I was killing it, hitting all these houses and getting at least a dollar each, and sometimes more. Pretty quick I upped my ask. Now it was "Would you like to donate five dollars to the cause of blah blah blah or whatever?" and some of them would go for it. But then I pushed it too far because my dumb overeager ass started hitting the same houses twice and this one dude was like, "Let me see me your credentials." I showed him my credentials and he said, "Something's not right about this. What the fuck are you doing, kid?" So I ran, and that was the end of the Poor People of America Fund. Before it was all over I made out with like seventy bucks, which was the most I ever got out of homeschooling because my mom was into it for maybe two weeks and then she was like, "This is too much work. I'm over this," and she quit.

She didn't teach me shit. Literally the only thing I can remember from my mother homeschooling me is addition, subtraction, and Hooked on Phonics. She'd sleep until two or three in the afternoon and I could only see my friends when they got home from school, so I'd wake up and fuck around the apartment with nothing to do—and the little kid who loved school because it was the one place where he could go and be a normal kid and hang out with other normal kids and make normal friends, that kid never loved school ever again.

ㅊㄲㅋㅋㅆ

One of the happiest days of my life was the day we took the bus to the courthouse in Rockville to the little chapel they have inside the government building: Tony and my mom were getting married. It was me in my Goodwill suit, Tony in a white button-up with a blazer, jeans, and cowboy boots, and my mom in a dress she'd bought at Tina's Consignments, plus this veil that she'd made herself that wasn't really a veil but more like Jesus' crown of thorns with all these fake berries and twigs and shit. I was their witness and the clerk married them and, like that, she was no longer Terry Lee Stone. She was Terry Lee Bransford. I had a stepdad again and I was so happy about it because I loved Tony so much.

It had been a strange road back for the two of them. At some point in the homeschooling years, we started taking those long bus rides to see Tony in prison again, first at Seven Locks and then to this other spot that was like a halfway house, called the PRC, the Pre-Release Center.

The PRC was in White Flint and to get there it was another all-day thing with a bunch of transfers, two buses and a train, followed by a super-long walk up and down a giant hill. We'd go once a week or when we could afford it. The PRC was basically prison lite. It reminded me of a giant cafeteria, and not in a good way; you wouldn't want to live in a cafeteria. Everything seemed cold. But at least here Tony wasn't behind glass. We could actually see him in person and sit at a table together and hang out and chat. Most trips, at some point they'd tell me, "Hey, stay right here," and leave me to go off and be by themselves for a bit. Tony had his own room. I don't think conjugal visits were allowed, but they probably found a way to do that anyway.

A halfway house full of semi-rehabilitated criminals probably isn't the safest place to leave a kid, but I'd been left in worse. They had food and a Ping-Pong table, which was cool. You'd go outside and everyone would be standing around smoking. Most of the inmates were nice, actually. I think they were just lonely and happy to spend a few hours entertaining some kid. I'd wander around and talk to them. One time this guy was playing chess and he asked me if I wanted to play and I told him I didn't know how and he said he would teach me. So I sat down with him and the guys he was playing with and they were the coolest dudes, patiently teaching me how all the pieces moved, and I just got it. I don't know why I did, but I did. For me, the moves and the strategy, I understood it and I liked it and I'd sit there and play with these convicts for hours. As much as I'd like to sit here and tell you I was Bobby Fischer, I was not. I was okay, but I learned. More than the game, I learned about myself, like how to think and be patient. Chess taught me that the more time you put into something, the more you get out of it, which would be helpful to me later on.

Tony moved in with us after he got out of the PRC. Kenny had been gone for a while by that point, but my mom was still technically married to him because she never bothered to get a divorce because she's fuckin' lazy. So she was still married to this white dude while Tony was living with us. I think that bothered Tony and they used to fight all the time, more than they ever did back when we lived in Germantown, and they fought a lot there, too. They would argue and yell, fight and make up, fight and make up. Tony used to tear her apart, but only verbally. He never hit her except once, and it happened totally by accident the time he was breaking into the apartment to hold us hostage.

The night it happened, she'd kicked him out after another huge fight. I'm pretty sure it was about drugs. There were times when they were sober, but they never lasted long, and at this point he was back on the drug shit and my mom was on her sobriety shit and she didn't want to deal with him being fucked up so she'd told him to leave. Which is what happens any time you get two addicts together. It works as long as they're on the same page. If they both want to get sober, they can take each other to meetings and it's cool. If they both want to go on a bender, it's not healthy but there's no friction about it. But when one of them wants to get sober while the other one wants to party, then it gets nasty. Each one is blaming the other for doing this or not doing that and whose fault is what and it's "You fuckin' asshole!" and "You fuckin' bitch!" and on and on and on.

So that's what my mom did to Tony. "I don't want you around my kid when you're drinking!" Which made sense, except that it was hypocritical because she'd been getting shitfaced with him the week before and she'd probably be getting shitfaced with him again the week after. But at that exact moment she was high on her self-righteous "I'm getting sober and giving myself to Jesus" kick, and Tony wouldn't stop drinking so Tony had to go.

But Tony wanted to stay. Tony wanted it to work. So it was pitch-black outside and my mom and I were in the living room watching *Sanford and Son* and all of a sudden we turned and we saw Tony pulling himself up onto our balcony. We were apartment 203, but the way the apartment numbers worked, we were actually three floors up from the ground. This fucker, stone drunk out of his mind, had climbed three stories of concrete balconies to get in, because that's who Tony is, fucking super-jacked and fearless.

He pulled himself over the railing and he started banging on the sliding glass doors and screaming my mom's name. *"TERRY LEE! TERRY LEE!"* Then he reached down and grabbed the handle of this sliding glass door and yanked it open like he was ripping a phone book in half. This door had one of those bullshit aluminum deterrent sticks that you put down and it keeps the door from opening from the outside. That shit crumpled like a Red Bull can.

My mom jumped up and tried to push the door closed, yelling, *"Tony! No!"* So Tony was trying to push one arm through the door as she was leaning in to try to close it and he jerked his arm back and he elbowed her in the face and busted her lip open and she started screaming and there was blood everywhere. I was scared, but I knew it was an accident because I knew Tony wouldn't hurt a fly. Or, Tony wouldn't hurt a woman or a child, let's put it that way.

He forced his way in, and my mom, blood running down her face, stumbled over to the front door to try to get out and he ran behind her and caught her just as she opened it and he pushed her out of the way and slammed it shut and locked it, trapping us inside.

So technically he took us hostage but when I say "hostage" I don't mean he held a gun to our heads. He just blocked the door and didn't let us leave for a few hours. Which is legitimate being-held-against-your-will kind of shit that 100 percent meets the legal definition of kidnapping, but to me it wasn't really "kidnapping" kidnapping, because I knew Tony was such a good guy. It was more of a *"Nobody's fuckin' leavin' till we fuckin' work this shit out!"* kind of thing.

From there the two of them went at it, yelling and fighting as usual. The only thing I remember is my mom screaming, *"The only dick I suck is my husband's!"* Which, you can sort of reverse-engineer what he was accusing her of, though since she was technically still married to Kenny at the time, I'm not sure what she meant by it. Whatever it was, they went at it all night. Eventually she coaxed him away from the door to talk in some other part of the apartment, leaving the door unguarded. Then she turned to me and shouted, *"Run, Bobby! Run! Run! Get the fuck out of the house and call the cops!"* I jumped up and ran to the door and opened the dead bolt and raced down the stairs to the neighbors', where I told them what was happening and the cops came and took Tony away.

I don't know if he went back to prison or he just spent a few nights in jail, but pretty soon after that, the divorce from Kenny came through and my mom forgave Tony for taking us hostage and took him back and that's when they got married.

After that, life was pretty good again for a while. It was almost like being a real family and having a real dad. Not long after they got married, Tony took me to the Montgomery County Fairgrounds to see fireworks for the first time. It was a hot summer evening and we walked there from our apartment and all the other kids were running around with glow sticks and I was sad because I wanted one but we couldn't buy one because we were broke, but then I found one on the ground and got all excited about it. Once we got there we found a spot and put a blanket down and watched this incredible show and Tony told me about how he used to be one of the guys who set off fireworks for shows like these, which to me was so cool. When the show was over, it was so late and it was pitch-black and we were in the middle of this throng of thousands of people packing up and walking home and even though there were all these people around us in the dark, I felt safe because Tony was holding my hand.

I always felt safe with Tony. I felt protected by him, and that was such a powerful feeling because I never felt protected anywhere else. I never felt safe. Ever. Only with him. Which is why I was so happy when they got married and why I needed him in my life, but of course when two addicts get married the end is pretty much inevitable and that's especially true when one of them is my mom.

The beginning of the end with Tony finally came the night my mom split his head open.

I was eleven for that one. They were having another one of their knockdown, drag-out fights, hollering and going at it for hours. Alcohol was involved. At some point, he'd had enough and he turned and walked away from her and she very cowardly reached for this cup she kept on her desk that she used as a pen and pencil holder. This cup wasn't like a ceramic mug or anything like that. It was a cup made out of cast iron, thick and heavy on the bottom and damn near razor-sharp around the edge. She picked it up and she chucked it at the back of his head and it hit him dead on his scalp, lacerating it and splitting it right open. You could see the flesh.

I could see that she immediately felt remorse, that she knew she'd gone too far. But for someone like my mom, in that situation the remorseful, empathetic side isn't in control. The part of her that couldn't admit a mistake, that's who was in control. So she kept going at him until somebody called the cops and then the cops showed up and my mom got hauled off to jail while Tony went to the hospital and got his head sewed up. It was one of many insane injuries that he'd experienced, but he handled pain like a fuckin' G, and obviously through a bottle as well.

Because Tony and my mom were married, he technically had custody over me as my stepdad. Since they shared the apartment and because she was technically the psycho in this situation, he got a restraining order against her and wouldn't let her back on the property. She legally couldn't go back to her own house or see her own kid, which was Tony's way of saying "Fuck you" over the cup thing.

So now I was living alone with Tony, which, as much as I loved the guy, was super–fucked up. It was pretty much *Groundhog Day*. He wasn't working. I was still being "homeschooled." So it was the two of us in the apartment all day watching cartoons and daytime TV. Every couple of days he'd go to the store to get beer and food, but that was about it. He wasn't paying the bills, and he wasn't cleaning up, that's for sure. Within a few days there was cat piss and cat shit all over the place from whatever cats we had at the moment. Meanwhile, he was drinking at least a case of beer a day and there were literally three-foot-high mountains of Coors and Bud Light cans from where he was chugging and tossing empties all over the floor, and it went on like that until one morning he was sitting at the breakfast table, barefoot, beer in hand, shitfaced drunk, and I was running around the apartment all happy, playing with these two toy guns I had.

Since I didn't have many toys growing up, when I had something I treasured it, and I fucking loved these two toy guns. They were plastic, but I'd colored in the orange parts with a black Sharpie so they looked real, like Glocks or Colt M1911s, and I was running around the apartment and pretending to be this little badass shooting stuff up and I sneaked up behind Tony and I yelled, "Tony! Tony! Look! BANG BANG! BANG BANG!"

Now, the responsible way for an adult to respond would have been to say, "Son, you should never point a gun at somebody, even if it's a toy." Etc., etc. But that's not what Tony did. The dude spun around so fast and grabbed the guns in his massive hands, twisting and squeezing them so hard that the plastic started cutting into my fingers. Then he shoved his finger right in my face and screamed, *"Don't you ever point a gun at anybody! Ever! Guns aren't fuckin' toys!"* Then he yanked the guns out of my hands and threw them on the cheap linoleum floor and he stood up and raised his bare foot in the air and it was like he was moving in slow motion because I could see what he was about to do and I screamed out, *"NOOOOO!"* as he brought his heel down on my favorite toy guys, smashing them to pieces.

But then karma showed up and was like, "Wassssup, Tony?" and right where Tony's foot had shattered the gun, this razor-sharp five-inch arrowhead of plastic broke off and buried itself in the fleshy center of his foot all the way back through his heel. The dude *screamed*.

"MOTHERFUCKER!"

This was the point where a sane, sober person would have called an ambulance, but Tony was so shitfaced that he reached down and grabbed this plastic shard and yanked it out and—like a scene out of *Kill Bill*—this plume of blood sprayed out across the kitchen and he passed out cold on the floor. The blood kept pouring out of his foot, collecting in a massive puddle across the shitty linoleum tile. I didn't know what to do, so I shrugged and went back to playing with my toys.

Eventually Tony came to, but he still didn't go to the hospital. He took some paper towels and duct-taped them around his foot and hobbled around that way for a couple of weeks. He also never cleaned up the blood. It stayed there and after a couple of days it dried into a flaky coat of brown paint; you could take a penny and scratch your name in it if you wanted to, and I had to walk around it every time I went into the kitchen to get a bowl of cereal. From there it was back to the same *Groundhog Day* routine it had been before, me watching cartoons while Tony built his mountains of beer cans and the cats pissed all over the house.

With one of my mom's shutters and the
linoleum Tony bled out on.

All told, I think it was just me and Tony like that for a month maybe. Eventually, I forget how, my mom ended up finding a way to get me. Tony hadn't pressed charges, which was nice of him, so when my mom got out of jail she went to live with a friend from the program. Late one night she called while Tony was shitfaced and out of it and said, "Come outside. We're coming to get you. We're going to be there in ten minutes. Don't bring anything. Don't do anything. Don't say anything. Just run. Run to the end of West Deer Park and we'll be there to pick you up."

I put down the phone and I looked over at Tony nodding off and I started edging toward the door and then suddenly he perked up. "Hey! Who you talking to? Where are you going? Come back here!" I bolted, made it to the door, and started fiddling with the lock as fast as I could, first the chain, then the dead bolt, then the knob. Finally it opened and I ran and Tony ran after me, this huge fucking guy barreling down the stairs like the boulder coming for Indy in *Raiders*. But his foot was still fucked up and I was too small and too fast and I ran out to West Deer Park and took off up the street. It was the middle of the night and I was petrified and freaking out and didn't know what to do. Then a car pulled up and slowed along the curb without fully stopping. My mom's friend was driving and my mom was in the back and she opened the door and said, "Get in the car! It's us!" Then she scooped me into the backseat and we sped off and we were living at her friend's house for a while, a few months maybe, which I only remember because that's where I crashed my skateboard and tore off my fingernail.

I didn't see Tony again for a long time. Maybe that's when they separated, or maybe they made up again and gave it one more shot. I can't say for sure; the details are fuzzy. They never got divorced. She stayed Terry Lee Bransford. By the time I was in eighth grade, he was gone because he was back in prison, probably on another assault charge. Then, the last time he went in, he didn't come out. He did some shit inside, maybe he mouthed off or put his hand on a guard, and the corrections officers beat him to death. They fucked him up so bad they put him in a coma and then he died in the coma.

I can't say Tony didn't deserve to get his ass whooped, because with his temper I'm sure he did something to set them off. But for them to beat him to the point of brain damage and put the dude in a coma was fucking tragic. He didn't deserve that. The world may think one thing about Tony Bransford because of his rap sheet and his problems, but the truth about Tony Bransford is that he probably saved my life because he was the only person I had growing up who taught me right from wrong and how to be a decent human being.

Tony was a fucked-up guy, but he taught me that you can be fucked up and still be a good person. He taught me that it's never okay to hurt people who are weaker or smaller than you are. In telling me how his dad beat him as a kid and how he'd never hit a kid because of that, Tony taught me that just because you've been treated like shit, you don't have to turn around and treat other people like shit.

Given who my parents were and how they didn't raise me and how most of my siblings turned out, I never should have made it to where I did. I made a bunch of poor decisions and mistakes because I was a kid. But in the grand scheme of things, knowing how to treat others and how I should expect to be treated, I learned the right lessons. When you're that young, you learn what to believe from people that you admire. I didn't admire my parents. I admired Tony. I became who I became because of him. Which sounds crazy since he was this violent alcoholic who was constantly going to jail for assault and shooting at the police. But it's true.

᠊ᠵᡭᡮ

One night there was a local news story about some girl who'd been kidnapped, raped, and forced into sleep deprivation as a form of torture by her rapists. Which is sick, but at the time I was a just a ten-year-old kid and I didn't really understand the gravity of the story or what it was really about and I said in sort of an offhand remark, "She couldn't stay up all night? That's not hard. I can stay up all night."

My mom flipped the fuck out, screaming, *"You don't know what you're talking about! You don't understand! I know what that girl went through because that was done to me!"* Then she went off about how she'd been raped and abused and sleep-deprived like this girl had been and how I was an ungrateful brat because I'd said what I'd said. "I'm going to *show* you," she said, "and you're going to see what it's like."

Then she grabbed me and made me sit in a chair and I had to sit there all night and she sat in front of me, staring at me, not saying a word, and every time I would start to nod off, she would scream, *"ROBERT! WAKE THE FUCK UP!"* at the top of her lungs and I'd jolt back awake and then I'd sit there some more and she'd sit there in front of me and eventually I'd start to fall asleep and she'd scream at me again.

I remember saying "I'm sorry" a lot that night. I remember crying and pleading with her, literally begging, because she was torturing me. "I'm sorry, I'm sorry, I'm sorry. Please. Please. I'm sorry." I said "I'm sorry" so much that by the end I didn't even remember what I was apologizing for.

It went on like that all night, and it wasn't the first or the only time she'd kept me up all night. That night was unique in that it was the first time the sleep deprivation was the actual point of the screaming and the torture, to teach me a lesson about mouthing off about sleep deprivation. Usually the sleep deprivation was more of a by-product of the screaming and the torture, which was happening for no reason at all. It'd be a random Tuesday night and I'd be in my room, jumping around and making noise past my bedtime and she'd decide I needed to be punished, so she'd call me into her room and make me stand there in front of her while she stared at me in this heavy-breathing silence and if I so much as twitched a muscle or opened my mouth to try to ask to be excused she'd fucking scream, *"YOU DON'T EVEN RESPECT ME, MOTHERFUCKER!"* and I'd have to stand there until she told me I could go.

It was literally torture, but through it all I never challenged her. Never. Not once. I never raised my voice to her and I never called her out. I never did anything like that ever, not like my sisters would, not like Tony had, and once Tony was gone and my sisters had moved out and I wasn't in school, it was just me and her and that was it. If you've ever seen the movie *Saw*, you have a pretty good idea what it was like. It was like being trapped in a padded room for seventeen years. It was like being in a one-person cult. I can remember thinking, "This sucks so bad. Why is this my life?!" I didn't understand the concept of suicide, thank God, but I just wanted to be the fuck out because it was prison. It had always been a prison, but the difference was that now, as I was getting older, I'd started to understand that it was prison.

When you're young, whatever your parents say, you just go with it. They create your world, and that world is normal to you, whether it's moving into an empty apartment with nothing but shadow puppets on the wall or making you sit and read the Bible for nine hours straight. Your parents do that, and you're like, "Okay. This is life. This is what we're supposed to do." So when you're in it, that's all you know and you don't get as upset because you don't know any different.

For me it was worse than that because I'd been brainwashed to believe that I was safer with my mom. The police were always in and out of our lives. The police knew Terry Lee like they knew Tony Bransford. Some disturbance would bring them to our door, sometimes once or twice a year, sometimes every month or two, and the cops always knew what was up. They'd see my mom and they'd see me and they could tell what the situation was and maybe some of them wanted to do something but probably most of them didn't care and there was nothing they could do about it anyway. *Technically* I had food and *technically* I had shelter and *technically* I was being homeschooled and all those technicalities added up to "We can't take him. We gotta leave him here."

Plus I'd been trained on what to say, how to say it, and when to say it whenever the cops or the social workers came around or whenever we had to go see a therapist so my mom could keep getting her medication. My mom would coach me. "If they ask if I hit you, you say no. If they ask if you have food, you say yes." And so I did, because my mom had put the fear of God in me, telling me shit like, "If they take you to a group home, they're going to rape you. They're going to molest you. They might even kill you." Which, she wasn't entirely wrong. Group homes and foster care, kids go into that system and come out super–fucked up. So I always lied when the social workers came around, which was once a year or more and all the different visits run together because it was the same shit and the same questions every time. Some '90s business-suit woman would show up and I'd go through the routine.

"Are you ever hungry?"

"Sometimes, but then my mommy gets me food."

"Do you ever see people you don't know?"

"No. Just me and my mom."

And at the end of every interview the social worker would give my mom this look that said, "You got away with it this time, but we'll be back." But they never took me because I'd learned what I was supposed to say to keep my mom out of trouble. "No, my mommy doesn't hit me. No, my mommy doesn't yell at me. My mommy loves me." Which is crazy, that I would actually willingly prefer to stay with her, but I did, and in my mind I was the smart one for telling my mom's lies for her. Any adult I didn't know was there to try to take me away, and I couldn't let them. That's how I saw everything, and I couldn't see any way out of it. I didn't know that I didn't have to sit there and read the Bible for nine hours. Most of the time when I had the Bible shoved in front of me, I didn't even understand what I was reading. I'd want to scream, "Bitch, please let me go watch *Ninja Turtles*!" But I couldn't. I couldn't leave. I was so brainwashed that I didn't know how to get up and leave. Because there was no getting up and leaving. Where would I go? I couldn't say "Fuck you" and go in the next room, because then it'd be her screaming and yelling and whooping my ass. I couldn't say "Fuck you" and storm out of the apartment. If I did, where would I go at six, seven, eight years old? Maybe I could go to a friend's house or go play at the park and I'd have a few hours of freedom, but then I'd be hungry and I'd have no money and I'd be wearing nothing but shit clothes and where the fuck was I going to go?

When they train lions in the circus, they start with the cubs. The trainer scares the shit out of the cubs, beating them with his whip, and as the cub grows, it doesn't realize it's a lion; it still feels like it's a cub, so when it sees that same trainer, with or without the whip, it succumbs. It won't try to fight back, because when it did fight back when it was little, it was overpowered every single time until it admitted defeat. So even as it physically grows stronger, inside it feels weak and will always feel weak because it was trained to feel that way. That's my relationship with my mom. I was so brainwashed I didn't even stand up to her the night she nearly killed me.

It actually started out a pretty good night. I was in my room being hyper and bouncing off the walls and jumping all over the place and running around and being loud and having fun and for whatever reason or more likely for no reason at all my mom just snapped and she came running in screaming, *"SHUT THE FUCK UP! SHUT THE FUCK UP! SHUT THE FUCK UP!"* and she grabbed me by the throat with two hands and pinned me to the wall in the corner.

It was like she was trying to murder me. It was like every ounce of force in her body was going straight through her arms and into her wrists and into her fingers and around my neck, like she was trying to pop my head and squeeze my brain out through my ears. I couldn't breathe. I couldn't speak. It was so quiet. All I could hear was the gritting of my mom's teeth. Right in front of me I could see the veins popping out of her neck, and then everything started to go blurry. Everything looked like it was underwater because I was looking through my own tears. I thought I was going to die.

Then, just as I felt like I was passing out, she stopped. It was like she snapped out of a trance and realized what she was doing and that I was her child. The empathy and the guilt kicked in and she wrapped her arms around me and embraced me and hugged me tight while crying, "Oh my God! My son! I'm so sorry! I'm so sorry!"

Once I stopped crying and caught my breath, I looked up at her and I saw that she was crying, so I hugged her back.

"Don't be sorry, Mom," I said. "Don't cry. It's okay. I love you."

PART II
BOBBY

The worst thing I've ever done in my life was spit in a retarded kid's Gatorade and give it to him and watch him drink it. And I know we're not supposed to say "retarded" anymore, but we were a bunch of little ten-year-old shits back then and that's the way we talked, so when this retarded kid ran onto the playground that's what we called him, "the retarded kid," and I don't want to pretend any different.

It happened during one of those times when we'd gone to live with one of my mom's friends from the program for some reason. This time it was a white chick named Heidi and she lived in a huge townhouse and at first you walked in and you were like, "Whoa, this is a *townhouse*." But then pretty quick you realized everything was dusty and cluttered and the floors weren't finished and you were walking on planks and it was creepy.

Heidi lived in Washington Square, which was the hood, so I spent most of my days running around the park with a bunch of these badass hood kids. It wasn't that bad. When you're a kid, even the most fucked-up, violent ghetto can be a fun and innocent place to grow up. There's all this violence and drug shit that's definitely going on, but nobody fucks with the kids. You're not scared because it doesn't involve you. So even though me and all these kids were in this neighborhood with drug corners and all the rest, we'd just run around and play.

One day we were in the park and this retarded kid we'd never met before showed up. He was a light-skinned kid with that reddish-brown hair and he had a big head and he was really sweet and he wanted to play with us. For whatever reason, one of the kids had brought a shit ton of Gatorades to the park that day, like a case of them—which, let's be honest, somebody probably stole them shits because who gives a kid a twelve-pack of multicolored Gatorades? So whoever had the Gatorades was handing them out to everybody and the retarded kid was like, "Can I have one? Can I have one?" So this one kid who was the main asshole of the group, the guy that everybody else looked up to, he got a bunch of us together down between these two cars in the parking lot and he took a red-punch Gatorade and he opened it, spat in it, and started passing it around, saying, "Yo, let's spit in this drink and give it to that retarded kid."

Everybody started laughing. I laughed, too, because I wanted to fit in. At first I was laughing because I was like, "Oh, this is so crazy that *you guys* are going to do this," because I didn't want to do it and didn't think I was going to have to do it. But as they passed the Gatorade around the circle and everyone took their turn, I realized that if I wanted to fit in I was going to have to spit in it, too. They passed the bottle to me, saying, *"Do it! Do it!"* So I did it. And because I was scared that they were going to think I was a chicken, I didn't just spit in it. I hocked a fucking massive loogie into it to prove I could be as cool as them. It was like the scene in *Eternal Sunshine of the Spotless Mind* when all the kids are yelling at Joel to kill the bird with the hammer and he does it and he feels terrible after and it's such a shameful memory that he hides it away forever. That's how it felt.

Then the kid who was the main asshole said to me, "Okay. Go give it to him." So I took the red-punch Gatorade with everybody's spit in it and I gave it to the retarded kid and I watched as he chugged nearly the whole thing, gulp after gulp after gulp. Then the kid stayed

and played with us. He was running around and having fun and everybody was laughing, but he didn't know they were laughing at him,
so he was laughing, too, like we were all laughing and having fun
together. At some point somebody told him what we'd done. "We
all hocked loogies in your drink, man!" But he didn't understand.
He kept laughing like we were all playing a game together, and I felt
like shit.

It started getting late and one by one the kids broke off and went
home and then it was just me and the kid, playing on the monkey
bars and swinging on the swings. It was one of those things that only
happen in childhood, where we were best friends in the world because we were playing together at that moment. Then it was time for
him to go and he needed to get through this fence and it was too tall
from him to hop over, so I lifted the chain-link up at the bottom to
let him under it. He gave me a hug and then he scrambled under the
fence and then he started to go but then he looked back and he said,
"Hey!" and I said, "What?" and he said, "I love you!" Then he turned
and ran off.

To this day, hands down, it's still the worst thing I've ever done
to another human being. To this day it makes me want to cry that I
did it. Because this kid had nothing but kindness and joy in his heart,
and I hocked the loogie of all loogies in his Gatorade just because I
wanted to be accepted by all of these piece-of-shit kids in this poor-
ass, fucked-up neighborhood.

ᛘ ᚠ ᚠ ᚴ

One afternoon when I was eleven my dad stopped by the apartment, which was rare, and we were talking and out of nowhere he said something about his kids. As in *kids*, plural. As in *his other kids*. I was like, "What?" and he was like, "Yeah, your brothers and sisters," and I was like, "My *brothers* and *sisters*?" and he was like, "Yeah." Like it was nothing. Like he was telling me about something he saw on sale at Target.

I was floored. My dad had never even mentioned them before. Not once. Never. My mom didn't know anything about them, either. It was like this bomb that he dropped out of the blue. He had two boys, Ralph and John, who are identical twins, and two daughters, Robin and Natalia. They were about ten or twelve years older than me and they were all living about thirty minutes away in Takoma Park. They'd been right up the road from me my whole life and I'd known nothing of their existence before that moment.

On the one hand I was pissed because I'd grown up feeling like an only child trapped alone in this apartment at the mercy of this crazy woman when really I had big brothers and sisters who could have been doing big-brother and big-sister stuff with me the whole time. But any feelings of resentment I might have had from not knowing were immediately drowned out by my excitement at discovering them. "I've got *more* brothers and sisters?!" I said. "Living here?! I want to meet them!" So I did. It was a whirlwind. One of the twins, Ralph, reached out to my mom and said he wanted to meet me and spend time with me because, up to that point, none of them had known I existed, either.

One afternoon my mom took me down and put me on the Metro and when I got off the train in Takoma Park, Ralph was waiting for me. He took me back to his apartment in the projects, which was some real hood shit, a bunch of basic brick-ass buildings, like a prison. Ralph's place was up on the ninth floor. We took the elevator up, and it was hella scary in his hallway with this nasty old carpet full of blood and semen and stank and piss. Ralph's apartment was actually okay. He ended up moving to a nicer apartment later on, when he started selling more drugs.

All four of the kids had the same mom, this Brazilian lady named Maria D'Souza who was always super-nice to me. Robin was the oldest. Robin had a bit of a Danny DeVito vibe going on. And I don't say that to be mean. That's just me keepin' it real. She's a big-boned girl.

Then there were the twins. Ralph and John were both tall, six-three maybe. Light-skinned with strong features and long hair that they did in cornrows. Not particularly swole, but lanky with some real power behind them. A couple of hood niggas, basically. The first time we hung out, they told me how they looked so similar in high school they used to see if they could fuck each other's girlfriends.

Then there was Natalia, who was still a teenager and the closest in age to me. Natalia was short and round with a DeVito vibe, too, only she started out small and then plumped up after her baby. Physically, she looked more Brazilian than black, light-skinned with Hispanic hair, the kind you could comb easy and throw in a ponytail.

They were all different but they shared a lot of traits, like they all had dark circles under their eyes, which they got from their mom. Everybody's teeth were fucked, too, like every tooth in each of their mouths was like Neo dodging a bullet. (And, again, that may sound mean but that's just how we talked to each other. In Maryland when you clown or you dis somebody it's called Joaning. "Man, why you Joaning on me?!" Ralph used to call me ugly to my face all the time. "Yo, nigga, you *ugly*." So the Neo teeth thing, I don't feel bad about it.)

I never got to know Robin that well because she was off with her own kids by that point. I hung out with Natalia a couple of times, but I learned early on that I couldn't fuck with her. I went to visit one time on my birthday and someone had given me ten dollars and Natalia, seeing I had this ten dollars, told me to come with her. She walked me five miles into the hood to buy some weed and we got to the weed guy and she turned to me and said, "Yo, let me get your money." I was a kid who didn't know anything, so I let her have my birthday money and she took it and got a blunt and smoked it while I was standing there. She didn't give me any of the weed or any change from my ten. So I never even tried to have a relationship with her. Whenever I went to visit it was mostly me and Ralph and sometimes John.

Ralph was like a real big brother, where John was more of an asshole—he was cool, but an asshole. He didn't talk to me. Mostly he just didn't give a fuck. Ralph gave a fuck. He took an interest. It was clear that Ralph and John were my dad's sons, only they'd learned opposite lessons from that experience. John had learned to behave like my dad, while Ralph had the self-awareness to say, "I know what it's like to be treated by a father who's an addict who's never around, so I'm going to make sure Bobby gets what I never got."

Ralph was a good dude. I mean, he was a drug dealer who'd sold crack to our own father and who was always doing shit like showing me the pounds of weed under his bed and letting me hold his gun and letting hood-ass motherfuckers come in and out of the crib while I was sleeping on the couch. But he was a good person.

That first trip I took to visit Ralph, he got me high. It was the first time I smoked weed for real. I'd hit it once before with this older kid in the neighborhood named Blue, but that was just a puff and I didn't feel high or anything. When I smoked with Ralph, I got *baked*. He had a girl at the time. I think it was Brenda or Deborah but I'm not sure because he had a bunch of ladies and a bunch of kids and to this day I'm not even sure how many nieces and nephews I have through him. But that weekend I was hittin' it like a fuckin' G with Brenda or Deborah or whoever it was. I told myself, "I smoke cigarettes. I can take big hits. Fuck it." I was doing shotguns and hitting it and holding it hard because I was trying to be that nigga. I got so obliterated. I was this eleven-year-old kid on this tiny balcony nine stories up, freaking out because I was scared I was going to jump off the balcony to my death. I kept asking them, "I'm not going to jump off of here, am I?" Which they thought was hilarious because I was scared of all the imaginary shit about weed you hear from parents who want to make you scared to try it.

After my first visit, I started going to stay with Ralph more and more. It wasn't all the time, but since I wasn't in school, I'd go and spend a week with him here and there. I think it was good for my mom, too. She could send me off to stay with my older brother and get me out of the house so she wouldn't have to worry about me for a few days and she could go and drink and fuck guys or whatever while me and Ralph would watch movies and play video games and hang out. Ralph did something special for me that no family member had ever done before. That dude spoiled me. He spoiled me with drug money. My dad never took me shopping aside from getting me a $3.99 Superman costume. My mom never took me shopping except at Goodwill. But Ralph bought me new clothes. He gave me fuckin' McDonald's and Popeyes chicken and pizza and Kool-Aid. He got me a two-way pager where you could text before texting even existed. It was some real hood-rich shit. He even bought me the new Razor scooter when it was out—maybe the off-brand one, but it was still dope.

Ralph took me under his wing and made me feel like I had a real big brother, someone who was going to look out for me. Sometimes he did other big-brother shit, too, like the time I turned thirteen and he and his girlfriend held me down and punched me thirteen times in my arm and left me crying like a bitch. So fuck them for that, but otherwise it was all good.

I didn't get to visit Ralph every weekend or anything like that. But for a while I was visiting every now and then and then less and less and then after a year or two it was not at all. We never had a falling-out or anything like that, but I was getting older and I had my own friends and my own life and this was before cell phones and texting, so we fell out of touch except for chatting a couple of times a year. But it was an experience I'll never forget because it didn't just feel like I'd found my family, it felt like I'd found my people.

Growing up, I understood that I was black. Sure, my mom was white, but my dad was black and all the men coming in and out of the house except Kenny were black and so were Jesse and Amber and Geanie. And while Gaithersburg and Rockville as a whole were racially and socioeconomically diverse, that wasn't necessarily true right where I lived, which was mostly black and Hispanic, and by Hispanic I mean Salvadoran. There were definitely a few ghetto-ass white people around on West Deer Park, but mostly I'd see white people at school. So it was all black and brown people and I took my cues from that and knew that's what I was.

My understanding of "race" was pretty simple but it was also weird. Like a horror movie, it was "the racism is coming from in-side the house." It was my mom calling me a nigger and then turning around and showing me Martin Luther King, Jr., documentaries to make sure I was proud of my heritage. So that part was confusing. But on the other hand, out in the street it was me and my hood-ass friends and even though my eyes were blue and my skin was lighter than theirs, I didn't look at them and go, "Oh, we're different." And it was never a big deal. We were kids. We weren't sitting around talking about race; we were playing tag.

We knew that race was a thing that existed, and people would make jokes about it. My friends would call me, "Hey, white boy!" or someone would joke during tag that the black kids ran faster because they had to learn to run from the cops, which is one of those things that's funny because it's actually kind of true. But it was all just whatever because we all knew each other. That was the other piece of it. Nobody left Gaithersburg. Nobody ventured out. Most of us never left the block. You didn't think in terms of "race" because it wasn't a world of "black" and "white" and "Hispanic." It was just Bobby and Mike and Richie, and we didn't think on it much beyond that.

Takoma Park was my first experience of venturing out and seeing a different part of the world. Before that, because I hadn't had any connection with my dad, I hadn't had any connection to my people. And for sure there's more to the black experience than poverty and drugs and hood-ass motherfuckers going to prison, but even if the hood isn't a universal black experience, it was my family's black experience. My dad's people weren't the black doctors and lawyers coming out of Howard. My dad's people were the people I found in Takoma Park. I remember playing on the playground in the projects one day and meeting this girl who was thirteen years old and had a baby. Out of nowhere she was like, "Oh, shit, I gotta go."

"Where?"

"I gotta go home."

"Why?"

"I gotta take care of my baby."

"Whaddya mean?"

"I have a baby."

She was telling me this shit on the playground. She was telling me this shit on the monkey bars.

"Aren't you thirteen?" I said, doing the math in my head and subtracting nine months from thirteen to get to twelve. "Aren't you too young for that?"

"Don't worry! I'll be back!"

"Okay, when?"

"After suppertime."

"All right!"

That was Takoma Park. Gaithersburg had some hood spots like Stewart Town and Washington Square Park, but Takoma Park was "the hood." It was the real shit. It was ghetto as fuck. It was thugs. It was dealers. It was killers. It was murderers. It was basketball courts with chain-link fences and the chain-link netting. It was thugs walking down the street and police driving by and chasing cars and all types of wild shit. But it was also a good time. It was a community of people who cared for and protected each other and loved each other. I'd walk down the street and people would remember me from my last visit and say, "Ain't you John and Ralph's baby brother?" People had houses, even if those houses had roaches. People had cars, even if they broke down all the time and weren't actually theirs because they stole them.

The hood is basically McDonald's. You love McDonald's. McDonald's is dope as fuck, and as long as nobody ever takes you to Mastro's or Nobu and shows you what real fine dining is, McDonald's stays dope as fuck. As a kid, I had a fuckin' blast. I wasn't thinking about the drugs and prostitution and the drive-bys at night. I was thinking about hanging out with DeQuonte from down the hall. I was thinking about Ashley the girl from C3 downstairs who was kinda fine and who took me outside in the bushes, where we kissed each other. I didn't have a worry in the world. I was hanging with the guys who were runnin' shit, or at least tryin' to run shit, and doing their own thing. I was eating like shit, which meant I was eating great. I was feasting like a king on Burger King and sodas and fuckin' fried chicken instead of powdered milk and my mom's bullshit. I was meeting girls and trying to have sex and do different shit that I shouldn't be doing. I was running around playing with all these black kids, and I *felt* black. I was like, "Damn nigga, I'm from the hood! I'm a hood-ass nigga! This is great!" I loved it because I was like, "Here are my people. These are my brothers." It made me feel more connected to the streets, more connected to the culture that I only had a taste of in Gaithersburg, and it taught me where I came from.

ⵝⵎⵣⵥⵯ

It was around nine-thirty on a random weeknight and my mom and I were watching *Training Day*. Because who lets a twelve-year-old watch a Denzel Washington movie about crooked cops smoking PCP and murdering people? But anyway. We were watching *Training Day* and the scene came on where Ethan Hawke's character finds these dudes trying to rape a young girl in an alley. They're beating her and punching her in the face and Ethan runs in and he kicks their asses and saves the day. So we were watching the movie and everything was cool and then this scene came on and my mom fucking lost it. She started bawling and crying and screaming at the television, going, *"Yeah! Beat his ass!"* Even as young as I was, I could put two and two together and understand that she was flipping out because what was happening to this girl was what had happened to her in real life and in real life there's no Ethan Hawke running in to save you.

Then, right in the middle of bawling and screaming at the television, she jumped up off the couch and said, "I need to go! I'm fuckin' leavin'!"

And she left.

She gathered up a few things, slammed the door behind her, and disappeared into the night, and I was left sitting there like, "Yo! What the fuck, man?! What am I supposed to do now?!" I'd just seen my mother bawling and screaming and crying over this rape, which I shouldn't even have been watching that shit in the first place, and I didn't understand what was happening and the next thing I knew my mom was . . . gone. She stayed gone for hours. I don't know what she did or where she went, but eventually I fell asleep and when I woke up the next morning she was there. She never explained and never apologized.

After that she started disappearing more and more, and for longer and longer. She called them her sabbaticals. She'd start losing her shit and she'd reach a breaking point and she'd yell, "I'm going on sabbatical!" and then she'd leave. The longest she was ever gone was two weeks. I don't remember what I did for those two weeks or how I survived but one thing I do know is with every year that passed, my mom got worse. I watched her get worse. I could literally see, month by month, how she was being reprogrammed by this disease that was taking over her brain. The weird obsessions got weirder, the drinking and the drug abuse got harder, and the violent outbursts got more and more violent, like when she put a cinder block through the sliding glass door to the patio the day Geanie had a birthday party for her daughter, Brianna, when they were back living with us for a while.

Everybody was shocked when Geanie got pregnant, but it wasn't so much that we were shocked that Geanie got pregnant, just that she got pregnant before Amber did, because the whole time Amber was a teenager the running joke in the family was "Oh, you *know* she's gonna be the first one to get knocked up." To me, Amber and Geanie were cool. They weren't exactly role models, but they weren't bad kids. Their biggest problem was having no respect for themselves when it came to men; our mom hadn't exactly modeled the best behavior for them in that regard. I watched men disrespect and abuse both my sisters my whole life, the same as they had my mother. The worst of it that I ever witnessed was the night one of my sisters and I were sharing a room and I was asleep in my bed and I woke up to sounds of her next to me in the same bed getting punched in the face while she was being forced to suck her boyfriend's dick.

The boyfriend was this huge fuckin' dude. Like six-eight. His name was . . . well, I'll just call him Charles. Charles sold drugs. The first time I ever held a gun, it was his gun, a 9mm Smith & Wesson with a black handle. I have it on video. We had a camcorder and I would record shit on my mom's old VHS tapes and erase all her infomercials and Bible movies, which pissed her off, and one day I had the camcorder rolling and I was holding this gun and trying to be all cool and pointing it at my head while it was loaded and nobody was saying or doing anything about it. When I was done playing with the loaded gun, Charles took it back from me and took the clip out and took the bullet out of the chamber. Then he picked the bullet up with his shirt, blew on it, wiped it, and put it back in. I asked him, "Why are you doing that?" and he said, "Fingerprints, my little nigga," and I was like, "Oh, shit. I don't know what that means." Now I know it was because he was out there fucking people up.

Charles was always getting the cops called on him, and a couple of times the people calling the cops on him were us. He had this one gnarly episode in our house where he went demonic because he was fucked up on PCP and he started screaming, *"I'm gonna fuckin' kill everybody here!"* He was usually coming or going, in and out of prison, constantly beating and sexually assaulting my sister. She'd get restraining orders against him and send him to prison and then she'd take him back. So Charles was a real piece of shit and on this one particular night I was asleep in bed and I woke up to these slobbering and slurping sounds, punctuated by my sister sobbing and crying, "Can I stop? Please? Is that enough? Is that good enough?" And every time she stopped she'd get punched in the face. "Bitch, I didn't say stop!" *Pop!* They weren't like Mike Tyson punches, more like openhanded slaps, but she was still getting checked pretty hard.

I was lying there, frozen. I was a kid and I sort of knew about sex but not really and obviously it was way more traumatizing for her than for me but it still fucked me up pretty bad because I was scared and I didn't know what to do. I felt guilty, like it was my fault because I was too small to do anything about it. Then, just as I started to understand what he was doing, she jumped up and ran out to the hallway, screaming, "Mommy! Mommy! Mommy!" And that's all I remember.

That was pretty typical of what went on in my sisters' lives. As young women in that fucked-up situation, being sexually attractive was the one kind of status and power they had as far as trying to get the love and acceptance they needed. So I get why they behaved the way they did, but it didn't lead them anywhere good, which is how Geanie ended up getting pregnant by this white dude named Ricky while my mom was locked up in a mental institution for six weeks.

The mental-institution thing wasn't one of her sabbaticals. She was gone, institutionalized. I don't know why or how and I want to say it was court-ordered but maybe one of her friends reported her saying she was a danger to herself and others. Either way, she was gone for six weeks, and for six weeks it was me and my sisters alone wreaking havoc at our house.

That was when my sisters introduced me to stealing. Not stealing money but stealing food, because we were hungry. Amber and Geanie and I would go to the Food Lion wearing big, baggy clothes and they would shove stuff into my pants and I'd be nervous the whole time and they'd be telling me, "Shut the *fuck* up!" while they kept shoving food into different parts of my body. Then we'd go to the front and pay for a few things but have way more stuffed under our clothes. We did that for a while. At first there was a part of me that was like, "Oh, no, you can't steal. Stealing is wrong." Then there was another part of me saying, "Well, we gotta eat, so you gotta do what you gotta do." Then pretty soon there was this other part of me going, "Okay, well lemme grab this Snickers bar while we're at it."

The great part was I ate better than I ever had. My mom was hella white. She could cook okay, but it was mostly white-people chicken with a hint of flavor in it. Amber and Geanie, they could cook. They'd be in the kitchen cooking with gizzards and all this wild shit. I loved it. At the same time they were both having a bunch of boys over and that was when Geanie got with Ricky. Then my mother came back and found out everything that had been going on and that Geanie was pregnant. So she kicked Geanie out but then ended up asking her to come back around the time Brianna was born because my mom was workin' the welfare system, not only claiming Geanie as a dependent but also claiming her daughter as well.

So it was Geanie's daughter's first birthday and it was the middle of the afternoon and we were having a party at our apartment and there was music and everyone was having a good time. Then out of nowhere my mom stormed out of the bedroom screaming, "What the fuck is this shit on my sheets?!" while she was waving around this bedsheet that had a shit stain on it either because the baby shat on it or somebody smeared the sheet while the diaper was getting changed. Which is whatever, right? That's what babies do. It's not that deep. But my mom was fucking losing it and Geanie was like, "Yo, chill out. It's all good. We'll clean it," and my mom was like, "Clean it right *now*!" and Geanie was like, "*Yo*. It's Brianna's birthday party. I'm not cleaning this shit right now. Put it in the basket, and I'll clean it later. What the fuck is wrong with you?"

But my mom wasn't having it. She kept yelling and going off, and the next thing I heard she was screaming, *"NIGGER!"* at the top of her lungs and this whole room of black folks stopped, turned, and stared. Motherfuckers were like, "What'd you say, bitch?!" and "Terry Lee, come on," and "You *know* you can't be sayin' that!" But my mom didn't give a shit. She got right in the middle of the living room and she yelled, *"Everybody get the fuck out!"* Nobody moved. The attitude in the room was like "Fuck you. We ain't leavin'. Yeah, it's your house, but fuck you. It's Brianna's birthday and you're not going to ruin this moment for this girl and her mother, so chill out."

But my mom kept yelling and everybody kept not leaving and so my mom went over to this stack of cinder blocks in the corner that she kept for bookshelves and she reached down and she picked up one of these huge fuckin' things and she screamed, *"Everybody! Get! The! Fuck! Out! Of! Myyyyyyyyy! House!"* and she hurled the cinder block through sliding glass door to the balcony and the whole shit just shattered.

Within minutes the cops showed up. I don't think it was anyone from the party who called; you never called the cops on your own until there was actual bloodshed. Probably it was the neighbors. While the cops went through and interviewed everyone and sorted out the mess, I got the fuck out of there and went for a walk. The cops had been to our house more times than I could remember, but this was the first time I was genuinely scared that they were going to take my mom away and I was going to end up in a group home getting raped and all the other horrible shit she had made me afraid of. I had tears in my eyes and I was walking around, muttering out loud, "Please don't take my mom. Please don't take my mom," like I was talking to the police or to God or to anyone who would listen.

After a while I wandered back home and my mom was there by herself, all fucked up and angry, with broken glass everywhere. It turned out there wasn't much to be worried about. The cops didn't give a shit, didn't want to be involved. They weren't going to take her to jail for destroying her own property, so they just sent everybody home. And even though I was in a house with no patio door and broken glass everywhere, I was relieved, like, "Hey, at least they didn't take her. It's another day I still have a home." Even though this woman was the single biggest danger and threat to my well-being, I still wanted her and needed her and was scared of losing her.

Geanie, on the other hand, was done. She figured out what my mom was doing by claiming her and Brianna as dependents and she wised the fuck up and said, "I'm going to go live on my own because I see what you're doing and now I can get that money myself and I can do it, too." So she did. Then she was off on her own and living on welfare and HOC and the whole cycle just started repeating itself all over again.

ⵣⵁ⤬ⴹⴽⵣⴽⴽ

Coming up in hip-hop, I got so much shit from people because I'd tell stories about my life and how I escaped this world of drugs and violence and food stamps and alcohol and people would hear me and say, "That's bullshit, man! You're from the suburbs! Gaithersburg ain't like that!" But that's coming from the person who didn't see what I saw because they didn't have to see or didn't want to see it.

Gaithersburg was a strange mix. It was the suburbs but it wasn't. It's an old Maryland farming town that got swallowed up by the suburban sprawl of D.C. It's got this big government center called the National Institute of Standards and Technology, which is this superscience place full of all these engineers and scientists who were well-off and had nice houses in nice neighborhoods. But that wasn't the part of Gaithersburg I was from.

I grew up on West Deer Park. There are definitely parts of Gaithersburg that are worse, like over in Stewart Town or off East Diamond Avenue. You tell people you live over there and they're like, "Oh, shit, you're in the hood." West Deer Park was more lower-working-class. It was about a 60/40 split: 60 percent of the people were responsible working families doing their best to earn a wage and drive a decent car and mind their own business. Then you had maybe 40 percent of people who were like my mom, getting by on some combination of welfare and food stamps and HOC, plus whatever minimum-wage bullshit they could cobble together. Wherever you've got that lifestyle and that culture, hood shit just comes along with it. You can build this suburban world that's all leafy green trees and white picket fences, but trouble's going to creep in one way or another. So when I say that I'm from the hood, I'm not from "the hood." I'm not from fuckin' Baltimore. I didn't grow up in the projects. But my apartment was the projects. My sisters were bringing home boyfriends who sold drugs, who were in and out of jail, who put guns in my hand and sat on the couch and wiped bullets and clips so they wouldn't have their fingerprints on them because they were fucking killing people.

On the bottom floor of our unit there were these guys who'd rented out all four apartments. They were cooking crack and meth in one apartment, selling it out of the second apartment, running prostitutes out of the third apartment, and living and sleeping in the fourth apartment. I didn't hang out down there too much, but I'd go down sometimes and it wasn't hard to figure out that shit was sketchy. One time I went down and went into the wrong apartment and was like, "Huh. Why is there no furniture in here?" And then the guys grabbed me and said, "Uh, yeah, let's go to the other apartment," and then they took me to this other unit that had nice furniture and an awesome TV. It was also impossible to miss all the unfamiliar faces coming in and out, either to buy drugs or to visit prostitutes.

The hard thing for a kid, especially for a kid from a fucked-up home who never wants to be at home, is that there's nowhere else to go. You're out with all the kids who think it's fun to spit in the retarded kid's Gatorade and you feel like you need acceptance from those kids because they're the only kids you've got. You have to hang with them if you're going to do anything besides play in your room all day. Probably the worst thing about West Deer Park was, because it was only sort of the hood, there were always kids trying to prove themselves by acting tougher than they were. Those are some of the most dangerous people, far more dangerous than real criminals. Real criminals do crimes for a reason, because they want money, not because they're trying to impress people. But the person who's walking around like they're a badass, going, "Yo, my cousin's from Southeast D.C.!" That person's lookin' for trouble because of whatever inadequacies they have, they're not being loved by their parents or they're not feeling taken care of or whatever, and that shit was everywhere in Gaithersburg.

I was never in a gang, but by the time I was eleven or twelve I was part of a crew of little shits who ran around causing trouble. There was Mike. He wasn't in my grade. He had to have been at least four years older than me and he was the nerdiest guy in the world, like Squints in *The Sandlot*. If you look up '90s nerd in a dictionary, it's this dude. Super-white. Super-skinny, too, but always wore baggy clothes because he was way into hip-hop. Mike loved black people. He was one of those white boys who was of the culture. He had fly gear, listened to Three 6 Mafia, loved rap music, said "nigga" all the time because he was one of those white people who just start saying the word and their black friends are cool with it because they're the ones pressing him to say it. Black kids will be like, "Yo, say it, white boy," and the white boy's like, "No, no, I'm not gonna say that," and the black kids are like, "You better say it. You white, but you my nigga. It's all good." So the white boy dips his toe in real slow, like, "Heeeey . . . my . . . nig-ga." But then he gets used to it and he uses it all the time. They're not the same as the brothers who actually know how to say it, but it's like white people who play jazz: Once you've proved yourself you're allowed to do it, which happens when you're in real life and not in some politically correct bullshit on Twitter.

I first met Mike by the pool when I was six. He lived with his nana because both of his parents were fucked up. Eventually his mom got it together and got a job; she was the one who worked at

Dunkin' Donuts and gave us the day-old donuts when we didn't have any food. But Mike's dad was a big-time alcoholic and a super-old guy—at least he looked super-old, which might have just been the drinking. He died when Mike was sixteen.

The weird thing about Mike was that he could make himself throw up. He'd be walking down the sidewalk in the neighborhood and there would be some fancy Lexus or BMW that didn't belong there, and Mike would be like, "Yo, check this out!" Then he'd puke all over their hood and there would be half-digested pizza and Pepsi and shit everywhere and it was crazy and disgusting and I was always super-jealous that he could do that.

Mike was probably my best friend but there was also Pete. Pete had a low hairline and he looked like a thumb. He also had yellow teeth and these hairy moles on his face and a little sister named Jennifer and an overweight mother who was out of it and weird. Pete lived in the same complex as me. If you walked out of my apartment and turned left up at the dumpster, he lived up on the corner to the right and they lived with a guy that everyone called Uncle Ramis even though he wasn't actually Pete's uncle, just the guy who was fucking Pete's mom.

Ashley was another dude, a black guy who lived opposite from Mike's place. Ashley was a handsome guy with a big ol' field-goal gap in his front teeth who was always going to jail and getting locked up for one reason or another because he was a hood-ass motherfucker. This one time when the lights in our stairwell were busted out, Ashley took a newspaper, put it in front of our door, squatted, and took a giant shit. I'm talking about a shit the size of that triceratops shit that Dr. What's-Her-Name goes digging through in *Jurassic Park*. It was disgusting and I was sitting in our apartment going, "It stinks up in here," and my mom was like, "Yeah, what the fuck?" and we went sniffing around for the smell and then we opened the front door and we almost stepped in it but we didn't. So that's who Ashley was. He was a fuckin' asshole, but when we'd hang out it was fun. He and my mom used to sneak off and go smoke weed in the woods and for sure he probably fucked her at some point.

My buddy Rashad was probably the straightest of the bunch. He was a bit older and he reminded me of Ludacris and I forget what his mom did but his dad was a schoolteacher and they were dope. They were the family I wished I had. They had everything I wanted, the PlayStation, the good snacks, the real Christmases. The funniest part is they were barely even middle-class. They didn't make crazy money; they were just responsible people who made good choices. But they were the exception.

There were a bunch of other kids, guys who were in and out and occasionally part of the crew. We'd ride our bikes and jump around in the creek and run through the sewer systems and play manhunt, which is this game that's a combination of cops and robbers and tag. We'd go out on West Deer Park and hide in the bushes and throw rocks and shit at cars. This one time we were out there and there were maybe fifteen of us and this one kid had a D battery and he took it and he chucked it at this car that was passing and we heard a windshield shatter and then, right after that, "WHOOP! WHOOP!" It was a cop car. We fucking scattered and I ran all the way to the far side of the apartment building and I could see the big flashing siren lights behind me casting a shadow of my body on the wall and I got away and it was awesome.

Mike was usually the one getting me to do the dumbest shit. We used to go up in the woods near the lake in Bohrer Park and take an empty two-liter of Pepsi and fill it with rubbing alcohol and then take a lighter and squish the bottle and make flamethrowers. One time Mike used his lighter to melt a rubber band that he was holding and it started dripping on his skin and seared into his flesh and then dried there and he ripped it off with his teeth. Mike was dumb like that. Another time, when I was twelve, we'd been watching a bunch of

WWE and he suplexed me. He jumped off a fuckin' dresser full blast and landed on me and it fucked my arm up and the paramedics had to come, but it turned out I was okay.

We'd steal shit, too. We'd go on missions to shoplift video games from Target. To get there from where we lived, you had to go through this insane tunnel under the interstate. So we'd crawl through that and get to the other side and then then we'd go fan out inside Target and steal video games and candy bars and whatever else. Which I was always scared to do, but I was with the older kids I wanted to impress, plus there were always girls who were going, and I'd have a crush on one of them and I'd be too scared to look like I was scared, so I did it anyway.

Because it's hard. Because you're around that shit all the time. Because you need to be a part of something. You want to belong to something, and if you don't have something positive to belong to, you'll belong to something that's not positive, especially if you're trying your best to be out of the house all the time because whatever's at home is fucked up. That was always the big thing I felt with my homies, too. None of us were getting the love that we wanted or needed from home, so we would get together and we'd end up going along with shit we knew we shouldn't go along with.

Throwing batteries at cars and stealing candy bars is wrong, but it's stupid kid shit and everybody does it and it's whatever. But the real danger was that me and these other kids were right on the cusp of that age when you start seeing the real gnarly shit. We were out in the neighborhood running into real gangsters and real thieves and real criminals, and the more we were around that shit and the harder it got, the more I felt "I don't want to be around this."

There was this other kid in my neighborhood I used to play with. This kid had everything, nice clothes, new shoes, and a brand-new PlayStation with all the PlayStation games in the world. He had so many that it seemed like he didn't care about a lot of them, so one day I went to his house when I knew he wasn't going to be there and

I opened his shit and stole a video game. This was burglary. This was breaking and entering. But I did it. His apartment was on the ground level and I knew he used to leave his bedroom window unlocked, so I went in and I took the game and I got it home and I played it for days on end, like, "This is awesome!" Then, a week or two later I was hanging out with him, and he was so sad, going, "Man, my video game is gone. I don't know what happened to it!" I went home and I tried to play it again and I felt so bad I couldn't enjoy it. So I took the game, put it back in its case, waited until the kid wasn't home, and broke back into his house to give him his game back.

This other time I was hanging out with Rashad and a bunch of these older Hispanic dudes. We always used to go and fuck around on the roof of my old elementary school Summit Hall at night. There was a certain way we could climb up the side of the portable class-rooms and get up on top and do dumb shit. I don't know what about it was so much fun, just the thrill maybe. So this one night we went over there and I was thinking we were just going to climb up on the roof like always, but then these older kids went straight to this one portable like they'd scoped it out beforehand and they were like, "Okay, it's this one. Let's get in there."

I looked in the window and inside on the teacher's desk was this huge jar of cash, and these guys wanted to steal it. The only window to climb in was narrow and high off the ground, so all the other kids looked at me because I was the runt and they were like, "Yo. Jump in this fuckin' window and go get that money."

I was nervous but they kept after me, being like, "Come on! Come on!" Basically being assholes to me on some prove-yourself shit. So finally I gave in and they jimmied the window open and pushed me up and I shimmied through and I jumped in and the second my feet hit the floor I heard this loud screeching "EEEEEEEE-EEEEEEEEEEEEEEE!" because of course there was an alarm. Everybody started to panic and I was like, "Oh shit!" and they were like, "Grab the money!" and I ran over to the teacher's desk and I grabbed the jar and I picked it up and I looked at it and I froze. Right there on the jar was this label that said the money was for some kid's cancer fund. All the guys kept yelling, "Take it! Don't be a bitch!" But I couldn't. Even with all the older kids yelling at me to do it, I couldn't do it. I stood there, frozen, with this alarm screeching in my ear, until finally they all gave up on me and said, "Fuck it! Let's go! Let's go! Let's go!" and they ran off and they left me. Except Rashad. He was the only one who stayed. I dropped the jar, ran to the window, grabbed his arm, and he pulled me through. It hurt like fuck because he was dragging my bony ass through this metal window frame, but I got out and we ran across the basketball courts and into this huge field where we caught up with the other kids.

By that point the police were already there, like a dozen cop cars racing up West Deer Park and into the school parking lot with their sirens blaring and lights flashing, and somebody said, "Quick! Lay down! Lay down!" We all dropped to the ground and started belly-crawling across this field toward the woods behind the school like we were Forrest Gump in 'Nam or something. It was wild. We made it to the woods and ran through and came out on the other side farther down West Deer Park and we all ran home.

I don't know why I didn't take the money. Everything about my parents and my childhood and the way I was raised would practically guarantee that I'd be the kid who took the money—and the kid who takes the money never makes it out of the hood. Maybe the cops didn't get us that time, but they always get you eventually. Which is why you'll never make it out without some kind of moral compass pointing the way, and for some reason I had one. I still don't know why or how, but I did.

⎯⎯⎯⎯⎯⎯

The worst sleepover ever was when my friend Richie came over and my mom got blackout-drunk and Richie saw her pussy and then she destroyed the television set.

Sleepovers were one of my favorite things as a kid, especially going over to other kids' houses. They had awesome snacks like Cheez-Its and they had all the video games and they had cool parents and if you made a bunch of noise it wasn't a big deal because they understood that you were kids. It was never like that with my mom. I rarely brought friends over to my house because it would always end up being such a shit show. We were a bunch of rowdy twelve- and thirteen-year-olds jumping around and banging on shit and laughing real loud and inevitably I'd hear my mom screaming from the other room. *"ROOOOOOBEEEEERRRRT! COME HERE!"* I'd have to leave my pals and go to her room and she'd do that thing where she made me stand in front of her while she stared at me, breathing heavy, with that "You're going to stay right there until I'm ready to talk to you" look. By that point my mom had stopped beating me, for the most part. I was getting too big for her and she was doing it less and less. But in my mind I was still the lion cub who didn't know he was big enough to fight back, so I would just stand there and if I moved to get up or if I tried to say a word it'd be *"SHUT*

THE FUCK UP AND SIT DOWN!" Then I'd start to panic because I knew my friends could hear her. Then, after ten minutes of the power stare, she'd point that finger at me and say, "If. You. Make. One. More. Noise . . ."

"But Mom. I'm having a sleepover—"

"SHUT THE FUCK UP!"

In a flash she'd be up out of bed, grabbing the Bible and twisting my arm and pulling me over to sit next to her. "THAT'S IT! COME HERE!" Then she'd open the Bible and we'd sit there and she'd force me to read passages from the Bible. Then she'd drag my friends in and force them to read the Bible, too. Either that or she'd send them home and then keep me up till four in the morning doing First Corinthians.

So this one night my buddy Richie was sleeping over. Richie was half Hispanic and half white. His dad was the Hispanic half. He was a nice guy but also kind of a super-tight-ass workingman who did manual labor of some kind. He wasn't around much because he and Richie's mom weren't together anymore and now Richie had two moms. They were both strippers and they were both smokin' hot. The fucked-up part, though, was that one of them had been raped while the theme song of *COPS* was playing in the background, so any time we were over at Richie's house and *COPS* came on we had to change the channel. But this time we were at my house and we were watching TV back in what should have been the master bedroom but at that point was really the living room because my mom had turned the living room into her master bedroom, and back in the master bedroom that was now the living room my mom had made these bookshelves out of cinder blocks, which were pretty much her favorite building materials when she wasn't throwing them through plate-glass patio doors. She'd even made herself a bunk bed in the living room out of cinder blocks, which she said she did because she wanted to be closer to God. I don't know how this bitch who was on disability and constantly complaining about her sciatica was able to build an Egyptian pyramid out of cinder blocks in our living room and somehow hoist an entire bed on top of it, but she did and her bed was up there and she put a desk and a chair underneath and I remember climbing up there on this shitty wooden ladder she'd found and thinking, "This is not safe at all."

But back in what was now the living room we had these bookshelves made out of cinder blocks and two-by-fours and the shelves were full of candles and Bibles and dictionaries and the TV was right in the middle of it. So Richie and I were watching TV and my mom was getting shitfaced in the other room and Richie went to get something out of the kitchen and on the way there he saw my mom. She'd passed out drunk on her bed in this long T-shirt nightgown without any underwear and he came back into my room laughing, like, "Yo, dude. I saw your mom's pussy, and it was gross!"

We both started laughing and joking about it because it was embarrassing but what else are you going to do? And because we were laughing and the TV was blaring, out of nowhere my mom came stumbling into the room, swearing and yelling about how we were making so much noise. We couldn't even tell what she was saying because she was barely using words and she reached up and she grabbed on to the end of these two-by-fours in the bookshelf and she ripped the whole thing off the wall and it came crashing down and Richie and I jumped out of the way and the TV and all the books and candles came crashing onto the floor. She started picking shit up and smashing it. It was the loudest, craziest, most insane thing you've ever seen and then, in the midst of all that, she snapped around and turned on me. She ran me into the corner and started beating on me, punching and kicking and landing haymaker after haymaker while screaming her fucking head off.

Then, like a passing hurricane, as quick as she'd come in, she turned and she was gone.

The next thing I remember was stumbling into the bathroom, my body hot with adrenaline and red all over from where she'd hit me. I was looking at myself in the mirror and Richie, who was the same age as me but taller, came over behind me and he put his arms around me and I broke down and cried and cried and cried. I was rocking back and forth and shaking, but he kept his arm around my shoulders and was like, "Shit, and I thought my family was fucked up." Finally I shook it off and stopped crying and we went back into the other room to sift through all the wreckage in the hope that the TV still worked.

Richie and guys like Mike were the only friends who ever saw my mom messed up like that. Nobody else knew because I wasn't exactly out talkin' to the kids in the neighborhood like, "Well, my mom is really suffering from some serious mental illness, so . . ." No. Every day it was just "Yo, man. Let's go ride bikes, bro." I was just trying to have a childhood.

In a weird way it was a blessing that my mother's condition was as bad as it was. I didn't spend a whole lot of time obsessing over how I could fix her or how I should deal with her because there was nothing to do but accept it. "I accept that my mom is fucked up. I accept that I don't have a dad. I accept that I don't have a real family. So, okay, cool. It sucks not to have those things, but what do I have? I have friends. I have a bike. I can go ride my bike with my friends. That's what I have." I chose to focus on the positive rather than the negative because the negative was beyond my control.

There probably aren't many twelve-year-olds who know the word "compartmentalize," but that's exactly what I was doing: putting my mom and all her crazy in a box and doing my best to leave her there so I could go out and be a normal human in the world. But given all the damage she'd already done to me, I could only do so much. Even as I was trying to cut those apron strings, I found that I couldn't.

Back at West Deer Park there were all these Salvadoran kids who loved to breakdance. These kids had a boom box and they'd put CDs on and they were usually out in front of Pete's house spinning on their heads on this big sheet of linoleum—that fake tile you see in ghetto kitchens that they probably got because their dads worked construction, which is what a lot of the Salvadorans who lived there did. I got into breakdancing with those guys and I would spin and do cool tricks and it was awesome and super-fun and great. Then one day I was breakdancing in my house, showing my mom this new move I was working on. I landed wrong on my shoulder and it dislocated for a second and then popped right back in and I felt this incredible rush of pain that quickly passed and my mom put my arm in a sling made out of some purple fabric she had. I thought I was okay. Then my mom left and went to the store and I had my first panic attack.

Panic attacks feel like you're having a heart attack or a stroke. You don't know what's going on and you're going crazy insane with this rush of fucking fear, like someone's got a gun pointed in your ear and they're going to kill your whole family—that's a panic attack. I felt like I was going to die. I couldn't understand it. Everything was all crazy. When my mom came home, I told her about it, and she said, "Oh, you had a panic attack."

After that first panic attack I started getting them all the time. It was pretty much any time I was out of my house or in situations with people I didn't know—and always when I was separated from my mom. In retrospect, I realize my mother did a lot of conditioning to me, to make me feel as though I needed her, and I think the traumatic experience of hurting my arm triggered something in my brain where all I wanted was for her to come home. I'd spent my whole childhood desperate for any chance to get out of the house, and now I was terrified to be without her for fear that it would bring on another attack.

It ruined sleepovers for me because the panic attacks started happening mostly when I was at friends' houses to spend the night. One time I was at this kid's house and we were watching *Saw* and there's the scene where they're cutting this dude's leg off and it was so intense that it started freaking me out and I ran to the kid's bathroom and my heart was racing and I was like, "I wanna go home. I want my mom. I want my mom. I want a safe place." Of course, my mom was not and never had been a safe place, but that's how fucked up I was. I had to have this kid's mom drive me home. Eventually the panic attacks started happening less and less, but that's how it was from then on.

It was a strange in-between time. Amber and Geanie had opened my eyes to the possibility of standing up to my mom, but I was still too young break off and leave like they had. I had this constant desire to get the fuck away from her but was having panic attacks any time she wasn't around. So I found ways to escape without going anywhere.

For a long time my only refuge from my mother's madness was television. That had been true since I was a toddler. I escaped into entertainment, distraction, whatever would tune the world out. I loved video games big-time, but we were so poor I was always three generations behind everybody else. When everyone had Xbox and PlayStation I was still getting by with a Super Nintendo. I'd listen to music, too, but music wasn't a big part of my life until I was fourteen maybe, so for a long time it was movies and TV. To this day I'm like a human *TV Guide* for the local Maryland broadcast affiliates in the late '90s. I can tell you the entire FOX 5 line-up: It was *Judge Judy* at five followed by a *Drew Carey Show* doubleheader at six and six-thirty, which was capped off by *The Simpsons* at seven, *Friends* at seven-thirty, and *Seinfeld* at eight. (And that's just FOX. I can still do ABC, NBC, CBS, UPN, and the WB, too.)

My other lifeline was skateboarding. When I was being "home-schooled," my mom would sleep until three, four in the afternoon and I would go to the skate park. I was there all day, every day. Most days I wouldn't actually go to the skate park itself because I couldn't afford the three dollars it cost for a day pass to get in. So I'd go to the skate park and stand outside and watch all the other kids skate and then I'd go to this loading-dock area around back where all the other poor kids would skate and I'd hang out and skate with them. But there was this woman who worked as the receptionist for the rec facility and her name was Bobbie and she was nice to me and she saw me coming every day and hanging out outside and not buying a pass, so one day out of the blue she said, "Here," and she gave me a season pass to the skate park and I was like, "Holy shit!" It was such an amazing moment, to have someone do something nice for me for no reason other than to be nice, and once I had that season pass, you couldn't get me to leave.

Skateboarding became my world. Where television only gave me an escape, skateboarding gave me a place to go and a reason to go there. Skateboarding taught me that I could be good at something and that, if I worked hard, I could get better at it. If I wanted to learn a trick and I dedicated myself to it and did the best I could and I practiced it over and over, eventually I'd get it right. Skateboarding was the first thing I'd ever done that gave me a feeling of accomplishment, something I'd never gotten from school. Every day I'd go to the skate park and I'd get better and I'd learn more tricks and I'd go home feeling better about myself for whatever cool new thing I'd learned how to do. Skateboarding saved my life. It gave me a place to go to get out of the house and kept me from getting into too much trouble with Mike and those guys. It gave me a sense of self-worth that kept me afloat until I met the two guys who introduced me to the thing that would not only save my life but give me a life worth living.

Robert Naples and Jesse Wideman were two older kids from the neighborhood. I met them one day when they were walking through Bohrer Park and I started following them, being like, "Yo, what's up?" and they were like, "Who the fuck are you, kid?" and I was like, "Yo, man, I'm Bobby Hall. Who the fuck are you?" They were in high school and I was this smart-ass eleven-year-old kid, but I amused them so they were like, "Yeah, we'll fuck with this kid—cool." We spent the afternoon getting Slurpees from 7-Eleven and after that we were tight.

Robert Naples was this super-tall, skinny, nerdy light-skinned black dude with an Afro. I'm pretty sure his dad was white, but I never met him because he was mentally ill and he wasn't in the picture. Robert was a kid who got bullied all the time, guys constantly jumping him and robbing him. Jesse Wideman was this super-white dude, kind of fat and really funny and weird. Jesse probably would have considered himself a chubby loser and a loner, but I thought he was awesome. The time I spent with Robert and Jesse was some of the best years of my life. Both of them were into so much cool, creative nerdy stuff. They showed me the world of creativity unlike anyone else. Jesse introduced me to Gorillaz, which was awesome. It gave me such a dark, fucked-up sense of humor. Jesse also had a guitar and he gave me some basic lessons on how to play.

Robert introduced me to stuff like anime and drawing and writing stories and cool video games that I'd never heard of before. He would write short stories and he would draw. He was a fantastic artist. Robert was also the first black guy who showed me there were different ways of being black. In my neighborhood, everyone was listening to the same hard-core hip-hop. It was always hood shit, and now here was this mixed black-looking dude who was into all this Japanese shit. He taught me that just because you look a certain way doesn't mean you have to act a certain way, which was dope. He introduced me to another way of thinking. He changed my life, and I don't think I ever told him that. He was the guy who first showed me *Cowboy Bebop*, which is one of the greatest sci-fi anime series of all time. I loved it. It blew me away. I think at first I just liked it because Robert liked it and I looked up to him so much, but in hindsight what it did for me was open my eyes to what I could do, which was be creative somehow, that I could tell stories. I'd always liked to draw and was always drawing *Dragon Ball Z* characters. Most of it was shit. But Robert was constantly drawing incredible, original stuff I'd never seen before, and it inspired me. I would try to copy him and do my own drawing and write my own stories and it opened my eyes to an entire universe of ideas and possibilities. It taught me that even if I felt trapped and scared and alone, I could escape my world by creating a new one.

ℙ𝕏ᾱᾱ∥

The summer before eighth grade, most days I was at the Gaith-ersburg Skate Park, which was right by the big public pool. There'd be all these girls who'd come to swim and then hang out at the fence watching all the guys skate. This one afternoon I was there and I was fuckin' killin' it, Tony Hawkin' it, in the zone, and there were these two cute girls watching.

In between tricks I walked over all hot and sweaty and super-cute and I was like, "Hey, ladies! How's it going?" and they were like, "Oh, hey! What's your name?!" and I was like, "My name's Bobby Hall." Everyone at the skate park used to call me Bobby Hall because there was a bunch of guys named Bobby around. The girls told me their names, and we started talking. I was on the fence between the two of them, my arm hanging from the chain-link, trying to do my best James Dean, spitting my game with my sweaty curls and my smile, and we hit it off.

The truth about me is that I was always a little flirt and a ladies' man. I was that five-year-old kid running around asking girls on the playground to marry me. One time when I was eight I was on the playground with the wood chips near the pool at West Deer Park with my buddy Rashad and his little sister, Shantelle. I thought I was being slick and I grabbed Shantelle's ass. It wasn't really even sexual at all; I was eight. It was more just "Ooh, I grabbed your butt! That's fun!" But it wasn't fun and she let me know it wasn't fun when she turned around and smacked the fuck out of me, socked me right in the eye.

So even though I was always flirting, I learned early on how to be a decent person about it and be charming but not creepy, thanks to Shantelle and also to my sisters. Being around older sisters and their friends is a much better way of learning about women than hanging out with a bunch of dumbass boys. My sisters had this one friend, a Spanish girl, Yolanda. She was like fifteen or sixteen. I thought she was super-smokin' and I thought I was this little player and any time Yolanda came around I'd be like, "Hey, baby, you're sexy." So one day Yolanda was over and my sisters were like, "You think she's sexy, huh?" and then they threw me in the walk-in closet with her. She was touching me and trying to hug me and kiss me, going, "C'mon, Bobby! Yeaaaaaaah! C'mon," like she was trying to fuck me but not really. All my cool-dude shtick, I dropped it. I got scared and I was banging on the door, like, "Nooooooo, get off! Nooo! Please, let me out! Let me out!" I never called another girl sexy again.

The truth was that for a long time I knew practically zero about the actual facts of life because of course my mom didn't teach me shit about shit. All she taught me was that it was shameful and evil and wrong. Once when I was around twelve I'd just woken up and it was morning and you know what happens for guys in the morning. My door was open and right across from my door was the door to the bathroom but lucky for me my mom slept until noon. So I was in bed, jerking off, doing my thing. This was back when I was so young I was shootin' ghostloads. I didn't even know what I was doing; I just knew it felt good. And I was right in the middle of it when: I heard the toilet flush.

I froze. "Oh, shit."

Ten minutes later, my mom called me into the living room. She was sitting on the couch with a Bible out in front of her and there were all these candles lit and this holy music was playing and she was *weeping*, tears literally falling on the open pages of her Bible. She looked at me and she took her hand and—swear to God—she made a jerking-off motion and said, through her tears, "Do you . . . ? You know . . . do you?"

I wanted to die. I did not want to have that conversation or have any part of whatever all these candles and music and shit were about. But I couldn't get away.

"Come over here and sit down," she said. "We're going to pray for your soul because you were masturbating."

So I walked over, sat down next to her, and we read the Bible. All . . . day . . . long. Twelve hours of Bobby's a sinner and he has to learn to hold back the sinning and who begat who and all this shit. Inside I was screaming, "Yo, I was just jerking off, man. Relax! It's not that big a deal. And besides, you fucked that dude from the bus stop two weeks ago!" But of course I couldn't say that out loud. So I sat there, reading and reading, and it sucked and I just learned to keep my mom's religious bullshit in its place so I could go out and mack on the ladies like I was doing with these two girls on that one afternoon at the skate park the summer before eighth grade.

Both of these girls lived down in Potomac, and after we hit it off they started coming to the park every Saturday. Both of them were crushing on me because I was the bad boy to them because I had curly-ass hair and I was skating and I was poor and they'd buy me Mike and Ikes from the snack bar because they cost like fifty cents and I never had the fifty cents.

Of the two of them, I liked one more than the other. The one I liked was bangin'. She reminded me of the middle girl in *Step by Step*. The other girl was pretty, too, but super-tall. I'm talking she could have been in tenth grade tall. I'm talking fucking Groot from *Guardians of the Galaxy* tall, with those same long, lanky arms and legs. Groot was definitely cute and nice but I was feeling the *Step by Step* girl more, so I started trying to maneuver to cut Groot out of it and have it be just me and the *Step by Step* girl hanging out and being boyfriend and girlfriend.

Now, the thing about me is that, even though I always try to be polite, I'm terrible with names. To this day I have conversations with people that go, "Hey, nice to meet you. I'm Bobby. What's your name?" "I'm Steve." "Hey, Steve. Great to meet you." Then I shake Steve's hand and walk away and five seconds later it's "Who's Steve?" So that's on me and it's a problem but it was a real problem with these girls because they both had basic white-girl names, like Susie and Vanessa or some shit. So one night I called up the girl I thought was the bangin' *Step by Step* girl but really I'd fucked up and I was talking to Groot. I was like, "Look, I think we should be dating. I want to be your boyfriend," and she was like, "But what about Vanessa?" Of course, when she said Vanessa she was talking about the bangin' *Step by Step* girl, but I thought she was talking about Groot because I didn't realize that I was talking to Groot, so I was like, "Nah, fuck Vanessa. It's me and you."

So then we got on a three-way call with the bangin' *Step by Step* girl, and me thinking I was talking to Groot I said, "Sorry, we're going to be dating now," and the bangin' *Step by Step* girl started crying, like, "Whaaaaat? Ohhh my God, noooo!" and I was like twelve and I was like, "Sorry." Then she got off the line and it was just me and the Groot girl who I totally thought was the bangin' *Step by Step* girl and I said, "All right, yeah, we should hang out." So the next weekend she and her mom came to pick me up to go roller-skating. They pulled up in front of our apartment, and I was like, "Oh shit! It's the wrong girl! It's Groot!" But it was too late for me to back out. And Groot was pretty, too, so I just went with it. I was like, "What the fuck else am I doing today? Why not? Second string. Let's go."

Groot's mom drove us down to the roller rink in Rockville, and when we pulled up outside, she said to Groot, "Sweetheart, why don't you go in and get the skates. I want to talk to Bobby for a minute."

So Groot hopped out of the car and ran in to get our tickets and our skates and her mom turned to me and looked at me.

"Now, Bobby," she said, "my daughter really likes you, so make sure you treat her with respect. Okay?"

"Yes, ma'am," I said.

"Okay."

Then she nodded and smiled and reached in her purse and pulled out a fifty-dollar bill and handed it to me.

That was the day I learned I was poor.

I'd always known that we didn't have shit. I'd always known that we were broke and most of the families around us had more than we did even if they didn't have that much. I'd always known it wasn't normal to be eating day-old donuts for dinner. I knew what it was like to feel embarrassed about dumpster diving. The West Deer Park apartments had these huge dumpsters, one for each block of units. People would throw out couches, desks, everything, and my mom was always stopping and rummaging through them. One time we found this desk and my mom was like, "Quick, jump in real quick and grab the other end of that desk." And there were lots of people around, other kids, my friends, and they were watching. But my mom didn't care. So I dove in and we pulled it out and took it home and that was my desk. Then one day my buddy Jose came over and it was Jose's desk so he knew for sure that I'd fished it out of the garbage. So that sucked big-time.

Still, you don't truly understand what it means to be poor until you have your first encounter with wealth, and that's what this was. Groot's family was wealthy. They lived at the end of this cul-de-sac in Potomac. I'll never forget the first time I saw that fuckin' house. I'm sure it was just a typical rich person's house in the suburbs, but in my memory it was this mansion. The trees and the lawn were so lush. It was like living in a rain forest, almost. I was like, "Holy shit. You have an orange tree. I can't buy orange juice, and you've got a whole fucking tree." I even remember the asphalt from her street because it was super-black and perfectly smooth, like they had somebody get up and go out and polish it every morning.

Groot's mom wasn't stupid. She could tell by looking at me that I wasn't like them. I didn't think she was being condescending by giving me the fifty bucks. I didn't feel like she was looking down on me. The vibe I got was that she was being kind. She knew I was going into this roller rink where all these suburban kids would have gobs of allowance money for snacks and video games and she didn't want me to be embarrassed because I couldn't pay for anything. She wanted me to be able to do something nice for her daughter. I was grateful and I took the money and I said, "Thank you," but inside I wasn't thinking "Thank you" at all. I was thinking, "Bitch, I'm about to spend barely any of this money on your daughter. I'm gonna maybe get her a candy bar and then I'm gonna go home and buy some groceries."

Groot and I ended up dating for like three months and it was fun despite the fact that she had nearly a foot on me; I was a runt, four-eleven maybe, and she was five-eight at least. She was super-athletic and I went with her to her swim meets and we'd ride bikes and hang out at her house. There were times when I'd go visit her in Potomac and then go back to my shitty apartment with my crazy mom and I'd think about how nice it would be if I could be a dog in a rich family. "Man, if I could be shih tzu or a Doberman in Potomac. Wow! I'd have my meals and people would love me and pet me and I'd at least get a solid twelve years out of it." I really thought that as a kid, and it's fucked up to sit around wishing you could be a dog in a rich family, but besides that, I was all right. Being poor sucked but it never turned into bitterness or rage that took over my life. Besides, the real problem in my life wasn't me being poor. It was my mom being my mom.

As with any girl I ever liked, I did everything I could to keep my mom out of the picture. I never asked girls to come over to my house to hang out. That never happened. Fuck, no. No way. But when kids get together, it's inevitable that the parents are going to exchange phone numbers and talk and sort of chaperone what's going on. At some point my mom was out at their house. Maybe she was there to pick me up or there was a party and somehow there was a dispute about something. All I know is it ended with my mom screaming at all these other moms, going, *"YOU MOTHERFUCKING COCK-SUCKERS! YOU THINK YOU'RE BETTER THAN US! FUCK YOU!"* Then she grabbed me and it was, "C'mon, Robert. Let's go. You can't see this girl anymore." She yanked me out the front door and there we were on their perfect asphalt cul-de-sac in the middle of Potomac walking three miles to get to a bus stop because they don't run buses where the rich people live.

And that's how it was. All through middle school and into ninth and tenth grade I'd have these two- and three-month relationships where I'd meet a girl, we'd dig each other, we'd start hanging out, and then my mother would come in and it'd be a big fucking scene that would turn into "You fucking cocksuckers!" and it would be ruined. The girl would go and tell all her friends and then I was the weirdo with the crazy-ass mom. She did that to every relationship I ever had and it all started with Groot and once it was over with Groot I didn't see her again until high school where I'd see her in the hallway be-cause you couldn't miss her because she was the size of a Verizon cell tower and she'd act like I didn't exist.

ᎭᎮᏆᎯ

The autumn after Groot and I broke up, I got dragged back to the special-ed program at Shady Grove to start going to actual eighth grade instead of my mom's bullshit homeschool eighth grade. The folks running the rental office at West Deer Park had been watching me skateboard in the parking lot all day and at some point they said to themselves, "Well, this doesn't make any sense." So they ratted us out to the social workers and my mom got caught for not doing the reports that she was supposed to be turning in to the state to document my "progress," of which there was none because for three whole years she didn't teach me shit. So the state basically told her, "You have to put him back in school or we're taking him away."

So off I went on the short bus back to Shady Grove, where they put me in eighth grade with a fifth-grade education. Which sucked, but I was happy to get out of the house because things were getting even weirder with my mom. She was going through another one of her yin-and-yang phases where she was going to rededicate herself to Christ, only this time she did more than go back to the super-Pentecostal, gay-people-are-going-to-burn-in-hell church. One day she randomly decided that the way she was going to rededicate herself to Christ was to start dressing like she lived in biblical times. She'd been deep in this goth phase of wearing all black all the time, and then out of nowhere she started wearing these flowing white garments made out of old sheets and duvet covers she bought at Tina's Consignments. She put all this shit on and announced, "I'm utterly and completely giving myself to the Lord now. I'm giving up my dark ways and I'm sacrificing my style to the Lord." I took one look at her in this getup and was like, "Bitch, you need to get some better medication."

She looked like some actress playing Mary Magdalene in one of those old Hollywood Bible movies. She wore that shit *everywhere*. She wore it to the doctor's office, to the grocery store. Everywhere we went, people would look at me like, "What the fuck is up with your mom?"

One day I was home and I decided to dress up in her Mary Magdalene garb and make a video of myself. I took our old camcorder and I was in my tighty-whitey underwear with this flowing thing draped over my head and I was dancing around the room like, "WoooOoooOoOO. I'm the Ghost of Christianity!" I was just fuckin' around and being stupid but then my mom stormed in and she didn't know she was being filmed and she started freaking out and yelling, "What the fuck are you doing?!" I used to play the videotape over and over and laugh my ass off and I'm glad I at least got one funny memory out of it because she wore that shit for like two years and it was fucking embarrassing.

So I was glad to be out of the house except that I was right back in the same special-ed class with the same hard-ass kids who'd treated me like shit three years before, only now they were bigger and meaner. They still bullied me and made fun of me, and I knew I couldn't fight back because I'd be proving the school's point that I had anger issues and I'd get put back in the rubber room. So I just let the kids bully me.

I hated every second of it. Thankfully it only lasted a couple of months because as part of reenrolling me they made me take another emotional aptitude test. I guess I did well on it because now they were like, "Oh, wait. He's fine. Huh. I guess he's always been fine." Then they released me to go back to regular school with the regular kids. I went back into normal eighth grade at Forest Oak Middle School, which was where a lot of the kids I knew from Summit Elementary had gone, so I was back with all the kids that I hadn't seen in three years.

Back in regular school I discovered that I'd become, like, popular. When I say "popular," it wasn't like I was a jock. It was more that everyone knew me. I was legendary because I was this kid who'd disappeared for three years and now I was back. There were all these whispers that I'd gone to juvie because I'd tried to hit a cop or some shit and I probably did a bit to encourage those rumors myself. I'd pass people in the cafeteria and they'd go, "Oh, shit, that's Bobby Hall." So even before I started rapping, people in Gaithersburg knew Bobby Hall. I had admirers and I had haters and it was cool.

After Forest Oak, I moved up to Gaithersburg High, and that's when all the problems with being pulled out of school and going in and out of this special-ed program started to fuck me up. I basically failed ninth grade three times. Technically I passed it the first time, but really the school was just passing me along because even though I was "in tenth grade," a lot of my classes were still ninth-grade classes and when kids found out about that, they clowned the shit out of me. "Oh, you're taking *that* class? That's a *freshman* class." Which made me not like school even more. But school hadn't given up on me yet, so I hadn't completely given up on school.

Outside of the classroom, everything was good. I got involved with the after-school ROTC program because the girls in it were hot and it looked like a really dope thing to do, learning how to do all those coordinated drills and marches and flipping rifles and shit like that. The head of ROTC was this black dude with a totally bald Milk Dud head. He was a hard-ass motherfucker. His name was Master Sergeant Beatty, but we all called him Master Beatty. He was a cool guy. We used to have these rallies, and I always wanted my mom to come, but she never came. Then, finally, this one time she came and of course the one time she came she embarrassed the shit out of me because she showed up in the full fuckin' Mary Magdalene garb. It wasn't even like I was one of the Muslim kids who's got their mom coming to school wearing a hijab and they feel embarrassed because other kids stare and make them feel different. My mom wasn't that. She wasn't a brown-skinned religious minority. She was just a white lady wearing a duvet cover.

The thing with ROTC is that you have to be able to march in lockstep. That's how you up your rank, and even though the kids who were juniors and seniors did better than me, I thought I did a decent job for a freshman. But my mom was like the dad who never said "Good game" or "Good job." The second we got home she started going off on me about how I wasn't good enough. "Didn't you see that other kid? You need to walk with passion!" And she made me do my drills over and over again in the living room to the point where I wanted to break down and cry because she was standing over me and shouting, *"No! Like this!"* and I wanted to scream, "Yo, go put your garb on and shut the fuck up! Why you gotta be trippin' on my walk? Why can't you support me? Why can't you be happy for me?" But of course she couldn't be happy for me because her newfound way of dressing holier than thou hadn't changed who she was at all.

Then one day, like with everything else, it was over. The Mary Magdalene duvet covers were just duvet covers on the mattress again, and she was back to blasting Nirvana and Chili Peppers and getting fucked up with random dudes she met at the bus stop and I was still just the poor kid at school with the fucked-up mom. But I was glad I did the ROTC because, unlike all the teachers who'd given up on me, Master Beatty actually cared. At one point everyone on the drill team was supposed to go away for an overnight tournament and I was so excited to go because this was the one thing in school I enjoyed and was good at. But then I got a D on a test, so my grades weren't good enough and Master Beatty had to sit me down to tell me I couldn't go. As he was telling me the bad news I started to cry and I could tell that this hard-ass, bald, Milk Dud–lookin' motherfucker was right on the verge of tears himself. Because he knew my situation. He knew my mom was the fuckin' crazy lady in the duvet cover. And on the one hand he knew I needed the help and support of something like the drill team and the camaraderie of going on this overnight trip, but at the same time he was a teacher and he had to enforce the rules and if I didn't have the grades, I didn't have the grades.

The biggest problem with school was that it made me feel stupid. Every day in class, I felt stupid. I couldn't do math. I still can't do math today. I can count money, but algebra and calculus and any of that shit, no way. I couldn't even do long division. Everything was a struggle, and because of that I hated it. I hated that there were things I couldn't accomplish that were easy for other kids.

I didn't give a fuck about school because I didn't know how to give a fuck about school. It had no relevance for me. It's not like I had dreams of going to college and all those dreams got crushed. It was more like I wasn't even conscious of the possibility that I would ever even graduate. My sisters barely knew how to read and had dropped out when they got pregnant. None of my siblings on my dad's side made it through, either. The only one of us who did was Jesse, and he was still off in California. And it's not like I was sitting around watching my buddies go off to college because the kids who were going somewhere weren't my friends.

I had a couple of teachers and counselors who tried to help me like Master Beatty did. One time two of the counselors took me out to get lunch at a dope spot to try to motivate me to do better. They were both sweet and they cared and they tried. But at the end of the day even the good teachers had their limits. They were getting paid like thirty grand a year, if that, and for what? To kill themselves over some kid who didn't want to be there in the first place? Their attitude was mostly "Look, we're going to do what we can, but it won't be enough for this kid with the fucked-up mom, so fuck it." I didn't give a shit because they didn't give a shit, and they didn't give a shit because I didn't give a shit.

More than anything these teachers didn't speak my language. We all spoke English, but there was a barrier. The majority of the teachers were upper-middle-class white women who wanted to "make a difference," but they didn't know how to communicate with poor black kids from the hood. They didn't know shit about our struggles or where we came from or how to connect with us. The only message I got from them was "You need to go to school!" and I'd think, "For what?" Which, to me, was just looking at things realistically. With or without a high school diploma, I was still getting the same shitty job someplace because who gives a shit if you have a high school diploma? Is anyone going to go behind you and fact-check it? No. You can just lie. I know. I've done it.

Nobody ever sat me down and said, "What do you actually like doing? Oh, you like video games. Why don't you be a video game developer? But if you're going to be a developer, you're going to have to know math and coding and all these other skills that we can teach you if you work hard." There was no moment when somebody came in and flipped a switch and turned a light on in my head. That shit never happened. So my whole attitude about school was A) I'm a fuckin' idiot and I'm not smart enough to do any of this shit, and B) There's no point and none of this matters and I don't want to fuckin' be here because these people don't give a shit about me. There was no one in my life to say, "None of that is true." Because none of it *was* true. But that's how it felt. To me, high school was a place to meet girls and hang out with my friends. So I started skipping and hanging out with Mike and skateboarding and rapping and smokin' dope because I was like, "Fuck school."

ᛂᚭᛆᛙ

By the time I got to high school, my West Deer Park buddy Mike and his mom had moved to Gaithersburg's Olde Town, in a place above the Diamond Drugs across from the Victor Litz Music Center, which if you love music and want to buy a new guitar or a drum set that's where you go. Mike's apartment was so shitty I couldn't believe humans lived there. He was eighteen years old and living on his own in what was literally a one-room box, a tiny studio across the hall from the apartment where his mom was living with some guy.

Mike and I had lost touch since he moved away. He'd been off doing his own thing, getting a little more hood, doing cocaine and robbing people and running around with guns, even though he was still the whitest fuckin' nerd in the world with the thick Coke-bottle glasses and everything. Then we reconnected and I started hanging out with him and these other homies of his. I was fourteen but I was scrawny, so I looked about twelve. My voice hadn't dropped yet, either, and any time I called the pizza place and ordered my pepperoni with extra cheese the pizza guy would be like, "Yes, ma'am." So I was basically a child hanging out with these criminals while they were running around robbing people and jumping guys. Mikey would always be like, "You're a good dude. You don't need to be involved in this shit." But then the next day he'd be like, "Yo, come with us! Let's do this shit!"

One time one of Mike's homies had a problem with this Spanish dude who was MS-13. Mikey's crew was like, "We're gonna go fuck him up," and they went after this guy with a baseball bat and fucked him up and I was there yelling, "Yeah, we're going to fuck this dude up!" But in my heart I was like, "I am not about to fuck this dude or any other dude up." I was just trying to be accepted and play the part, but it was never me, because I knew it was wrong. Point being, I was always tagging along with Mikey and these guys and one of these guys was this white boy, Josh LaFrance, who was crashing with Mikey in this shithole over the Diamond Drugs, so when I started getting cool with Mike again, I got cool with Josh.

Josh was this cool older dude who'd just turned eighteen, tall and lanky with biggish ears and brown eyes and thick brown hair. He was that guy who smoked lots of weed and talked about wanting to go to Amsterdam all the time. It was 2004 and everybody was smoking bullshit weed out of cans and apples and tinfoil pipes. Because of my mom I was weird about drugs and alcohol. Especially alcohol. Except for having a couple of drinks and falling asleep at this party this one time, I didn't touch it until I turned twenty-five. I smoked weed every now and then, like when my brother Ralph got me high, but in general I shied away from it and I always got shat on by my homies because of that. They'd be like, "You're such a *pussy*. You're such a *bitch*. C'mon, c'mon!" And I'd think, "Fuck you. You can say whatever you want, because I'm looking at my mom and I'm also looking at your mom because both our moms are in the program, and all I know is that's not going to be me."

Still, I'd hit it every now and then, and one afternoon I was with Mike and Josh in Mike's shitty apartment and these two hood-ass black dudes came over and sold them weed and we smoked and Mike and Josh were being assholes about it. That was one of the other things I hated about drugs. Everything had to be extreme. Guys would be like, "Hit that shit!" and they'd make me hit it and hold it and shotgun it and just get obliterated instead of taking a small hit and feeling a good vibe. The problem this time, though, was that I'm pretty sure the weed was laced with PCP, because as soon as I smoked, I felt horrible. Not like "Oooh, I'm a little paranoid" horrible, but more like "Oh, shit, call an ambulance" horrible. I was so fucked up I crawled into the kitchen in the dark and curled up on the filthy linoleum floor between the fridge and the oven and went to sleep and had the craziest dreams. At some point I came to and saw the same dudes who'd sold us the weed creeping back into the apartment and going through Mikey's shit, like they'd dosed us on purpose so they could come back through and rob the place. It was some super-weird shit.

When I finally sobered up, Mikey was taking a shit and throwing up in the tub at the same time. Josh was all right, for the most part, so we were hanging out and I don't know why but I felt a bond with him, a real big-brother vibe. For whatever reason, Josh fucked with me, too. We became friends. For a while it was me and Mikey and Josh, but then there was some pussy shit between the two of them and they started fighting and I stopped talking to Mike out of my low-key fear of and reverence for Josh. Not long after that Mikey got super-drunk at a party one night. I wasn't there but he was showing off his trick of how he could throw up on command and he was throwing up off the third story of some apartment building and he flailingly fell off the balcony and hit the ground and snapped his back and had all these problems and never walked right again. From then on it was just me and Josh.

When I met Josh the thing that impressed me about him was that he seemed like such a big fish in the small pond of Gaithersburg. He was always carrying guns and listening to Three 6 Mafia. He had Berettas and .22s and rifles. At the time I looked up to him as this badass hood motherfucker. Except that he wasn't that at all. Josh had grown up in a loving, stable middle-class family. They had two cars, a three-story house, the whole bit. Mary Jo, his mom, was the kindest, most loving woman. Bernie, his dad, was an engineer who designed satellites for the government. But Josh, like my mom, was a drug addict with serious mental-health issues. Long before I knew him he was having outbursts at school, stealing shit from his parents, and just being an asshole. Once they had to ship him off to Utah to this facility for troubled teens. But that shit didn't work. He came back and he graduated high school and was like, "I'm not going to go to college; I'm going to take a year off." Which is what a lot of kids say right before they fuck up their lives.

A big part of it was Josh being this suburban kid from a nice home watching *Scarface* and listening to gangsta rap and thinking he was that. That's a real thing. That's a lot of people back in Maryland, honestly. You meet nerdy white guys like Josh and Mikey and they've got this badass posture and you're like, "Yo, you're not this dude. You're not some hard motherfucker." What's crazy is they do it long enough that they actually become it. That's what was happening to Josh. He used to walk around with a sawed-off shotgun in his trench coat. The dude was a gangster motherfucker for sure. He was, but he wasn't. He was a suburban white kid living in a delusion, but the fact that he acted it out made it real.

He used to take me out with his other homies and we would ride around doing dumb shit and bustin' guns and Josh would be like, "Yo, come shoot this gun. Don't be no bitch," and I would be like, "Yeah! Fuck yeah, dawg!" But at the same time I knew it was fucking stupid and wrong and I didn't want to be doing it. I'd be thinking, "Why the fuck am I, at fourteen years old, riding around shooting guns? Why am I with these people?" Of course, in hindsight I know exactly why I was with those people: because I had to do everything I could to get out of my house and have a family outside of my house. Once I met Josh, I was at his place all the time. And he lived a couple of miles away, at least. I'd hoof it over there in the dead of winter and I'd hang out and stay for dinner and do whatever I could to stay there, even when Josh wasn't home, which was increasingly the case.

In Josh's room, holding one of his guns,
with a tin foil grill on my teeth.

Josh would have these bouts of "I'm fuckin' out of here!" and he'd storm out for a couple of weeks and go stay somewhere else. Then that wouldn't work out and he'd go back home until everything blew up and he'd leave again. Then the summer after my freshman year he finally lived his dream and told everybody to fuck off and he went to Amsterdam and did lots of mushrooms and acid and absinthe and shit. When he got back he wasn't the same person. He was obsessed with absinthe and got way into the color green. Everything was green. He was always talking about the Joker, saying shit like, "I am the Joker!" I loved him, but Bernie and Mary Jo weren't having it, so Josh came and lived with me and my mom at West Deer Park. That's when he got my mom smoking weed again. Then we all started getting high together.

Smoking weed with my mom was only a little bit strange because at that point she and I had been smoking cigarettes in the house together for over a year. After trying my first cigarette at five and hating it and getting in trouble for it, I didn't really start smoking again until I was eleven. Whenever my mom and I walked to the store or the bus stop she'd smoke one of her Marlboro Light 100's and then she'd throw the butt and I'd pick it up and take a few hits. Then I started dabbling and smoking on the sly with my older sisters and my homies and finally I just told my mom I was doing it because I didn't want to hide it anymore. The fucked-up part was that when I told her, she was cool with it. It was the addict in her, letting her child do this unhealthy thing so she could enable her own habit. And since she let me smoke around her at thirteen years old, I became an addict, too. I used to smoke in my room, which is disgusting to think about now, but back then I thought it was cool, and as fucked up as it was, getting high with Josh and my mom was actually really cool, too, because she loosened up and we bonded a little. Then after a few months she snapped back and kicked Josh out and started going to church again.

But Josh, for all that was crazy about him, changed my life. We were brothers. We really did love each other and he saw something in me that I couldn't see in myself. At the time I was still deep into skateboarding. That and video games, but mainly skateboarding. That was the thing that kept me sane. It wasn't rap at all. I mean, I liked rap. When I was growing up in the 1990s and early 2000s, everybody in Gaithersburg liked rap. Whenever you'd get together with your friends somebody was always rapping, making up rhymes and goofing around. I wrote my first rap ever when I was seven years old. "Yo, what's up? / It's little Bobby / But they call me B / I'm a young MC from the streets of MD." So I was rapping that kind of shit with my friends and my brothers and sisters down in Takoma Park. But it was never that serious. I wasn't any more into rap than any other kid in the neighborhood.

Then I met Josh. Josh was like my mom in that he'd go through these phases. It'd be nothing but Marilyn Manson and Nine Inch Nails for months and then that would be over and it would be something else. The year I met him he was way into rap, listening to Wu-Tang and Three 6 Mafia, pulling out all these obscure albums and deep cuts that I knew nothing about. He was the guy who introduced me to all of that shit.

That was around the same time I saw Quentin Tarantino's *Kill Bill* for the first time. My mom wouldn't let me watch it because of the violence that the media was going crazy about, but I got a copy on DVD and I watched it alone while my mom was gone and it was a revelation. The story, the fighting, the action, the dialogue—and the soundtrack. When I started listening to the soundtrack, learning that it was composed by RZA from the Wu-Tang Clan, it was like everything I loved in life came together in one package: it was hip-hop plus Japanese anime and swords and action movies and kung fu movies and all the other stuff I'd picked up from my friends Robert Naples and Jesse Wideman.

The effect *Kill Bill* had on me was insane. It was a catalyst. I watched it a million times. The story made me want to write a book, and I did. I took my old laptop and I wrote the craziest *Kill Bill* rip-off story about some chick from Japan whose parents were killed when she was seven and she went to this warehouse to train alone in kung fu. The soundtrack made me want to create music, so Josh and I started rapping together. I was Hit Man and he was Lone Wolf. We were recording crazy shit on my old laptop and fucking around and that's when Josh said the thing to me that changed the course of my life.

"You are so much better at rapping than you'll ever be at skateboarding," he said, "and you don't even have to try. And the reason is that when you rap, you commit to rapping, but you don't commit to skateboarding."

Commitment is a term that's used in skateboarding. If you're going to drop down on an eight-foot half-pipe, you have to commit. You have to commit to gravity and throw your body out over a slab of concrete. You have to be willing to fall the wrong way over and over until you get it right, and there's always the chance you could break your neck. And that was something that I was never willing to do. I did some crazy shit skateboarding, twisting or spraining an ankle here and there. But I always held something back out of fear.

Setting up my first Myspace Music page
with Josh (left) and Dylan (right).

There were kids way younger than me who were tre-flipping and kick-flipping thirteen stairs and shit and I'd look at them and be like, "Nope. Sorry." Because I didn't want to hurt myself.

What Josh noticed was that when I rapped I didn't hold back out of fear. I took the leap and let myself fall with the confidence that I would be able to land. As fucked up as he was, Josh saw me better than I could see myself. My parents never gave a shit about anything I'd ever done. They never encouraged me to do anything creative. Same with the teachers at school, who saw me as this problem kid who was probably going to drop out anyway. The first person who ever gave me an ounce of encouragement to follow a dream was Josh LaFrance. This mentally unbalanced, drugged-out, white-boy tough-guy wannabe was literally the first person in my life to tell me what every kid ought to hear: "You're good at something. You should do the thing that you're good at."

So I did.

기군장비

Halfway through my tenth-grade year I had to change schools because we left West Deer Park and moved back to Germantown. My mom never told me why we were moving. All I remember is packing up and not wanting to leave and feeling fuckin' bummed out, because I liked where we lived. It wasn't like my mom was moving for a new job or to be in a relationship; she was moving to be alone on welfare in a different place. And to be closer to my sister. Germantown was where Geanie had settled and she had two kids now, Brianna from the time she got pregnant with Ricky and now Daisjha with Donnie, who was about to die from a heroin overdose.

There was no acknowledgment from my mom that maybe ripping me out of my school and taking me away from all the friends I'd ever known wasn't in my best interest. She didn't care about that at all. I think it was mostly that she'd lived in this place for ten years and she was always "starting over" with her different phases and she'd probably started over as many times as a person can start over while staying in the same place and she wanted something new. Of course if you're bringing the same shit from one fucked-up apartment to the next fucked-up apartment, nothing's going to change. But good luck telling that to my mom.

One day a friend of hers showed up in a white moving truck and while we were packing I accidentally dropped my laptop. For most of my life, the idea of getting a computer would have been crazy, but technology was advancing fast and computers were getting cheaper, so more and more kids had them and their parents were always getting them new ones and my mom always knew these families with money through the program, which was how I got my shitty old laptop, but even though it was a shitty old laptop it was still my most prized possession and I freaked out when it fell. Then I opened it up and the screen was cracked and I almost lost it, but then I realized I could still plug it into a monitor so I ended up getting one of those old gigantic dinosaur monitors that are the same color as a manila folder, like one you'd find in an elementary school library in 1987, and I started plugging my laptop into that.

The place we moved to in Germantown was this apartment complex called Grey Eagle Court, which was where Geanie lived. It was a bit of an upgrade from West Deer Park in that it was newer and didn't have as much wear and tear on it, but otherwise it was the same white floors and beige carpets and linoleum kitchen tiles as everyplace else. My mom took over the living room and set up all her shutters and her dance mirrors and her cinder-block shelves. I took the bedroom and set up my crappy desk and my laptop and my enormous manila-folder monitor and then I jumped in midsemester at my new school, Seneca Valley.

All I knew about Seneca Valley High School was that when I was at Gaithersburg High School, people would say, "Everyone at Seneca Valley has AIDS." When I got to Seneca Valley, people would say, "Everyone at Gaithersburg has AIDS." So that's how it was. The school itself was cleaner and newer and definitely nicer. It was fucking gigantic, too, thousands of kids. But it was the same as Gaithersburg in terms of being extremely diverse, everything from rich kids to poor kids, black kids and white kids and lots of immigrant kids. So it was the same shit, minus the familiarity.

I mostly remember feeling alone and unhappy. I didn't make any friends, not like my real friends back at West Deer Park. I didn't feel safe. As a kid I'd been around all the gangster shit and the hood shit but I always felt protected because of that weird code that nobody messes with kids. But the protective feeling was starting to erode because I wasn't a kid anymore. I looked more and more like the teenager I was. I started seeing other kids my age getting jumped after school, so I started bringing a knife to school, this fillet knife with a twelve-inch blade, like the kind you'd use to gut a catfish. I had no intention of ever using it, but I'd take it with me everywhere and I had all these stupid ideas about how if I got jumped I'd pull it on the guy and tell him to get lost. It made me feel safer, but only because I was too much of a fuckin' idiot to know that bringing a deadly weapon into school didn't make me or anyone else safer at all and it didn't matter anyway because I was there maybe five months before they kicked me out.

Since I hated the place, the few friends I did make were the burnouts, like this one Indian kid Jay whose mom worked during the day, so his house was empty. I would skip and go hang out with him and this Shrek-looking ogre motherfucker who was the school bully. We'd smoke weed and rap on instrumentals on YouTube and fuck around on Myspace and that was about it. After a few months of that, one of the counselors called me into his office and said, "Look, you're barely showing up. Your grades are terrible. You're out of here."

I can't say they hadn't warned me. They'd been telling me for months, "You need to shape up. You need to come to class." But I was so ignorant I wasn't thinking about the repercussions. The only thing that was crazy was that it hadn't come with any kind of intervention or outreach. There was no "Is everything okay at home? What's going on in your life? Why is it that you're not coming to school? Are you scared to come to school?" There was none of that. It was just "Clean out your locker and don't come back." In hindsight it pisses me off that they didn't try harder for me, but at the time I didn't argue because I didn't care. I already knew I wasn't going to college. Even if I'd had the grades, I didn't have the money. So when this counselor told me to pack up and leave, I wasn't mad at all. I was kind of like, "Cool. Fuck it."

I went home and told my mom that I'd been expelled. She didn't care. I mean, she cared a little, but it was like when you tell someone, "Oh, it might rain tomorrow." They're not thrilled with the news, but they don't get that worked up because what are they going to do about it? She didn't call the school, didn't fight to get me back in, nothing. She was like, "Okay, fuck it. You don't seem happy and I'm still getting my check for you from the government, so it's whatever."

So now I was expelled, hanging out with my mom with nothing to do and my days and nights got totally fucked up because I'd sleep all day and stay up all night fuckin' off and watching *Conan*. After a month or two of that Josh came by one day and said, "'Yo, I'm going to Florida. Wanna come?'"

Josh had this buddy down in Florida named Vince. Vince was a skinny guy with diabetes and Josh always talked about how they used to be best friends, and that week Josh was in one of his moods where he was like, "Fuck y'all in Maryland. I'm going to Florida to stay with Vince because fuck it." He asked me to go with him and because I was a stupid sixteen-year-old kid who didn't know not to get on a Greyhound bus with a mentally unstable drug addict and travel nine hundred miles to another state, I said, "Sure. Lemme ask my mom." So I asked my mom, "Hey, can I go to Florida with Josh?" And instead of doing what any sensible parent of a sixteen-year-old would do and say, "Absolutely not," she was like, "A'ight. Cool."

Which was weird.

So one morning I packed up this ghetto-ass suitcase I had with some snacks and a change of underwear and my busted old laptop and my Discman. The whole thing was completely insane, because I was still a kid—and when I say "kid" I mean I was terrified of the world. Other than a few trips here and there, like going to Ocean City one time, I had never been twenty minutes outside of my own area code. I had maybe twenty-five dollars on me for the trip. I didn't even know where in Florida we were going. Miami, Tampa, the Panhandle—I didn't know the difference. To me it was all just Florida. I was looking up to Josh like he was this big brother who was going to protect me, having no idea that this was a dude who wouldn't have thought twice about leaving me on the side of the road anywhere at any time. So one morning Mary Jo drove me and Josh down to the Greyhound station in D.C. and Josh bought our tickets and we jumped a bus.

It took us two days to get to Florida because there was so much waiting in different bus stations and transferring from one shitty Greyhound to the next shitty Greyhound and it all looked the same. When you're on a Greyhound you're either in the middle of nowhere or you're in some shit area on the shit side of town and the back part by the bathroom smells and everyone's sketchy and you maybe talk to someone if they're sitting right next to or across from you but for the most part you keep to yourself. The thing that sucked the most was not having money. My twenty-five dollars ran out pretty quick and I had to ask Josh to buy me snacks, which he seemed pissed about having to do.

The whole ridiculous scheme started to unravel the minute we arrived in Florida. We showed up on Vince's family's doorstep and they were all excited to see Josh but then they took one look at me and were like, "Who the fuck is this?" At which point it was immediately obvious that Josh hadn't told them I was coming.

So there we were: a mentally ill nineteen-year-old drug addict and this sixteen-year-old minor with no parents and no money. This family had no idea what to do with me. They invited me in and told me stories about alligators and were fairly accommodating, given the circumstances, but it was clear from the jump that they didn't want to be responsible for me. I was so pissed at Josh because I felt like he'd used me and manipulated me. He hadn't wanted to ride down by himself, so he'd dragged me along to have someone to talk to and boss around, but he didn't care what happened to me once we got there, and other than seeing a palm tree for the first time, which was awesome, what the fuck had I gotten out of it? It made me feel dumb. Had I really been stupid enough to think I was going to live in some random family's house in Florida with no money? How could I not have had enough sense to see how insane that was?

I stayed maybe three days max. The only thing I remember other than the palm trees was they took me to this house where there was this old white dude in his fifties with a buzz cut who was sitting around ranting about "something something something niggers." I heard that and I froze. I didn't know what to do. He kept going on about killing niggers and he didn't know who he was talking to because I was this little black dude in a white kid's body and to this day I feel like I was a coward because I didn't stand up and say, "You can't talk about black people that way" or "Yo, *I'm* black." But I was sixteen years old and weighed about ninety pounds and I was alone in this strange place with this psychopath skinhead who probably had a gun. The whole thing was crazy and scary. It was also the moment when I realized "I have to get the fuck out of here."

At some point Vince's family must have called my mom and sorted things out because the next day they were buying me a bus ticket to D.C. to get me out of their situation. The mom bought me some snacks for the trip, like Pop-Tarts and shit, which was cool, but I didn't have any other money left so I asked Josh, "Can I have some money?" and he said, "No," and I said, "How am I supposed to go back with no money?" so he said, "I'll buy your laptop for twenty bucks." Shitty as it was, my laptop was totally worth more than twenty bucks even with the broken screen, a couple hundred at least. It was the most valuable thing I owned, my prized possession, but I didn't have any choice, so I sold it to him and he gave me twenty bucks, which I thought was really fucked up.

I climbed back onto a Greyhound by myself with some Pop-Tarts and the twenty dollars from my laptop and I was terrified and alone with a bunch of weirdos and creeps and I got scared again. But the trip wasn't a total loss because Josh had bought me some new Wu-Tang albums as well as the Roots' *Do You Want More?!!!??!*, which was an album that really hit me.

Josh, for all his fucked-up bullshit of dragging me to Florida and ripping me off for my laptop, was still the guy who'd buy me music because he knew I couldn't afford it. He was still the guy who'd take me through the music store, pulling different CDs out of the racks, going, "Here's this and here's this and you need this and this and this," and he never stopped pushing me and telling me, "You need to be rapping, you need to be rapping, you need to be rapping." For the whole rest of the ride home I did nothing but huddle by the window, staring out at the highway, plugged into my Discman, listening to the Roots and to Wu-Tang and memorizing the beats and thinking up rhymes in my head.

FOURTEEN

When I got back from Florida, I walked into my mom's apartment and, as I was talking to her, out of nowhere, my brother Jesse, who I hadn't seen since I was four years old, popped out of the back bedroom where he'd been hiding, yelling, "Surprise! What's up?!" I couldn't believe it. I was definitely surprised. For a minute it was all happy and we were all hugging each other, having this fun moment catching up, but then suddenly he got on this weird older-brother trip where he was like, "Yo. I heard how you been treating Mom."

"What do you mean?"

"You been disrespecting her, not listening to her."

Which meant, obviously, that while I'd been in Florida my mom had been in his ear with all her lies and bullshit about how nobody loved her and nobody helped her, and now he was defending her to try to get back on her good side after being away for so long. That lasted about two weeks and then he came into my room one day and was like, "This bitch is crazy! I gotta get the fuck out of here." So that was cool and from then on we were able to bond over how fucked up our mother was. For a while it was me and him together against the world, and then he couldn't take Terry Lee anymore and he left to live with Geanie and her babies in the apartment across the way and

With Jesse.

then it was me and my mom again and I realized I wanted out, too. I wanted a change, something different, just like Josh wanted something different in Florida and my mom wanted something different in moving to Grey Eagle Court.

More than anything, for whatever reason, I felt this urge to have my dad back in my life. I wanted a real relationship with my father. I wanted a dad to go fishing with and to play catch with, as stupid as it sounds. I wanted that because I'd never had it, and I was still too young to understand that I was never going to get it. Because my dad was who he was, would always be who he was, and had always been who he was my whole life, which I was too young to understand.

Maybe I should have figured it out when he left me in the backseat of a car outside a crackhouse. Maybe I should have figured it out the time he stole my cubic zirconia earring off of my naked body to pay for drugs. Or maybe I should have figured it out the time he stole my identity. That was a new one. I like my name and I'm proud of my name, but when it comes to protecting your identity and your credit rating, it isn't a good idea to be named after a crack addict. My dad's name is Robert Bryson Hall and mine is Sir Robert Bryson Hall II and because he knew my social security number, he stole my identity and took out five or six credit cards and maxed them all out. The only cards he was able to get all had low limits on them, so it was only a few grand, maybe. But it was a few grand my mom couldn't pay back. We didn't even find out about it until a couple of years later when we started getting calls from collection agencies and by then my credit was already fucked.

Everything about my dad was a lie. My dad would play me music and lie about it being his. He'd pull out a CD and pop it on and say, "Yeah, this is me from back in the day." And he'd play the shit, and it would be obvious even to a sixteen-year-old that the guy singing wasn't my dad. I'd be like, "Yo, this isn't you. You're playing me this and you're swearing to me that this is you and it's so evidently not you."

The thing about my dad was that he did have admirable qualities. He was a talented musician and a smooth, silver-tongued dude. If he wanted something he could get it, and I inherited that from him. The difference is he only used his powers for evil, to hustle and manipulate people so he could skate by without doing shit. Which is the funny thing about lazy people. They're not lazy. They put so much effort into doing the least amount of work. If you've seen *Ocean's Eleven*, my dad was like the Danny Ocean of laziness. He'd go above and beyond and cook up all these crazy plots and schemes to do nothing. If he'd just had a regular fuckin' job, he'd have been further along than he was. But I didn't see it back then. I didn't see it when I was sleeping in the car outside the crackhouse or when he stole my earring or when he stole my identity. I looked past all that because I still wanted a relationship with him so much. When I got back from Florida, I wasn't in school and I didn't have shit going on or any friends living nearby, so one day I announced to my mom, "I don't want to live with you. I want to live with my dad."

At the time my dad was living down in Fireside in an apartment that was way worse than any I ever lived in with my mom. You walked in and you were in the living room with the carpet that probably looked good in 1982 but now had so many stains and spills that it was mostly covered up with throw rugs. It always felt dark in the house, too, even if the windows were open and all the lights were on. In the corner was a TV up on a big stand next to the sliding door out to the porch where I would smoke, and in the middle was a coffee table and one of those big '90s leather couches that was always cold when you sat on it and it was nasty and dirty because it never got cleaned.

My dad's brother, my uncle Mike, was living with him at the time. Uncle Mike was super-cool and he worked at Nordstrom Rack. Immediately to your right when you walked in was a door to this tiny room that was barely more than a walk-in closet. Uncle Mike slept in there on a mattress on the floor. Then past that was the kitchen and then the tiny bathroom and then my dad's room. I didn't have a bedroom. I slept on the nasty leather couch that was always cold, which is probably why to this day I hate leather couches.

So I was living with my dad for a minute, watchin' TV and cookin' fried eggs with Old Bay on them to make sandwiches. My dad sort of had his shit together at that point, so it was difficult to know if he was using or not, but I know for sure he was pimping because he took me with him to do it one day. I guess he saw it as like a fun father-son activity.

The girl wasn't one of his girlfriends. Donna the Cryptkeeper was gone by that point. I don't know how or where to. And my dad hadn't yet met his third wife, Debbie, the one who he cheated on while she was in a coma and then divorced as soon as she got out of the coma. So the girlfriend he was seeing when I stayed with him was this woman Bridget. Bridget was attractive for a crack addict. She was like a ditzy, dumb blonde with big breasts and she and my dad were fucking for a while, but then she ended up getting with Uncle Mike, which is so gross if you think about it. She left the master bedroom to head down the hall and sleep on the floor in the little ghetto bedroom with Mike.

The girl my dad was pimping out wasn't Bridget. It was some other girl. He took me and we picked her up and drove deep in the hood, way out into Takoma Park, and when we got to these apartments behind some random supermarket my dad parked and said to her, "So, he's up there?" and she said, "Yeah," and my dad said—and I'll never forget this—he said, "All right. When you come back, you make sure you give me that money." She got out of the car and we watched her walk up some alleyway behind the supermarket. Then we drove to McDonald's for a bit, and while that girl was getting pimped out I got my all-time go-to standard McDonald's order. (Number 1 Big Mac, medium, with a Coke and a Spicy McChicken on the side in case the Big Mac sucks. Because the Big Mac is always a roll of the dice, but the Spicy McChicken, you can't fuck that up.) Then we drove back to the apartment behind the supermarket and the girl came down and got back in the car and gave my dad some money and I was like, "Damn, was I just part of a prostitution exchange?"

So that was that and then Bridget moved down the hall and that's when Debbie first showed up. My dad met Debbie in A.A. She was this blond woman and she wasn't skinny but she wasn't fat and she had her teeth. She was from Atlanta and from money but now she and my dad were addicts together. When they were clean and doing well, they were clean and doing well, and when they were using they were using. She had two adult kids, and they were both drug addicts and alcoholics, too.

I didn't like Debbie at first, but she turned out to be the sweetest woman ever. I wouldn't call her a mother figure but she was a good person when she was clean and she was clean most of the time I was there. This one time, my dad came into some money he probably stole and we were at the shoe store and he was buying himself all these shoes and I was standing there in my ratty sneakers with holes in them but my dad didn't care because he was so focused on himself and Debbie was like, "Buy your fuckin' son a pair of shoes. What's wrong with you?" I always liked that about her. They got married and then she OD'd and fell into a coma and while she was in the coma he was running around cheating on her, but all that came years later.

Other than pimping that one girl out and shifting gears between Bridget and Debbie, I don't know what the motherfucker was doing with his life at the time besides bossing me around. There was literally zero parenting going on. He never cooked a single meal for me; I had to fend for myself. The only parentlike thing he did was say that if I was going to live with him I had to go back to school, so six months after I'd been expelled from Seneca Valley, he went down and enrolled me back in Gaithersburg High. The fall semester had already started and I missed the first few weeks and technically I was a junior but really I was still somewhere between flunking and passing ninth and/or tenth grade. I did all right, all things considered. I reconnected with some of my old friends, which was cool. But I didn't give a fuck about school. More and more, the only thing I was into was music. Lying on my dad's shitty leather couch late at night with just the light shining in from the bathroom or the window, I would put on CDs and stare into the blackness until all the light disappeared and there was nothing but me and the music. I would listen to Wu-Tang tracks over and over and over, and as I listened, I started to train my mind to strip the words out of the songs, making an album in my mind of Wu-Tang beats without any Wu-Tang raps. Then I'd close my eyes and imagine my own raps set to the beat. I'd do that for hours, just me alone in the dark.

I fell in love with rap for several reasons. Part of it was that I was actually good at it; it was the only thing anybody had ever given me positive feedback on and encouraged me to pursue. Part of it was that I looked up to older guys like Josh and liked what they liked because I wanted to be like them. But I also know a big part of it was wanting something I could share with my dad. We'd never go fishing together or play catch together, but we could record music and go to open mics together, and we did.

Living with my dad was when I first started recording raps. He knew some guys with a legit studio. And by legit studio I mean there was this self-storage unit in Gaithersburg where these hood motherfuckers—and I mean like real killers—had rented a unit and turned it into a recording studio. We'd go there and take an elevator up and find this storage unit and go in and record. Some days I'd go in and rap for fifteen minutes straight because I had three notebooks full of a million raps.

My dad took me with him to open-mic nights and radio-station contests and shit like that. A lot of them were scams, because you'd have to pay to perform and then you'd have forty people performing and each of them gets two minutes and they think they're going to get up and be discovered or whatever. You'd be there for hours and whoever put the thing on would walk away with all this money and nobody ever got discovered ever. But my dad would do them with his band and I'd go along.

My dad was a good entertainer. He didn't have the best voice, but he could hold a tune and had a lot of charisma. There was this one open mic we went to that was at this bar. Debbie was there and my dad had his whole band set up and toward the end of their set I got up and rapped with them. It was one of my first times on a real stage. I didn't know what I was doing, but it was exhilarating. I just got up and went crazy with these insane raps, veins popping out of my forehead while I shouted, "I'm gonna murder this rhyme" and "I'm gonna kill this beat." Everything was hard-core. Everything was about death. But it was dope.

I've got pictures of me and my dad performing together, which is special. I'd go with him to these things and before our sets we'd smoke cigarettes in the stairwell outside and then we'd go back in to perform. We shared this deep love for music and it was awesome and I loved it and, in hindsight, I think I mistook that for affection. It wasn't like going fishing together or playing catch together because it was all about him. It was never about us and it certainly wasn't about

Performing with my dad.

me. If we showed up late to an open-mic night and there was only one slot available, he'd take it. If it was a choice between me getting an opportunity or him getting the opportunity, it would be him every time.

My dad was a fifty-year-old crack addict who'd been hustling in the local D.C. music scene for thirty years getting nowhere, but in his mind he was still going to make it. The big break, the lucrative record deal, they were always right around the corner. A less selfish person might have recognized, "Hey, this music thing hasn't worked out for me, but my son has an interest in it so let me get behind him and maybe help him grab the spotlight." Which is what Joe Jackson did with Michael and the Jackson Five. As abusive and exploitative as Joe Jackson was, he at least had the self-awareness to know that the kids were the meal ticket. My dad was too selfish to exploit me as his meal ticket, because that would have meant giving me the spotlight he thought he deserved for himself. He wasn't particularly abusive or mean, just selfish and indifferent. He didn't like to share.

My dad is the type of nigga where if there was ice cream in the freezer and he saw me going for the kitchen, he'd be like, "Don't eat up all my ice cream, now," and I'd be like, "I can't have *any*?" and he'd be like, "Nah, fuck you. That's my shit."

And that's the way it was.

ㅈ룑룑ㅈㅈㄲ||

It was late in the fall semester of my being back at Gaithersburg High and as usual I was skinny little Bobby with the curly hair, skipping school and macking on all the girls, and I'd met one girl in particular, a Salvadoran girl, Christine. She was a freshman and I was head over heels in love with her and one morning at school I asked her if she wanted to be my girlfriend. She said yes, and that afternoon I decided to skip the rest of the day after lunch, blowing off my classes and leaving school to walk back through Bohrer Park to my dad's place down in Fireside.

Two things were true about me in high school: A) I was too poor to afford new clothes, and B) my favorite color was blue. I only had a few outfits and I wore them all the time and since blue was my favorite color pretty much everything I owned was blue. So I had on this blue tracksuit I loved and I was walking home through Bohrer Park and I started to hear these footsteps behind me. But whatever. I didn't give it any thought. I kept walking and walking and the footsteps started getting closer and quicker and the second I thought to think something was wrong I turned to look behind me and *BAM!* I got sucker-punched, cold-cocked in the temple just behind my right eye.

I stumbled and hit the ground hard and my arms shot up around my head as a reflex and before I could even look to see who did it I shouted, "I ain't got nothin' on me!" Because I thought I was being robbed. Then I looked up and I saw this guy, dark-skinned and way tougher and bigger than I was. Not so much taller, but super-jacked. He was wearing a football jersey, so I knew he played ball, and even as I kept saying, "I ain't got nothin' on me!" there was this look on his face like he didn't care. This dude had malice. He wasn't trying to rob me. He just wanted to fuck me up. He was coming after me for a reason, but I had no idea why. I hadn't done anything. I went in my backpack where I had my catfish knife, but as I was pulling it out I fumbled the handle and it fell down in the leaves and I couldn't see it and I panicked. I was like, "This dude is going to kill me. I have to run away."

So I did. I jumped up and I ran. For a long time, when I told this story, I was ashamed to say that I ran away, but when I explain what happened, people always say, "Oh, no. That dude was trying to murder you. When someone is trying to murder you, you should totally run away. You did the right thing." Which is nice to hear, but at the time I wasn't thinking about what I should or shouldn't do. It was instinct, self-preservation. I ran through the woods and through my old West Deer Park apartments and at some point I lost the guy but I still kept running across the street to Summit Elementary where I jumped the fence and ran into the field full of teachers and kids having recess where I knew I'd be safe. But then I was the sixteen-year-old dude with a bloody face running through a field full of kids, which was weird. A teacher flagged me down and said, "Are you okay?" But I was in shock. I could barely speak and I stammered something about this guy who was trying to fight me but it didn't make a whole lot of sense, so I kept running and running, past Robert Naples's old house, down through to Fireside, where I hopped over this fence and landed in the yard of my dad's apartment complex and who did I see but the fuckin' guy who'd just fucked me up. He was maybe a hundred feet away, but thankfully he didn't see me. He walked right into my dad's apartment complex and went into one of the buildings.

The dude was my fuckin' *neighbor*.

I ducked into my dad's apartment, locked the door behind me, and curled up on the couch, overwhelmed by these feelings of anxiety and panic and complete fucking terror. When school let out, Christine came by and she saw my black eye and was like, "Oh my God! What happened to your face?!" I told her I was okay and not to worry but secretly I loved that she was so worried about me and—I'll be honest—I totally played it up for sympathy. My dad, on the other hand, didn't give a fuck. When he got home I told him what had happened and he was like, "Can't let them niggas push you around!" and that was pretty much all he had to say.

I couldn't articulate to my dad or to Christine why I was so shook. I didn't fully understand it myself. I'd been in fights before. I'd been pushed and punched and knocked down and gotten bloody, but that was just kids being all "See you after school, bro!" where you know the worst that will happen is that you might take a few hits before the teacher breaks it up. I'd been in some shady situations with Mikey and Josh, but always on the sidelines. There had never been anything in my life to make me look over my shoulder. This was different. Maybe this was some random thing and it would never happen again, but there was something about the guy that made me feel powerless and weak. My whole life, the danger had been coming from inside the house, from my mother. Being out in the world, skateboarding and riding bikes and hanging with my friends, that was where I'd felt safe. Now, in the blink of an eye, that feeling of safety had been stolen from me. It was like I grew up and became an adult in that moment, not because I was older or wiser or more mature but because my entire relationship to the world around me had changed. Now I wasn't safe at home or away from home. I wasn't safe anywhere, and I was terrified.

I barely slept that night. It was all I could think about, knowing that this dude was in the building across the way. The next morning

I walked to school on the lookout for this guy the whole time. Most of the day was uneventful. Lunch came and I sat with Christine and her friends in the cafeteria and everyone asked about my black eye. I told everyone what had happened, playing down the fact that I'd run away and generally acting like the whole thing was nothing. But then the bell rang and lunch was over and Christine and I walked out into the hallway, which was like a New York City sidewalk at rush hour, hundreds of kids running back and forth to get to their lockers and get to class, and in the middle of this throng of kids rushing past, I saw the guy. He was standing there, completely still, staring at me with this look that said, "I am going to fuck you up." He reached up and rubbed the side of his face. I had no idea what he was doing but then I realized he was gesturing to where he'd hit me and where my bruise was, to remind me what he'd done, like he was tormenting me.

I felt sick. I ducked into my science class, and the whole lecture I sat there, not thinking about anything except "This guy is a killer and I weigh ninety pounds and I'm fucked." This guy wasn't even a known bully. He was just somebody who wanted to fuck me up and I had no idea why. Months later I was telling this story to somebody who was with the Bloods and they told me, "Yo, that dude is a Blood, and since you're always wearing blue he probably thought you were a Crip." Which, I don't know if that's true, but it makes as much sense as anything given that I didn't know this guy, didn't share any classes with him, and didn't run in the same circles. So there was nothing else I could have done that made him have this vendetta against me.

When the bell rang I ran to my next period—and by "ran" I mean I Usain Bolted the fuck down the hall to art class and got in there and the whole period I sat in a panic until I was suddenly overcome with this feeling that I had to get away. Not for the afternoon but for good. Not just from school but from this neighborhood. I needed to go home. I needed to go back to my mom's. "I can't do this," I thought. "I have to leave and never come back here, ever." The second class was over, I ran out of the school and never went back. I ran home to my dad's, trying to think of how I would tell him that I wanted to leave and go back to live with my mom. I was too ashamed to tell him the truth because I knew he wouldn't understand why.

Then, as soon as I got back to my dad's, I got a call from Jesse.

"Hello?"

"Yo, it's Jesse."

"Yo, what's up?"

"Yo, man. Mom got stabbed!"

"What?!"

"Yeah. She fuckin' got stabbed!"

"The fuck are you talking about?"

"Some dudes in the park. She was with them late last night and she was doin' whatever, drinking and smoking and getting high and all this dumbass shit, and she called somebody a nigger and they stabbed her ass."

"Oh, shit."

"So get the fuck over here!"

It was the most fucked-up, crazy, yet also weirdly serendipitous thing that I'd ever experienced. There I was, needing an excuse to move back home, and lo and behold my mother conveniently gets stabbed. I ran in to tell my dad.

"Dad. Yo. Mom got stabbed. They're bringing her home from the hospital. I need to go home. I have to go back to be with her. I need a ride back to her place."

Then came the moment that finally opened my eyes to who my father was and always would be.

"If you wanna leave, leave," he said. "But I ain't gonna drive you."

"Huh?"

"Take the bus."

"Take the *bus*?"

"Yeah, take the bus."

"But that'll take hours. Mom's been stabbed."

He got all mad. Like it was a personal insult that I was leaving. "You wanna leave?" he said. "You don't wanna be here? Fuck you, nigga, go. But don't ask me to drive you."

"But . . . but Mom just got stabbed. She's in the hospital. I have to go. You can't give me ride?"

He still refused. I couldn't believe it. And it ain't like he was doing shit. He was just sitting in his room, and he still wouldn't take me. I was so angry that I wanted to yell, "Mom just got *stabbed,* you fuckin' piece of shit!" But I only yelled it in my head because I was too small to stand up to him and I didn't have the vocabulary to express myself, so I packed my shit and walked to the bus stop.

Two buses and nearly two hours later I made it to Grey Eagle Court and went straight to Geanie's apartment, where my mom was fresh out of the hospital. Walking in, I was terrified. Terrified of what I was going to find and what it was all going to mean. The first thing I remember seeing was the blood-soaked gauze wrapped around her stomach and ribs. She was definitely fucked up, but the most striking thing about her was that she was quiet. I'd seen my mom in pain before, but that was always her crying and screaming, in hysterics. Now she was somber, shaken. Jesse and Geanie were telling her what to do, "Lie down here," "Rest your head there," and she was doing what she was told, not arguing with anyone, as docile as a baby deer. After a bit, we walked her back to her own apartment.

For the next few weeks it was my job to take care of her. I had a washcloth and a tub of water and twice a day I'd clean her wounds and sutures and change her bandages. The stab wounds were dotted along the sides of her rib cage and her back. Each one was about the size of a dime and looked like it was crusted over with dried grape jelly. I'd seen my mom naked plenty of times because she was always passing out drunk without any clothes on, but this was even more awkward because she was stone-sober and awake, and there I was, her teenage son, cleaning her stomach and her back with swabs of rubbing alcohol.

It was strange getting used to this new, obedient Terry Lee Miller Bell Stone Bransford. In my mind, for such a small woman, my mother was gigantic. She was the devil incarnate whenever she was enraged or in pain, and now here was this frail creature who needed to be taken care of and nursed back to health. It was bizarre to feel stronger than she was, because I'd never felt that way before in my life.

Needless to say, it didn't last.

For most people, getting stabbed would be a near-death experience, a New Year's resolution on steroids. "I'm gonna change. I'm gonna do better." My mom didn't do shit. Her feelings of sadness and fear quickly turned to the same bitterness that had always been there before, and soon enough she went right back to being her old self. My own feelings swung between pity and anger. One minute I'd be thinking, "You didn't deserve this. Nobody deserves this." Then, a minute later, I'd think, "Bitch, you one hundred percent deserved this." Because, let's be honest, this was a forty-five-year-old woman hanging out with a bunch of fucked-up hood-ass teenagers—kids that I went to high school with—and she was getting drunk with them and probably having sex with one of them for drugs and then she called one of them a nigger. I suppose it was less that she deserved it and more that it was inevitable. You can't be throwin' that word around or you're going to get stabbed up.

ᎯᏔᎲᎼᎧ

A few weeks after the stabbing I was walking my mom across the Grey Eagle Court parking lot when she saw some black dude walkin' along, minding his own business, and she grabbed my arm and pulled in close to me and said, "Oh my God. He's *black*."

Part of me was like, "What the fuck is wrong with you? Two of your husbands were black. All of your kids are black." But then another part of me was like, "I get it. Some black dude stabbed you, so you've got post-traumatic stress and you're freaked out and paranoid about black people." But what's fucked up is the reason I understood it was because I was feeling it myself. My mother's stabbing had been so overwhelming, and I'd been so busy taking care of her, that I'd never stopped to reckon with my own assault. I was suffering from wicked PTSD, too, and it had royally fucked me up.

From the day I got attacked and my mother got stabbed, whenever I left the apartment and I would see people of, let's just say, "a certain demographic," it scared me. I would feel a panic attack coming on. It fucked me up to where I started perceiving black people a certain way. For a time I was like, "Is my mom's racism fuckin' with me? Is her racism incepting me?" But then I realized it wasn't racism because it wasn't black guys I was scared of. It was shady motherfuckers in general. It was hood-ass white dudes and shady Hispanic dudes and thuggish dudes of any color. I'd see them and I'd feel this intense panic and I'd cross the street or duck around the corner and run home as fast as I could.

What was setting my panic off about these dudes wasn't the color of their skin but the way they were looking at me. They weren't looking at me like the twelve-year-old boy I still felt like inside. They were looking at me like the teenager I was, like the Blood in Bohrer Park had. They were sizing me up to see if I was going to be a threat to them, which made them feel like a threat to me, which was something I'd never felt before.

And those kinds of dudes were everywhere. All those motherfuckers with Nike Foamposites and Jordans and jeans and dreadlocks and all that shit, those dudes were most of my friends. I started looking at everything differently. I developed this intense anxiety where I saw risk and pain and death in everything. Where I used to look at a set of stairs and see a handrail to grind, now I looked at it and saw a place I might trip and smash my nose through my septum and into my brain. Everywhere I went, I was scared that I would be hurt or robbed or punched. Everywhere I went, I saw pain and death and hurt.

Then my everyday fears started to collide with all these bigger fears about life and my future. I'd been kicked out of school. My dad was an asshole crackhead. My mom was an alcoholic insane person. My brothers were gangsters and drug dealers and drug addicts. My sisters were all on welfare with different babies by different men. That was my reality and I was looking around at my reality and I was like, "I'm done for. My life was over before it started. There's nothing that's going to happen for me."

I stopped leaving the house. I never went anywhere that I didn't absolutely have to go. If I had to go to the store or run an errand, if my mom said, "Go to the store and buy milk," I'd be like, "*Fuck.* All right. Please, God, let everything be okay." Then I'd go out, buy the milk, and come right back. My mom had always been terrified of the world, and now I was, too. Together the two of us never left the house. Most days I just stayed in my room.

It sucked for Christine because I'd basically asked her to be my girlfriend the same day I got assaulted and moved back to Germantown and got too scared to leave my room. We ended up having this strange long-distance relationship, talking on the phone and AOL Instant Messenger. She was patient and kind and she stayed with me through it all and she managed to get me to go out once or twice. She and a girlfriend would have one of their moms drive them up to Germantown and we'd go out to see a movie or something. But that was about all I could handle.

For that whole year, AOL and the Internet were my only connection to the world. I'd picked up another janky piece-of-shit laptop from somewhere and, just like I only ever had janky piece-of-shit laptops, I only ever had janky piece-of-shit Internet, too. This was back when you could walk into pretty much any store and they'd have the CD-ROMs for America Online with the free monthly trial. You could pick one up and then put the code in and you'd have Internet for a month and then it'd cut off and you'd go back to the store and get one of the million other CDs and you'd put that code in and get another free month. It was shitty and it was slow as fuck, but it saved my life.

All I did was rap. I took my old computer and a microphone I'd gotten ahold of and I set up a booth in my closet—and that was my whole year, just learning lyrics and how to paint visual pictures and stitch punch lines together. A friend of mine had given me all these *How to Be an MC* CDs, which were discs with a bunch of instrumental tracks that you could rap to and write lyrics for, and I was writing and recording all night long. But none of it would have gone anywhere without the Internet. Through my computer I could reach out into the void and connect to everyone out there who was like me and who knew more than I did.

Since I didn't know the first thing about software or how to properly record myself, I started talking to people through Yahoo! Messenger in this chatroom for music. I just went on there and was like, "Hey, does anyone know how to record?" and some dude was like, "Yeah, use this thing called Cool Edit Pro," and I was like, "Okay, I don't know how to get that," and he was like, "Don't worry, I'll give it to you right now." Then he passed me the file for it. Nowadays it would take about two seconds, but back in 2006 on my shitty dial-up connection it took all night, and this random person I'd never met stayed up to watch the transfer to make sure this file went through from his Yahoo! Messenger to my Yahoo! Messenger, which was the beauty of what the Internet made possible.

So now I had this program Cool Edit Pro, which later turned into Adobe Audition. I learned how to take beats and load them into the program and then record myself and use compression and all this other stuff. That shit was dope. It was crazy to me that I could just do this in my bedroom. Then I saw somebody in this Yahoo! chatroom link to a website called Spokenvswritten.com, which was this site where people could battle-rap each other through written rhymes. The interface was actually pretty sleek for back then, mainly black and gray with simple text. You created a name and posted an avatar. Mine was LORD_SUBLIMINAL. "Yo, I'm Lord Subliminal / A criminal in the hyminal byminal." So cheesy. But my avatar was a picture of Bruce Lee, which was tight.

I'd post up in one of these forums and challenge someone to a rap battle. If they didn't respond, they'd lose points. You picked certain people to challenge and dunk on. You picked other people to up-vote because they were influential and they'd get votes for you later on. It was one of my first experiences with understanding that you gotta know whose dick to suck to get ahead. I did it daily, for hours, and after a couple of months I got voted number one. It was the first time I'd ever been number one at anything.

If I hadn't had rap and the Internet that year I don't know what I would have done because other than rap it was just me and my mom in the house all the time, me up all night and sleeping all day and my mom in the next room being my mom and not giving a shit that her son wasn't in school but at the same time really concerned that I was cursing so much in my lyrics. I remember I watched the original *Star Wars* for the first time, and that Michael Bay movie *The Island* with Ewan McGregor and Scarlett Johansson, but other than that the whole year is a blur. It was lonely. Sometimes I'd watch TV with my mom or she'd want to sit and read the Bible, but I was mostly just alone in my room.

Jesse would come around, too. He was getting into working out, and he tried to get me into it. I was still a twig, but I was doing push-ups and shit. But Jesse wasn't really coming around to work out. Mostly Jesse was coming around because he and my mom had started smoking PCP together just like me and her were smoking cigarettes together, with the primary difference being that this was

Trying not to be a twig.

fucking PCP, which is damn near embalming fluid, like legitimately. It's like vodka, which doesn't freeze at the same temperature as water, so people keep it in the freezer to keep it cool and then they dip the ends of cigarettes in the fluid and light up and smoke it like that. In Maryland they called it "boat," as in "smokin' boat," and that whole smokin' boat phase was crazy. Jesse would come over, and he and my mom would smoke together and get obliterated, mother and son, and whenever it wasn't Jesse it was this other dude who fucked my mom in the ass in the living room. He was a young guy, black, early twenties, and this dude would spend the night and shit and I could hear them getting wasted and fucking in the other room and I know it was anal because she told me about it the next day and I was like, "Why am I the one who has to hear about this?"

Then, like always, my mom went cold turkey and went back to Jesus. The dude stopped coming around and Jesse stopped coming around and pretty soon after that Josh showed up and that's when everything finally went to hell.

ꭻꮊꭽꭶ

J osh had come back from Florida. Mary Jo and Bernie wouldn't
    let him live at home because he was using and Bernie was doing
    his tough-love thing, so my mom said he could come stay with
us for a while and he did. By that point my mom was so fucked up on
booze and PCP and prescriptions. I'd definitely become a target for
her because it was just the two of us in the house besides my brother
coming through and the occasional random dude she was having sex
with. Before, I'd been this kid she was supposed to take care of. Now
I was just some dude who was eating all her food and not working
and not contributing, never mind that she was getting money from
the government for my being there. She was always on me for the
fact that I wasn't doing anything—"You're just sleepin' all night and
all day!"—even though she was doing the exact same thing.

A few weeks after Josh arrived, one night it all came to a breaking point. I don't know why that night was the breaking point or why
it hadn't come on any of the other hundreds of nights when she beat
me or choked me or called me a nigger, but for whatever reason this
night was the night. It was around four in the morning and Josh came
in and shook me awake and said, "Bro, your mom's bleeding and
naked."

"Huh?"

I went out to the hallway to find her standing on a stepladder next to the door of the laundry closet, which was one of those cheap-ass folding doors that slides along a metal track at the top. Something had gone wrong with the track and she was up on a chair, totally shit-faced and completely naked from the waist up, trying to jimmy the door, but she'd fucked it all up and lacerated her hands on the metal and she was screaming and cursing her head off and still trying to fix the fucking thing with all this blood streaming down her arms and smeared on her face.

It wasn't a good look. Meanwhile, we had company in the next room.

Josh knew full well how crazy my mom was, but I was still morti-fied at the idea of him seeing her like this. I snapped. I couldn't take it anymore. I'd had enough, and I laid into her. "What the *fuck*?!" I yelled. "What the *fuck* are you doing?!"

I had never talked back to my mom that way before, never in my life. But like my sisters before me, I'd run out of patience and found the strength to stand my ground. I was an adult. Still a teenager but grown. So we started getting into this argument and it was "Don't tell me what the fuck to do!" and "But Josh is here!" and "Fuck you!" and "You fuckin' cunt!" and "Don't you talk to me that way, you fuckin' nigger!" Then it was nigger this and nigger that and all the same bullshit I'd been hearing my whole life. And we just kept going. It was all nonsense. It was about the broken door but it wasn't. It was her taking out all her anger and rage at her life being a massive pile of shit and me taking out all my anger and rage of seventeen years of taking her abuse. Because I'd taken it and taken it and taken it until finally I couldn't take it anymore.

At some point Josh wandered out of the bedroom with an ex-pression like, "This bitch is crazy." He stood there, watching us go at it, back and forth, like a tennis match. Fed up with the scream-ing, I turned and ran to my room and grabbed a baseball bat and came back out, yelling at her and waving it in her face, like I was going to hit her with it. But that was the one thing I could never do. I couldn't put my hands on her. In spite of everything she'd done to me, I couldn't hurt my own mother, not in a million fuckin' years. So I kept screaming and she kept screaming and all this rage was boiling inside me and I didn't know what the fuck to do but there was a ceramic lamp on the table next to me so I choked up on the bat and I swung and smashed it and yelled, "BITCH! SHUT THE FUCK UP!"

And the bitch shut up.

And it felt good.

It felt so good and I just kept going, all the way around the living room, her whole kaleidoscope of mirrors, one by one.

"FUCK YOU!"

Smash!

"I FUCKING HATE YOU!"

Smash!

"YOU FUCKING CUNT!"

Smash!

"YOU AIN'T RUNNIN' SHIT NO MORE!"

Smash!

By the time I was finished, the living room looked like a tornado had come through, shattered glass all over the floor. I looked up at her and she was shook. She had never seen this from her little boy, her baby. She didn't know what I was going to do next. She was afraid because she realized she couldn't control me anymore, and I was like, "*Yeah,* you motherfucker." Because I'd put that fear in her. She was feeling what I'd felt every day of my life, and I wanted her to feel it. For the first time I had power over her and that power felt good and I wanted more of it.

But I didn't like it. I didn't like that it felt good. I didn't like that I wanted more of it. I didn't like putting fear into somebody, no matter how much I felt at the time that she deserved it. Because she didn't deserve it. Because she wasn't evil. She was sick. The manic depression, the addiction, whatever other mental conditions she had—there was a human being trapped inside, being tortured by those diseases. Year by year, I'd watched as all that sickness had beaten her down until it finally broke her. Only a broken person could have done what my mom did to her own children.

The crazy thing looking back is that, after seventeen years of her abuse, she hadn't broken me. She'd broken my brother, she'd broken my sisters, but she hadn't broken me. I was damaged. There were pieces of me on the floor, but the core of me was whole. It hadn't been shattered. I think a lot of people would have been driven completely insane by this woman. They'd have flipped out and killed her. But I didn't. Even at the angriest, most rage-filled moment of my life, I still had a moral compass inside me, pointing me in the right direction. I had the self-control to take it out on the furniture and not put a hand on her, because I knew that that would be wrong.

And I don't know why. To this day I don't know why I came through with my sense of self intact. To this day I don't know why I survived. I don't know where I got these adamantium bones that couldn't be broken. I don't know how I managed to navigate my way, whether it was God or common sense—I have no fuckin' idea. I was just a hurt kid who wanted to feel something other than scared, which is the same thing my mother wanted to feel every day, and that's why she acted the way she did. I never could have articulated that at seventeen the way I can now, but even then I felt it. I understood it, and that's why I didn't like what I was doing to her, and I've never done it to her or to anyone else since.

I looked around at the shattered glass all over the floor and my mom shook and cowering in the corner, and I chucked the bat aside. I didn't want it anymore. And my mom, with no idea how to deal with me or what to do, just screamed, *"Get the fuck out of my house!"* Then she threw on some clothes and ran out the front door. I didn't know what was about to happen, but I turned to Josh and said, "We better get the fuck out of here," and he was like, "I feel you."

We started looking around in the mess for the cordless phone to call Bernie and Mary Jo to come get us and that's when we realized my mom had taken the phone. We were standing around, wondering what to do next, when suddenly my mom came back in. She wasn't yelling and screaming anymore. She was just not looking at me and not paying attention to me, and then out of nowhere there was a knock at the door.

There's a certain knock that only the police know how to make. The second you hear it, you know, especially if you've heard it a million times like I have. That's what this knock was. I heard it and I was like, "Oh, fuck." The cops came in. There were three or four of them. The second they stepped inside, my mom launched into this teary-eyed sob story. "I don't know what's happening and I have no idea why he's acting this way and I didn't do anything to him and I was minding my business and he came out of his room and he went crazy and destroyed everything and he's threatening me and I don't feel safe and I'm afraid for my life."

The cops looked around the room and they looked at me and now I was the bad guy and my mom was the victim. The main cop, who was one of those real asshole types of cops, started busting out his handcuffs and that's when Josh stepped up and said, "Yo. He didn't do anything. She broke all this shit."

The cop stopped. I could see him doing the math in his head. He knew Josh was lying. It was obvious I was the one who'd smashed everything up, but it was also obvious that my mom was fucking crazy. What this cop wanted, more than anything, was not to be dealing with poor people's bullshit at four in the morning. He didn't want to have to arrest me and haul me down to the station and send me to juvie and spend the next six months filing reports with social services. Josh's lie gave him the pretext not to have to do any of that. He could let everyone off with a warning, finish his shift, and go home and go to bed. So this asshole cop put his cuffs away and looked at me with his asshole face and said, "I'd take you in right now if it wasn't for this witness. But she says you've gotta get out of her house, so get your shit and go."

I was like, "All right, man, cool, whatever."

The cops left and I turned to my mom. "We're going to leave," I said, "but I need the phone to call somebody to pick us up."

"No," she said, "you can't call anybody. Just get the fuck out!"

"Yo, that's ridiculous. Give me the phone."

"GET THE FUCK OUT OF MY HOUSE!"

She took the phone and jammed it in her back pocket and turned and ran out the front door. I ran after her as she was storming down this hill and since I knew she was partially deaf in her left ear I ran up on her left side and snatched the phone out of her pocket and turned and booked back up the hill toward the receiver to get a signal. I started dialing Mary Jo's number and of course she was asleep because it was still ass-early and I left her what must have sounded like the most insane voicemail of all time, going, "Mary Jo, my mom's fuckin' crazy! She called the cops on us! I need you to come here and get us," and on and on and on. Then Josh and I gathered up all our shit and we sat waiting on the curb, hoping that Mary Jo would get the voicemail and come get us, which she finally did. We climbed in the backseat of her car and as we drove away I knew in my bones that I was never coming back, that this wasn't my home anymore, that I was never going to see my mother again. I knew that I was leaving everything, taking nothing but my memories, the good memories and the bad memories, the ones I'll never forget, the ones I don't want to forget, and the ones I've tried to forget but for the life of me I just can't shake, like the memory of this one night when I was eight and my mom was making me watch her old movies like she always did. Some of those movies were cool but a lot of them were boring and stupid and full of stuffy old white people I didn't care about but on this night she made me watch *The Miracle Worker* and for some reason it's followed me and stayed with me and I remember everything about it, every little detail in every scene in the film and everything about the night that we watched it, too. It was late and it was raining and thunderstorming outside and completely dark in the living room except for the black-and-white glow of this old movie on the television. I was curled up there with my mom on the couch and I was hungry as shit, literally starving, because it was the end of the month and it was one of those months when all the cash went to cigarettes and alcohol and we had barely anything to eat, just some powdered milk and a few things that came out of cans.

The Miracle Worker is the story of Helen Keller, about how she went from being born deaf and blind and dumb to learning how to read and speak and be a person thanks to her teacher, Anne Sullivan, who was played by Anne Bancroft. At the start of the movie, Helen is this girl who basically lives like an animal even though her family is rich because her parents have no idea how to handle her. Her father's given up on her; he doesn't give a fuck. But the mom refuses to give up. She hires Anne Sullivan to come in and do shit like hold Helen's hand under the water pump to teach her to spell W-A-T-E-R in sign language. Once Helen learns how to communicate she goes on to learn more and she graduates from college and writes books and makes her own way in the world.

At the start of the movie we're in these rich white people's house. There's like nine black folks in the background as the help and it's some real "Yas, master"–type shit and I'm sitting on the couch going, "What the fuck is this?" But then there's this famous scene after the Anne Sullivan character shows up, the breakfast scene. The whole family is eating breakfast at the very long white-person table, and while everyone's trying to eat Helen is going around the table like a blind dog hunting for scraps, going plate to plate and picking up everyone's eggs and bacon with her hands and eating them like a slob and dropping them all over the floor. The other kids are ignoring her and the dad's reading his newspaper and everybody's like, "Well, that's Helen!"

Anne Sullivan sees this, loses it, and orders everyone out of the room. Then she takes Helen, who's kicking and screaming and thrashing around, and she forces her to sit in a chair. Helen kicks the chair over and Anne forces her back in the chair and puts a spoon in her hand. Helen throws the spoon, so Anne grabs another spoon. Helen throws that spoon, and then another one, and another one, and another one. Finally Anne forces Helen to dig into the eggs with the spoon and put the eggs into her mouth and Helen looks up at her and—even though the bitch can't see—she spits it all in Anne's face and then Helen tries to run and she knocks the plate off the table and all the eggs are all over the floor. Anne runs after Helen and she grabs this little fucker and they're fighting and Anne gets her and puts her back in her chair and she's forcing Helen to eat her eggs and Helen won't eat the eggs and fucking eggs are going everywhere and they're all over the floor and nobody's eating them.

Meanwhile, I was sitting there watching and I was *starving*. I was so angry because those black-and-white eggs looked so good and I wanted to eat them so bad and I was watching this fuckin' brat throw her food on the floor and I wanted to scream, "Eat your fucking eggs! Use your spoon! I'm so hungry and you have eggs and I don't, so why don't you eat your fucking eggs!"

Finally they cut to the mother and father outside the door listening to all this and the fighting dies down and it's quiet and Anne comes to the door and she opens it and her hair is fucked up and she's out of breath, but Helen is sitting at the table and Anne says, "Helen ate with a spoon and folded her napkin."

And it made me cry. To this day I think about that scene all the time and it still makes me cry and for the longest time I thought the reason it made me cry was because it reminded me of that night, of being so poor and how hungry I was and how much it sucked living on nothing but powdered milk and canned food at the end of the month. But then I realized it wasn't that at all. The real reason that movie had such a powerful effect on me was because I was her. I was

Helen. I wasn't literally born deaf and blind, but every baby is born helpless and crying and scared and it's your parents who teach you how to be a person, like how to eat your eggs and share your toys. I didn't have that. I didn't have parents, not in any real sense.

My parents gave as many fucks about me as the dad in the movie who was happy to let his daughter scrounge for food like a dog. Nobody ever put my hand under the pump to teach me how to spell W-A-T-E-R. Nobody ever taught me how to tie my shoes or ride a bike. I had to learn all of that myself. The closest thing I had to a Miracle Worker were those few moments with guys like Tony teaching me to be kind or Jesse and Robert showing me *Cowboy Bebop* or Josh encouraging me to rap. That was all I had, and I'm so happy that I did because those few precious moments were the difference between me finding the strength to run out of my mother's house and me being that little girl eating eggs off the floor for the rest of my life.

And that movie's stayed with me for as long as it has because it's been there to remind me of something I needed to never forget, that if this girl who was born in ignorance and couldn't see or hear or speak, if that little girl could learn how to fold her napkin and go to college and even write a book, then just imagine what I could do.

PART III
LOGIC

Mary Jo LaFrance was everything my mother was not. She was kind and sweet and beautiful and so full of love for everyone and everything. She was just this jolly woman who reminded me of Hagrid from *Harry Potter,* which wasn't so much a weight thing but the fact that she had long dark hair and she dressed like a queen-witch with these long flowing garments and turquoise and silver jewelry, and she had a loud, cackling laugh that sounded like the Count from *Sesame Street. "Vone! Two! Tree! Ah hah-hah-hah!"* It was hilarious.

The first time I met Mary Jo was back when Josh and I started hanging out. I don't think her impression of me was a particularly good one. Josh had come into some money. It was nothing crazy, like a thousand dollars maybe. He said he inherited it but he probably fuckin' stole it. We were in a pet shop and I saw a snake and thought it was cool and he was like, "Do you want me to buy you this snake?" and he bought me the snake. Then he took me and the snake by his house and Mary Jo was like, "Why are you buying this kid a snake? What is wrong with you?" Which, in hindsight, she was probably right because the snake died; I went somewhere and I forgot about it and I came back and that shit looked like fried chicken.

But I started showing up at their house more and more and we hit it off and I learned how kind and caring Mary Jo was. Pretty soon I felt like she might be too kind and caring. I was worried that once she got to know the whole story with my mother she might reach out to social services or the police to try to help me. So one day I sat down with her and said, "Look, you're going to see some shit. But you have to promise me you won't call social services because no matter how bad it gets, know that I'll be okay." She promised she wouldn't, and the fact that I could have that deep a conversation with her told me I could trust her.

It was the first time in my life I'd met a grown-up I could trust.

After Mary Jo picked up me and Josh outside my mother's apartment at four in the morning, there was no question for her what was going to happen next. "You're coming to my house," she said. "You can stay with us, and we're going to figure this out." She let Josh back in and let me sleep on the couch.

That lasted maybe a week because Bernie laid down the law and told me I had to go. Bernie already didn't want Josh back in the house because he was trying to do the tough-love thing with him, and now Josh was back with some other kid? No way.

I did the only thing I could think of. I called my dad, figuring he would let me crash. Not because he was suddenly Father of the Year but because he'd get extra social security and extra food stamps if he could count me as a dependent. I was right. He said I could and I went over there and stayed for a couple of months and everything was cool until the motherfucker told me I had to start paying rent and I was like, "Fuck you. You want me to pay rent on top of the extra social security and welfare checks and food stamps you're getting because I'm living here? You want to double-dip on your own kid? And never mind the welfare and the food stamps. Where's my eighteen years of child support?" Because by that point I'd done the math, and a few hundred dollars a month times twelve months times eighteen years came out to around a hundred grand, so I threw that back at him. "Where's my hundred grand, Dad? Why don't you pay that, and then we'll talk about me paying some rent." That pissed him off and he dug in and I said, "Fuck this," and I left and, thankfully, Mary Jo let me back in. She'd convinced Bernie to go along because now they could put me up in Josh's room in the attic because he'd fucked off somewhere for a bit.

Living at Mary Jo's was one of the best times of my life. They lived in this funky old house on Chestnut Street right at the center of Olde Town and I got to take over the third-floor attic. It was only half-renovated and most of it wasn't drywalled and all these rafters were exposed and it was the bomb. I put hip-hop memorabilia and posters up everywhere: Redman, Wu-Tang, the Roots. There was a closet that was like a phone booth with no door and I put a mic in there and I was hanging up blankets and sleeping bags and old clothes and socks and that egg-crate-foam stuff, anything I could to get the sound right.

Everything about my life up in Mary Jo's attic was music. Kanye had just dropped *Graduation* and I was playing that over and over and over and rapping over the beats and having a blast recording the most ghetto shit ever of all time. Every single day was hip-hop for me. I was doing my homework. This was back when King Tech and Sway Calloway had their morning show and they had all these artists like Immortal Technique and Atmosphere coming by. I would study their interviews, gleaning any bit of insight I could. I was listening to old Stretch and Bobbito radio shows from the '90s, when they had Biggie and Eminem and all these people in the studio. I was in it. I lived and breathed it every waking moment.

When I wasn't rapping I could head downstairs and hang with Mary Jo and she and I would joke around and laugh and I'd be grabbing her and hugging her, going, "Damn, girl, you so *sexy*!" and she'd be laughing and screaming, "Get off of me!" Then Bernie would walk in the room like, "What the fuck is going on?!"

Bernie was the dad I wish I had. Bernie was Mary Jo's second husband. She'd been married before, to this super-abusive guy, and she had her daughter, Rosemary, with him. Rosemary was older than Josh by a few years and she was around. She worked at Kodak, developing film, and she'd develop pictures for me for free. She'd been through some gnarly shit as a teenager, having an abusive father and being a lesbian coming out of the closet, but she got through it and for me, after years of running around the playground saying, "That's gay" and all the "homosexuals will burn in hell" shit that my mom had raised me on, it was cool to meet someone like her who helped me understand what it meant to be a strong gay woman.

Bernie's day job was building satellites for the government. He would go out to Alaska and Japan and all over the world to see his satellites shooting off. He had a 3D printing company on the side and he loved gas-powered go-karts and he'd go and race them all around the country. Dude could build or fix anything. He loved working with his hands and was always puttering around the house in jeans and flannel shirts.

There was something very Mr. Rogers about him, even though really he's a hard motherfucker who calls it like it is and doesn't give a fuck what other people think about him. He's bald and wears glasses and has this lanky pasty-white body that I got to see plenty of because the dude would literally walk around the house wearing nothing but tighty-whities, giving you that "keep it down" look because he was the king of the fuckin' castle.

It was the polar opposite of how I'd grown up, in that everybody worked. Mary Jo was working her job cleaning houses and Bernie was working for the government and I went and got a crappy part-time minimum-wage job detailing cars and cleaning the bathroom at the Jiffy Lube around the corner. Then I got a second part-time job across the street at a flower shop working for this Korean couple, Mr. and Mrs. Ahn, taking orders and dethorning roses and learning about birds-of-paradise and these other different kinds of flowers.

With the little money I made, I paid Mary Jo rent. I actually wanted to pay rent since she had taken me in voluntarily and hadn't skipped out on eighteen years of child-support payments. She gave me chores, too, cleaning the bathrooms and folding the laundry and tidying up and taking out the trash and helping with the lawn. Which was awesome. I mean, I hated it at the time; no kid wants to do chores. But I'm glad I did it because it gave me the satisfaction of doing my part. It was like I finally had someone putting a spoon in my hand and showing me how to eat eggs and be a functioning human in the world.

So the chores were cool, but the bathrooms at the Jiffy Lube were fucking disgusting and Mr. Ahn was nice but he was always looking at me like I was some white kid who couldn't do anything right, so after a few months I quit both of my jobs because I only wanted to make music. I didn't tell Mary Jo for a while because I didn't want her to get mad and kick me out for not being able to pay rent, but then I told her and she was okay with it and she just gave me extra chores around the house and even started taking me with her to clean houses and paying me by the hour to help her. So things were good. I still had my long-distance thing going with Christine and I was skating and rapping and hanging out and—other than the fact that I still had crippling anxiety and PTSD that kept me from leaving my room unless it was absolutely necessary—it was music, music, music and life was cool.

It wasn't like I felt like I finally had a "home." I'd never felt like I had a home. I felt safe. I felt taken care of. But it wasn't home. I was never going to be their kid. I couldn't fuck it up by bringing the cops to their house or anything like that. Still, it was fuckin' dope and not long after I moved in, I convinced Bernie and Mary Jo to let Jesse come and live in the attic with me. I figured they might say yes because I had learned something new: I wasn't the first kid they'd taken in, and I wouldn't be the last. It was like Mary Jo was running an orphanage. Not in any official foster-care capacity, just her helping kids who needed help.

In my day, there were at least five of us in and out and different times. There was me and Jesse. There was this kid Dylan who lived across the street. His mom, Theresa, was best friends with Mary Jo, but his dad wasn't in his life so Mary Jo was always helping him out. There was also Redhead Mike. Redhead Mike's parental situation wasn't great, either. He was always trying to get high and he couldn't keep a job and one time we set him on fire after watching *Jackass* too many times. We were fuckin' stupid. Redhead Mike was like, "Yo, set me on fire! Pour some alcohol on me and it'll burn really quick!" and we were like, "Okay!" We did it a couple of times and it worked and the alcohol burned off and he was fine, but then the last time somebody poured on too much and we hit him with a match and then we couldn't put it out and we were trying to stomp out the fire on his skin and we were kicking him in the face in the dirt and then we all ended up rushing him to the hospital with third-degree burns on his neck.

Dylan was also friends with this kid Willy, who I'd known back at Summit Hall Elementary. I'd seen Willy a few times since, but we'd lost touch and I didn't know him that well anymore. He was a sweet and funny guy, but his home life was terrible. My shit was bad, but his shit was dark. He wasn't a bad person or anything. He just had a lot of demons, so he was always hanging around looking for the same love and support the rest of us were.

Mary Jo's house was definitely like the island of misfit boys. Some, like me, would move in for months at a time; others would crash for a few nights when they couldn't go home. Bernie was like the fire marshal, corralling the kids and not taking shit from them. Mary Jo was on a crusade. She didn't have much else going on at that point. Her own kids were grown. Her husband worked. She loved her stories and she'd go with Dylan's mom to the Laredo Grill on Thursdays for margaritas, but other than that, helping her boys was her life.

With most of the kids Mary Jo could only do so much. They didn't magically become doctors and lawyers and their lives were still pretty fucked up, but she helped some of them get sober and hold down steady jobs, which was a big step forward. The one true success story she had was this one dude from before my time. She'd taken this kid in off the street and helped him and he finished high school and went to college and got a job and fell in love and had kids and lived in a real house, like with a yard. I remember living in her attic and hearing about this dude and dreaming about being him. I wanted to be that guy so if any other kids ever came through there after me, they could look back and look up to me the way I looked up to him, because I would feel good about that.

But you can't save everyone. We lost Willy. He ended up committing suicide by jumping in front of a train by the fairgrounds on Chestnut Street. It was all very weird, because who jumps in front of a train? He wasn't drunk. He wasn't high. He and Dylan were walking alongside the train tracks and out of nowhere Willy leaped out onto the tracks. He was only seventeen. Mary Jo was devastated. We all were, especially Dylan, because he'd watched it happen and it fucked him up and he became a major alcoholic for a long time after.

A few months after I moved into the attic, Josh came back from wherever he'd fucked off to and by that point, like with my mom, I was watching him deteriorate in front of me in real time. He got worse and worse month by month as the drugs ate away at his brain. He was fighting everybody, being fucking horrible to his parents. He'd scream at Mary Jo and steal money and cigarettes from her purse and call her a fat, ugly bitch. And she had the easier time of it, honestly. I truly believed that Josh was going to kill his father. I remember looking out the window one day and Josh and Bernie were in the backyard and Josh was punching Bernie in the face and wrestling him to the ground. At one point I told Mary Jo, "Y'all need to stop lettin' this nigga live with you, because he's sleeping with guns under his pillow and walking around with butcher knives and one day he's going to kill you. He's going to walk in your house and blow your fucking heads off or walk into your room at night and stab you in your sleep with a soldering iron."

Bernie and Mary Jo were always back and forth about what to do. Bernie would go storming around screaming, "I can't live in this fuckin' house! Either he's gotta go, or I gotta go!" But Mary Jo always chose Josh. She would always take him back, no matter what. I'd put my parents out of my own life because they didn't deserve to be there. But I know it's not the same with a kid. I don't know what it means to cut someone off after you've raised him and wiped his ass and had the love that comes with that, and that's the position they were in. Mary Jo was and is the kindest, most generous, bighearted person I've ever met, but there's always been a darker truth behind that: She was trying to save all the lost boys in the world because she couldn't save her own son.

All I know is Josh had everything that I ever wanted in my life — family, parents, clothes, money — and all he wanted to do was act like he came from the fucked-up world that I came from. It's weird, but it always felt like Josh turned out as though he'd been born and raised in my house with my parents, and I turned out as though I'd been born in his house and raised by his parents. I know Bernie wishes my story could have been his son's story, and that's the way it should have happened, honestly. For a kid to come from such a warm, loving home and wind up the way he did is a tragedy, and for a kid to come from a home like mine and end up where I am today, frankly, it's damn near impossible that it happened.

Josh would still fuck off and come back and fuck off and come back. Then eventually he was just gone and I wouldn't see him because, like Tony, he'd be in and out of jail on some bullshit. I actually have audio of Josh on one of my old songs, calling from the phone in jail, talking about "Yeah, I never snitched on nobody!" like he's all gangsta.

Then he wasn't in jail anymore because it was prison. He stabbed this dude and split his stomach open and the dude's intestines spilled out all over the sidewalk while he was still stumbling around, alive. Which is gnarly but, in Josh's defense, he only did it because the dude had hit some woman in the face and Josh got in the middle of it and came to the rescue. But he didn't need to take it as far as he did and he ended up doing some real time behind that. He was supposed to do fourteen years and was in for maybe four or five.

But for all the fucked-up shit that Josh has been through and done, he's still a beautiful person. He's just a sick person, like my mother. Whether that's because of chemicals in his brain from birth or something induced by the drugs that he did, I don't know. All I do know is that even though he's not in my life anymore I'll always love him, not only for changing my life by inspiring me in music, but for being there for me when nobody else was.

As for Mary Jo, I can't even begin to sum up what she did for me because she's still doing it, because that's what a parent is.

One night I was up in Mary Jo's attic with this buddy of mine Steven and we were talking about rap and producing songs and he said, "Yo, if you're going to do this, you need a real name, and not some gimmick like that Wu-Tang shit."

Steven was a guy I'd known since eighth grade. He was an older kid, African dude, a bit of a hustler. He was always working odd jobs, looking for a way to make a buck. He knew I was into hip-hop and, like Josh, he was a guy who wanted to help out. At the time I was making a ton of music, but I was just making it. I had no place to release it other than Myspace. I had no way to make a living from it, either. Steven didn't know anything more about that shit than I did, but he did know the people around Gaithersburg who booked open mics at bars. He also knew enough to know that if I was ever going to be a rapper, I'd need a better name.

When I got to Mary Jo's, I'd been through so many different alter egos. I'd been Lord Subliminal and East_Koast_Killa. Sometimes I was still trying to be Hitman: "Yo, I'm Hitman / I've got the hits, man." They were all terrible. So that night Steven handed me a dictionary. "Go through this," he said. "Take your time, and look for a word that you think best describes you as an MC."

It took me two minutes of flipping through and I found it: Psychological.

"That's it," I said. Because that's where the raps came from, the brain. Everything in hip-hop is mental and verbal swordplay. It seemed perfect.

Around that same time, I was on the phone with Geanie a lot and one day we were talking and I said, "I want to come live with you. That would be fun." So I did. I packed up and moved over to her place. I don't know why I left Mary Jo's except for the same reason my mom left West Deer Park when she did. Poverty gets boring pretty quick. It's the same shit every day because you can't afford to do anything else, and sometimes you just want to switch things up, even if it isn't necessarily the smartest decision you could make.

It was not the smartest decision I could have made. I was set at Mary Jo's house. It was safe. It was supportive. I had nothing but great times there. Meanwhile, Geanie's situation was fucked up. She'd moved from Grey Eagle Court over to a complex in Montgomery Village where she was in a townhouse and she had all her kids and her baby-daddy drama and her crack-dealing boyfriend to deal with. But it was new and Geanie was family and I can't say I regret moving there because you reach a point where you have to think everything happens for a reason, and it turned out to be a dope time in my life. Jesse and I were hanging out a lot. I saw Amber more, and the three of us would hang out. Still, I was definitely more on my own there than at Mary Jo's. Geanie wasn't there to be a surrogate mom or to take care of me. She cooked dinner every night and I got to piggyback off of that and steal her cigarettes when I needed to, but other than that I was on my own.

Since there was no more tagging along with Mary Jo to help her clean houses, I was back to needing a job and I went to work in the bakery at the Safeway that was a couple of miles from Geanie's townhouse. Now I was walking three miles a day back and forth to the Safeway and I had to make the donuts and all the other shit and my boss was some Ukrainian woman who had this hairy mole and talked like a Bond villain and was angry all the time. So I quit that and I got a job next door at Wingstop, where it was pretty much the same thing except with wings instead of donuts, which is better because you can eat a day-old wing and get some sustenance out of it but you can't with a donut. Also the boss didn't yell at me like a Bond villain, so that was cool.

Instead of being up in Mary Jo's dope attic, I was now down on this twin bed in the basement trying to get to sleep while it sounded like people were getting murdered upstairs, only it wasn't actually people getting murdered. It was my sister's baby daddy freaking out from smokin' boat. The dude was cool, though. He did a lot of drugs and he probably definitely cheated on my sister, but out of all the men in Geanie's life, he was all right. Although he was selling drugs out of the house with kids upstairs, which kind of makes him a fuckin' idiot.

He was the guy who taught me how to cook crack on the stove. One night I was recording in the basement and he came down, gun in his waistband—he kept a lot of guns in the house—and he was like, "Yo, I'm going to show you how to cook crack tonight."

"A'ight," I said, trying to be all cool, when really I was like, "Yo, this is going to be *sick.*"

I followed him up to the kitchen and he started showing me the whole routine, the baking powder and the measurements and the mason jar with the crack rocks in it and boiling the jar and letting the cocaine harden and then cutting it with some other shit. I'll never forget the smell. The only way to describe what crack cocaine smells like is to say that it smells like crack cocaine, and that stench was coming off the stove in these billows of smoke that were wafting up to the vent and the air ducts that led to three little girls' bedrooms upstairs. I couldn't believe this shit was happening in the same house, but it was.

Watching him do it, I was like, "Whoa." But at the same time I was thinking, "Why are you showing me this? Why are you showing me you cooking crack with a gun in your waistband?" But that was the life. He was doing it to feel cool, like, "Lemme show this kid something."

The best thing about being at Geanie's was that Jesse and I really connected. We spent all day in the basement making music. He taught me how to produce and we recorded a lot of songs. Like, a lot of songs. Most of it was me learning by doing, by imitating. It was me doing my best impressions of Kanye and Kendrick and J. Cole and Wu-Tang and everyone in between. I was developing the skills that would ultimately make me the rapper I became: a chameleon. Gangsta rap, trap music, boom bap—I learned it all. I was like an X-Men character. I was Mystique. I could do anything, become anyone.

Ten years later a lot of those songs are so cheesy they make me want to cut my face off. Even the best ones are just a kid showing he could do some rappity-rap shit; they weren't real songs with real stories. Still, a lot of them are actually okay for an eighteen-year-old high school dropout who was recording on a busted piece-of-shit laptop in his sister's basement in the middle of Gaithersburg, Maryland, which is about as far from the music world as you can be.

At that moment, I had no money, no income, no connections, no real understanding of the music business, no idea what a master was or what publishing rights were. But I knew rap was what I wanted to do. Hip-hop was always a pipe dream, except that it wasn't. Being a rapper didn't feel attainable, but it also didn't feel unattainable. I just knew I was pretty good at this thing and it was the *only* thing I had ever been good at, so I didn't want to stop doing it. You can call that delusional, but when you're staring at the reality of making it out of the hood on $7.25 an hour with no high school diploma, being a rapper was as plausible as any other option I might have had.

Ultimately me being a rapper was less about a career choice that hinged on making it or not making it. It was the only thing I had in the world that made me feel like I was any good. It was who I was. I do this, therefore I am this. That was true no matter what. And in the end, the thing that finally pushed me to go for it had nothing to do with the realism of it. While I was at Geanie's, Christine and I broke up. My anxiety and my PTSD ended up being too much for her to handle and she got tired of the fact that I never wanted to leave the house, and she had her own issues being confused about who she was and what she wanted and it was always on-again, off-again and the rejection was too much for me and finally I ripped off the Band-Aid and said, "I can't do this anymore."

I was so damaged from my childhood and so desperate to find love and a home that I know I would have married her if she'd been down for it, but she wasn't. And what I took away from the experience was that no matter how much time, effort, love I put into another human being, I wasn't guaranteed to get it back. But whatever time, effort, love I put into my craft, I got it back in spades. Every second, every minute, every hour of every day that I spent on music, I saw improvement little by little. My music was something that would never leave me. So I chose music.

At an open mic with Jesse.

As I was going through the breakup, Steven was taking me around town to open mics and shitty low-level gigs. I was this skinny, white-lookin' kid who didn't even know how to dress, but the one thing I could do was rap. I'd wait offstage, all nervous and excited, but once I got that mic, boom, I would just *go*. After a few months of that, I started making noise in this small pond of Gaithersburg and ended up with a spot opening up for Ghostface Killah from Wu-Tang at this place downtown called the End Zone. Ghostface was just there getting his money, and they needed somebody cheap to open up for him, and Steven knew a guy who knew a guy who knew a guy, so I got the call.

I rolled up that night and I was pumped. I was feeling like Rabbit in *8 Mile,* thinking, "This is my one moment, my one opportunity." Then we got to the door and the owner said I couldn't get in because I was underage. I begged and pleaded, but the guy gestured over at the cops who were there for the crowd and said, "No."

So I went over to the cops and I talked them into letting me do it. I gave them the whole sob story about how I came from this poor family and I didn't have anything and I was doing rap so I could be somebody in life and all this other bullshit and the cops bought it. So now I had a police escort walking me from the front door right to the stage. I got up, killed it, and then they escorted me offstage. I didn't even get to meet Ghostface or stay for his show. They took me right back out the door and it was freezing outside and I had to crane my neck to try to see Ghostface onstage through this plate-glass window.

And that's when I met Lenny.

During a break in the show I walked around to the back on the side by the train tracks to have a cigarette and I was smoking and this guy walked over and said, "Hey, man. You Psychological?"

I looked up and it was this dude. A big dude. Like, a *really* big dude. He reminded me of Kingpin from *Spider-Man,* but with brown skin and jet-black hair.

"Yeah, that's me," I said.

"Cool," he said. "Nice to meet you. I'm Lenny."

We started talking and he was cool and we hit it off. Sometimes you meet people and it's like, "Oh, yeah. We're going to be best friends now." And that's what this was like. Lenny wasn't anybody who was part of the music scene. He lived with his cousin in College Park and worked as a land surveyor for an engineering firm up in Germantown and he loved hip-hop. It was funny because as we were talking, the subject of race came up, as it almost always does because of how I look. I was telling him the whole story, black father, white mother, etc., and I said, "So, what about you?"

"I'm Indian."

"Oh, word," I said. "What tribe?"

"No tribe," he said. "I'm an actual Indian. Like, from India."

I don't remember which one of us suggested we hang out some time, but before I knew it, he was picking me up from Wingstop and we were inseparable from that moment on.

The next gig that came my way was for this music festival at the Montgomery County Fairgrounds off Chestnut Street in the summer of 2009. Pitbull and Ludacris were the headliners. They were on around nine or ten p.m. I got a slot around three-thirty in the afternoon, playing while people showed up to set up their chairs and shit, but that was cool with me. This was the realest thing I'd ever done. The big hip-hop station WPGC was there and everything.

I decided to cut a mixtape to sell at the show. It wasn't the first I'd ever made. Technically the first was this one I did called "Finding Logic," which I made in my sister's basement around the same time. But I wanted this one to be more polished, so I put time into recording and producing the songs and printing out three hundred CDs with "Psychological" on them for the day of the show.

Since I was on the same bill as Pitbull and Ludacris, I could say that I opened for them, but in reality my only interaction with them was seeing them walk down the hall and going, "Oh, shit. That's Ludacris! There's the back of Pitbull's bald head!" I was so nervous I can't even remember most of the day except I did get to meet Inspectah Deck from Wu-Tang. He was super-cool and that was a big moment for me because Wu-Tang was everything to me and I got to be the fan that I meet at every show now, going, "Bro, you changed my life, man! You don't even know what your music means to me!"

I did my set and it was cool and then I went out to try to sell my CDs to the crowd and I didn't sell shit because I was too nervous to go up to people and say, "This is my mixtape. Can I have a dollar?" By the end of the day, I'd managed to sell maybe forty of them, so I just started handing them out and I learned a lot about having to force myself to get out there and promote myself and I also learned that maybe I needed a new name because I kept trying to get the crowd going with "PSY-CHO! LOG-I-CAL! PSY-CHO! LOG-I-CAL!" and that shit didn't work.

There was no real "eureka" moment when it changed. But after knowing me for a few weeks, Lenny didn't want to keep fucking with "Psychological." He called me "Psycho" a few times, but that didn't take, and then one day he called me "Logic." Then the next day he called me Logic again, then again and again and again. I started hanging around with him and all his cousins and he always introduced me as Logic and they started calling me Uncle Logic and it was easy and rolled off the tongue and it stuck and that's how it started. Then one day I decided, "Duh, I'll go by that instead," and to this day it's super-cool that my best friend gave me my name.

�᚛᚛ᚷ

The last time I ever saw my mother was outside the End Zone. I was performing that night. I'd ditched Psychological and this was my first real show as Logic and it was me and this other cat named Knowledge, which is a funny double bill to have: Logic and Knowledge. Knowledge was a fat white dude with a patchy beard and he had a fine-ass black girlfriend who looked like a thicker Ashanti but eventually they broke up.

I first saw my mom when I walked out of the club. I don't know how she found out about the show or who told her about it or what. I don't even know if she actually saw me perform or if she showed up late and was waiting outside, but I like to think she saw me. I like to think she came because she thought what I was doing was important because that would have been cool. But I honestly don't know. At the time, all I knew was she hadn't gotten any better because Jesse was still bringing me news. A few months before she'd started smoking boat again and one night she had a party and all these strangers showed up because that's what addicts do: They find each other. Jesse spent the night talking to this one girl he'd never met, and over the course of the evening this girl kept looking over at my mom, sort of cocking her head with this furrowed brow and this bewildered expression.

Jesse was like, "What is it?" and the girl kept staring. Then Jesse was like, "What's going on?" and the girl kept staring. Then finally the girl turned to Jesse and was like, "Yo, I think I stabbed that bitch."

One addict nearly kills the other in a violent assault, and two years later they're back partying together again. If there's any story that better illustrates the self-perpetuating and self-destructive cycle of addiction, I've never heard it.

So there my mom was at my show and the memory stands out not just because she was there but also because that was my first brush with the business of what fame would be like later on. It was a small show, seventy-five people, maybe. But even at shows that small you've got a dozen or more people clamoring for your attention and wanting to talk to you. You walk out of the club and everybody has to wait around to get their five minutes with you and then they're pissed because they only get five minutes but there's nothing you can do about it.

My mom was out there on the sidewalk, being sweet but fuckin' weird, and it was strange her being one of this small crowd of strangers waving to get my attention. "My son! My son! Sir Robert!" I'm sure I was nice to her and gave her a hug. She's my mother; if I saw her today, I'd hug her. But I was still keeping her at arm's length, emotionally, so I didn't really engage and I was so distracted I don't even recall when she left or how we said goodbye, and that was that. That was last time I ever saw her.

From that point on, what little family I did have started to fall away. They weren't a part of the new life I was making. I did have this one cousin, Troy. Troy reminded me of André 3000 of OutKast. He had the braids and he had the swag and he was always dressing real bizarre for the hood. Nowadays you'd call him an innovator, but back then you'd just say the nigga be wearin' pink shirts and shit.

Troy wasn't always around; he was a barber who worked in D.C. and up in New York. But when he was around, he was there for me and encouraged me. He always said positive things about the music

I was making. He took me to see Lupe Fiasco, my first concert ever, which was amazing. Troy gave me a copy of *My Beautiful Dark Twisted Fantasy* by Kanye on CD. He gave me clothes and cut my hair. More than anything he was the epitome of a guy from the hood who knows it, talks it, and walks it, but never chose it. He never allowed it to define him. In that regard, he inspired me by showing me there's always a better way, and he still does the same for Geanie's and Amber's kids to this day.

So Troy was there, and Jesse was in and out depending on whether we were getting along, and Geanie was letting me stay with her. But that was it, really. Then, less than a week before Christmas, Geanie told me I had to move out. She came downstairs and said, "I want you to leave. I don't want you to live here anymore." I was like, "What?" and she was like, "I don't want you to live here anymore. Get your stuff and get out of here."

She was kind of bitch about it, too. Later on she would tell people, "No, I didn't kick him out. It was because HOC was coming to inspect and he couldn't be here." But that's bullshit, because if that was the case, why didn't she tell me to beat it and lie low for a few days and then come back after the inspection?

I don't like to complain about it too much, because Geanie did let me live with her rent-free for a decent amount of time and I'll always be grateful for that. But she did kick me out the week before Christmas.

She actually did that.

So now I had nowhere to stay. I called Mary Jo, but Bernie was back on his "We're not raising all these kids!" thing, so I couldn't go there and I sure as shit wasn't calling my dad again and Amber wasn't an option with all the weird dudes in and out of her house. Which meant that I was homeless.

It wasn't the worst kind of homeless. It wasn't the living-under-the-overpass-in-a-cardboard-box kind of homeless, but I didn't have anywhere to go so I was sleeping wherever I could, sneaking into friends' houses after their parents went to bed or crashing out in the stairwell outside someone's crib. Occasionally I'd sleep in cars. But there were definitely nights when I couldn't find anything and I'd sleep outside on a bench under a pavilion and it'd be freezing because it was fucking January. Luckily, after a few weeks of that, Mary Jo finally got Bernie to change his mind and they took me back in, only they were renovating the attic so I had to move down to the guest room and this time they put a limit on it and by "they" I mean Bernie. Mary Jo would have let me stay until I was a senile old man, but Bernie was like, "These fuckin' kids in my house, they keep coming back!" So when I moved back in, Mary Jo had to be firm. "You get one more year," she said. "And then that's it. You'll have to go." I agreed and I moved back in.

And that's when shit really started to happen.

When I got back to Mary Jo's, everything was different. Josh was gone. Dylan and Redhead Mike weren't around. I was on the outs with Geanie because she'd kicked me out and I was on the outs with Jesse because he was being an asshole and Christine and I had broken up and Lenny wasn't around because his father had died and he was taking some time for that. So for a while it was just me and Mary Jo and Bernie.

And the Internet.

Online, everything had changed. It was like a switch had flipped and the Internet of AOL and Yahoo! chatrooms was transforming into something else. I remember stumbling across this video of J. Cole that was going around YouTube. It was right around the time he'd put out his *Friday Night Lights* mixtape and signed with Jay-Z's Roc Nation, but you could tell from the video that there was nothing professional at all about how it was made. It was just him in the studio recording a rap and then getting in a car with his crew and rolling to Krispy Kreme, where he was like, "Hey, baby girl, you got any strawberry milk for my donut?"

It killed me. Even though J. Cole was this big rapper on the come-up with all the talent in the world, watching the video felt like he was hanging out with his friends and his friends felt like they were my friends. The reason it felt like we were all friends was because there was no professional camera crew. It was just some guy with a handheld Canon, and everybody's comfortable around him because he's their homie from the hood who's only on the squad because he knows how to run a camera.

The DMV, as the D.C./Maryland/Virginia metro area is known, has a thriving local music scene but it's never been an industry hub the way New York or L.A. or Atlanta is. At that point, the only major rapper ever to come out of the DMV music scene was Wale. He started blowing up around 2006. Wale claimed D.C., but really he was from Maryland, which made him the dude who let me know I could make it out of Maryland. He grew up not far from where I grew up. His high school played my high school. His music was amazing. His mixtapes were album-quality shit. He was working with Mark Ronson. He was doing it different, and he made me want to do it different. Still, I had no idea *how* he had done it.

Then I started seeing more and more of these real-life, day-to-day videos from famous and up-and-coming rappers and musicians online. I saw Mac Miller doing "Kool-Aid & Frozen Pizza" for the first time. I saw Wiz Khalifa doing videos of him and his friends. The thing that was so exciting was that in these videos they were just being regular folks. Incredibly talented, sure, but also everyday, relatable dudes. When I was listening to Wu-Tang and the Roots and Kanye and Biggie and Nas, I revered those guys. They were up on a pedestal, untouchable. There was no connection, no bridge between me and them. Now there was. Everything I'd been doing, writing bars and recording on my shitty laptop, it was all a bunch of hard work and talent and potential with nowhere to go. I was writing and recording and hoping for . . . something. But I had no idea what that was. Then I started seeing these videos with Mac and Wiz and Drake and J. Cole and Kendrick and Big K.R.I.T. and Kid Cudi. None of those guys were that much older than me. Some of them were the same age. Mac Miller was even younger. He was just this white kid from Pittsburgh who put out his first mixtape when he was fifteen. I started following all of these young rappers on Twitter and YouTube and 2DopeBoyz and it wasn't just "I want to be these guys." It was "I *could be* these guys."

That was the moment when everything went BOOM! Here was a blueprint. All of a sudden my dreams weren't delusional at all. All I had to do was exactly what these guys were doing, which meant the first thing I had to do was make a mixtape. A real mixtape, not like the one I threw together to hand out at the summer festival the year before. Mixtapes have always been the key to getting serious attention in hip-hop, going back to the day when they were passed around on actual cassette tapes. You make a free album and give it away to promote yourself and build a fanbase and make enough noise to be recognized by a major label, which will hopefully sign you and give you a budget to create a real studio album.

By that point I had hundreds and hundreds of songs on my hard drive, but I didn't want to do a bunch of songs and raps thrown together. I wanted it to be a cohesive project from start to finish, a real thing that I could put a cover on and press into CDs that would live forever. That way I could perform at open mics and say, "Yo, I just dropped this mixtape and here's where you can download it," rather than, "Yo, you've never heard me before, but here's some raps I did over an OutKast beat." It would be more legitimate, more professional, more real.

It needed to have an identity, too, and that identity was Logic. Rappers create alter-ego MCs for the same reason kids love superheroes. You get to be something more magnificent and powerful than yourself. Bruce Wayne is Bruce Wayne; that's just Christian Bale in a fancy suit. But Batman is fucking Batman. He gets to wear dope body armor and kick the Joker's ass.

What Logic and Hit Man and Lord Subliminal and all the various aliases I'd come up with had in common was that they were a way to be something I wasn't, something I wanted to be and wished I could be. When I got on the mic, I could escape myself and my reality by playing this character. I could live in another universe. I could rap about having millions of dollars when all I had was dozens of food stamps. I could rap about chilling in Cabo when really I'd never left Mary Jo's guest room.

In that room, I'd set up my monitor and my laptop and my microphone on Mary Jo's spare desk. Right under me, in the space where your legs are supposed to go, was where she kept her cats' litter box. It was one of those giant kitty-litter houses, and she would not let me move it. She was always like, "You do *not* move that litter box! That's where the cats go!" So I always had my legs spread-eagle around it with the wafting of shit in my nostrils as I was recording "Yeah, I'm the motherfuckin' man!" and rapping about being the shit sitting next to the shit.

Straddling the cat shit in Mary Jo's guest room.

While working on the mixtape I'd met this guy Castro on Facebook. We were both into hip-hop and both couch-surfing around Gaithersburg because we had fucked-up families and couldn't go home. So I was hanging with him a lot and he hooked me up with a job bussing tables at Joe's Crab Shack, which was cool because I needed the money. He was in and out and we'd rap together, but I think for him hip-hop was mostly a way to have fun and goof off. I was always the one sitting there straddling the cat shit going, "Bro, you gotta take this *seriously*."

Because I did take it seriously. Even though this character I was playing in the songs was the furthest thing from the truth of the litter box under my chair, I had to visualize what I wanted to be and then be that on the album. It was the only way I could make the music. Bobby Hall is just Bobby Hall, some skinny, poor half-black kid from Gaithersburg who grew up on welfare. Who would be interested in listening to him? Bobby Hall would never have been able to get on the mic and have the ego to demand that millions of people listen to him and pay attention to him. But Logic is Logic, and Logic was—or was going to be—one of the greatest MCs in the history of hip-hop.

Logic was also a person for anxiety- and PTSD-ridden Bobby Hall to be in public. At some point that year, Lenny was back around more and he started telling me about college radio and the station at the University of Maryland, WMUC, and how there were shows that would play unsigned artists and you could get your shit on there, so we sent in one of the tracks we were working on and: They actually played it. We couldn't believe it. I had Lenny call back the next day and be like, "Hey, uhhhhh . . . could you play that Logic joint again?" The DJ was like, "Do you know him?" and Lenny was like, "Nope!" and then he hung up. It was such a minuscule victory, but for us it was everything.

There was this one guy we always used to listen to at WMUC named DJ BossPlayer. He had a show called *The Hip-Hop Corner* where he'd do this segment called "Bump It or Dump It?" He would play shit from unsigned and local artists and ask this panel, "Would you bump it or would you dump it?" So one week I sent in my tracks "Nothing but a Hero" and "Growing Pains" and they bumped it. BossPlayer thought my shit was dope and he called me and invited me into the studio and I went down there with Castro and Lenny and I went on the radio for the first time with my terrible Maryland accent, going, "Yo, what's up? I'm Logic. Hip-hop artist from Merlin." (Which is how you know somebody is actually from Maryland. Because every time they say "Maryland" it sounds like "Merlin" and you're like, "Why is this nigga talkin' about wizards?") BossPlayer and I chatted a bit and then I freestyled so hard on the mic and fucking killed it and after that he was like, "Let's kick it," and we started hanging out.

DJ BossPlayer's real name was Thomas Agbonyitor and he was this sweet and generous African dude from a strong African family with the hard-ass African dad. His mother had died of cancer some years back and he was still struggling and dealing with things because of that, which is why he was twenty-six and still an undergraduate. But the dude loved hip-hop and I think he saw this kid who could spit and he wanted to help out and be a part of what was happening. He helped me reach my first real local fans, playing my songs on his show and inviting me into the studio to do freestyles and taking me to different clubs where I could jump onstage and perform. He even bankrolled me for a bit. He'd come into some money when his mother died and he spent at least a couple grand helping me print business cards and buying me clothes and a couple of pairs of Jordans so I could look decent enough to go onstage. He even bought me meals. This nigga took me and Castro and Lenny to IHOP all the time and he would always open his wallet and pay for everything.

DJ BossPlayer also helped me deal with my social anxiety and my fear of leaving the house. Not because he was a therapist but because the dude looked like and was roughly the size of Shaquille O'Neal. So while I still couldn't leave the house without feeling waves of panic, my love of getting onstage and rapping was enough to make me want to leave the house, and having this big-ass dude rolling with me was enough to make me feel safe. Plus Castro and Lenny usually rolled with us. I had these three big, tall guys I could hide behind if any shit ever went down. Which of course it never did, but I still worried that it might because that's how anxiety works.

At the time I was twenty years old, about to turn twenty-one, and I hadn't been back to Washington, D.C., since my mother nearly abandoned me on the Metro platform on the way to the National Zoo and my father actually abandoned me in an empty car to go get high in a crackhouse. But DJ BossPlayer was pushing me to start going to open mics at the Everlasting Life Cafe down in Southeast and at Bohemian Caverns on U Street, and I knew I was with Shaquille O'Neal so I felt pretty good about it.

The first night he took me and Castro to Bohemian Caverns, I met these two University of Maryland students, 6ix and OB. Together they were a production duo known as the Official. I didn't get to "meet them" meet them, but Castro had started working as my hype man, and after the two of us did a set I had my business cards with my name and my email and my Twitter on them and I was handing them out to everyone and I gave one to 6ix and he said thanks and then once I left he turned around and threw it in the trash.

After that I started running into them at different beat battles and open mics. Rappers would get up and freestyle and DJs would play beats back and forth, and I noticed that the beats that got the best reaction from the crowd were always from 6ix and OB. And they would see me rapping, and they were like, "Damn, this guy can spit." And so we connected online and they sent me a bunch of beats and before I knew it we were working together.

OB's real name was Owen. He was this African dude who looked like a real dark Ninja Turtle. Sweet guy. Funny guy. Happy drunk. At first I spent more time working with OB. His beats were better than 6ix's because 6ix had only just started making beats. 6ix was this skinny, hairy super-nerdy Indian kid who was premed at UM even though he didn't want to be premed at UM because he came from one of those hard-ass but loving immigrant families where you had to be premed. But premed wasn't 6ix at all. He had this long stoner hair. Smoked dope constantly. I'm pretty sure his concept of air is weed smoke; he's almost always high, but functionally high. Very smart. Good with numbers. Really kind and funny and sweet and, back then, quiet and timid and awkward. 6ix went by 6ix because his real name is Arjun and his friends all called him June, which is the sixth month of the year, which is how he came up with 6ix.

Even though 6ix was doing the premed thing to make his family happy, his real passion was music. But not hip-hop. He mostly played guitar and drums in metal bands. It was only when he got to college that he met OB and OB got him into making beats and that's how they became the Official. So at first it was mostly me and OB, but then he got busy with school and 6ix sent me this fucking huge batch of beats and I liked only one of them. It had this snare roll in it, and I was obsessed with this snare roll because J. Cole used to put this same snare roll in his songs, so I was like, "Oh my God, this sounds like some J. Cole shit. I love it." So I took that and it became the beat for my song "Love Jones" and I started to fuck with 6ix and he came out of his shell more and we got close and from there, things started to snowball. Everything I'd been doing haphazardly over the years came into focus on what would become my first real mixtape: *Young, Broke & Infamous*.

As we were wrapping up production and getting ready to drop it online, I decided to quit Joe's Crab Shack. I didn't exactly quit. I did but I didn't but I did. I had two managers and one of them was this guy Rob, who was super-cool, but the other one was an asshole and you were supposed to have this specific type of rubber shoes and I'd never bought the shoes because I needed the money to pay rent to Mary Jo. Then, out of nowhere, this manager was like, "You have to buy these shoes," and I was like, "I don't have the money to buy these shoes because I've barely got money for the bus to get to work," and he was like, "Buy the shoes or don't come in."

I didn't buy the shoes.

The shoes were the fork in the road. I said, "I don't need to buy those shoes because I'm never going to work another job ever again." And I never have.

Young, Broke & Infamous dropped in December 2010. We loaded up to DatPiff, the music-sharing website that hosted everybody's mixtapes for download back in the day. DJ BossPlayer paid to print up about a thousand CDs, and we had a launch party at some club with maybe fifty people there. It was Castro and Lenny and Lenny's brother Benny and some girls who were out of our league and everyone was drinking except me.

Those were the purest days. It was just about the music. I was getting mentions on local blogs and we were printing and handing out CDs and doing local shows that DJ BossPlayer got me through his connections at WMUC. It was rough going at first. One of the worst gigs I ever played was this talent show at University of Maryland, opening for Dead Prez. I was up onstage looking out at this sea of people and rapping my heart out and they were all just standing there, staring at me. I was giving it everything I had, shouting, "Hands up! Hands up!" and maybe three people had their hands up because nobody had heard of me and they were all there to see somebody else.

I got another gig opening for Mac Miller at this shit club in Virginia. It was one of those gigs where there's a million opening acts and the crowd has to wait a million years for the person they actually came to see and by the time you get on they're angry and drunk and hostile. I was the last act to go on before Mac and DJ BossPlayer went out and said, "All right, the man you've all been waiting for. He's the illest white boy in the game . . ." Everybody was like *"YeaaaaaaaaHh-hhhHHahahahHH!"* and then I started walkin' out right as he yelled, "LOGIC!" and everyone screamed, "NOOOOOOOOOOOOOO!"

Which sucked. But I just said, "Yo, Mac's gonna be out in a couple of minutes. I'm the last motherfucker you gotta deal with. Let's turn up!" And it was the shit.

We started making videos, too. 6ix and OB knew this Peruvian guy named Orlando who went by the name GRVTY and we shot this video of me walking around on the Maryland campus freestyling and trying to be J. Cole in his "Simba" video and GRVTY edited it and we put it out and it got maybe a hundred views. Not even. But it was a start.

Then, right when we were starting, Bernie put his foot down. My year at Mary Jo's was up. I didn't have any place else to go so I begged Lenny to let me stay on the couch in his mom's basement. In hindsight, it was an absurd leap of faith for him to take. I couldn't pay rent or even buy my own groceries. I was a high school dropout recording inside a closet. My producer was a drummer from a metal

Shooting a music video on the University of Maryland campus.

band who'd only started getting into hip-hop two months before he'd met me. I had no agent and no manager and no nothing.

Still, it made a weird kind of sense because we were actually already doing it. It seemed like every week something new was happening: little breakthroughs, some blog posting my music, more followers popping up on social media. Between GRVTY and OB and 6ix and Lenny and Castro, if we wanted to shoot a video of us recording a track and then rolling to Krispy Kreme to get strawberry milk with a donut from baby girl and post that shit up on YouTube, we could do it. I had access to the same tools and the same platform that J. Cole and Mac Miller did. Which, compared to what had existed only a year before, was insane. I knew if I was ever going to make anything of my music I needed to be taking advantage of that, not buying the right shoes to bus tables at Joe's Crab Shack.

So why not give it a shot?

I said to Lenny, "Yo, give me a year. I know it's asking a lot. I know I'm twenty-one and I'm supposed to be a grown-ass person and I'm basically asking you to feed me and clothe me and you just lost your father and your family's just getting by as it is, but please trust me that we're on to something. All I need is one year."

And Lenny said, "Okay."

せ ス ✕ ナ Ⴈ ፚ

When *Young, Broke & Infamous* started making noise
around town, I got noticed by the guys at 368 Music
Group, which at the time was the biggest independent
label out of D.C., Maryland, and Virginia. They had all the big local
artists, like Chaz French and Phil Adé, and everybody wanted to be a
part of what they were doing.

368 was spearheaded by Raheem DeVaughn, a legendary soul
singer who's pretty much the Don Corleone of the DMV. I don't remember how, but I got introduced to Raheem and we started texting
and he was talking about maybe signing me and then, one night out
of the blue, I was out with Lenny and I got a text from Raheem: "Hey,
brother. I'm gonna be at Stadium tonight. Meet me there."

Stadium is *the* strip club in D.C. I'd never been to a strip club before, and we had no money. Lenny was waiting on payday, and I was
the unemployed kid living in a basement with grimy carpet where I
slept on a ripped-up couch next to an old weight set that never got
used. Lap dances were not in our budget. But we were like, "Fuck it,"
and we drove down to the city in Lenny's beat-up old GMC Envoy
Denali. We pulled in to Stadium and parked and Raheem pulled up
behind us in some brand-new dope-ass candy-apple-red sports car,

and he got out and he talked like Prince and he was like, "All right, brother. Come with me."

We followed him in and we had no idea what was going on. All we knew was we totally didn't belong there. There were these monster security guards and all these women were lined up chilling and Raheem walked right through like he's the biggest star in the world. He went up to the front desk and came back with two handfuls of cash, fat stacks, four or five grand at least. Meanwhile I was standing there in my blue tie and the only button-up shirt I owned, this scrawny kid standing next to big-ass Lenny. We looked like some skinny-fat duo, like binary code or some shit.

Then Raheem took us around to this private area away from the main club and Dre the Mayor was already there and he had a table. Raheem sat down and I sat down next to him and I had no idea how to handle a business meeting, no idea that you're supposed to hang out and have fun and then, maybe, talk business for five minutes at the end. That was a foreign concept to me. So I launched right in with Raheem, like, "Hey, man, you know I'd love to sign to 368 and I want to be on the label and . . ." and he was like, "Chill, brother, just enjoy yourself," and I kept at it like, "Yeah, but like listen . . . like for real . . ." and he had to cut me off again like Prince, going, "Brother . . . we'll talk about it. Chill."

So Lenny and I tried to chill, but there's only so much you can chill in a strip club when fine-ass black girls with fat-ass titties are grinding all over you but you know you don't have any money. We were recycling the "make it rain" money, picking singles up off the floor like nobody would notice, and doing the best we could to fit in but mostly we sat there kind of uncomfortable and not knowing what to do and at some point this girl came over to Raheem and she took some ice cubes and put them in her pussy and popped them into a highball glass. That was like her party trick, I guess. But the funny thing was she did it and he wasn't looking so it was awkward and she had to wait until he was looking again and then she did it again. He took one look at the glass, then looked at me and said, "Delicious."

We had a couple more meetings and it was like I was running with them and they wanted to fuck with me, but then they didn't and it didn't happen and couple of months later, the first week of March 2011, I went to this event they had every year in D.C. called the DMV Awards, which was like the Grammys for local DMV artists and which, to put it charitably, was the most ghetto shit ever.

To get nominated for a DMV Award, they had this online system where people could vote for their favorite artists. At the time I had started to make a very small name for myself with *Young, Broke & Infamous*. Between Twitter, Facebook, and YouTube, I had a couple thousand people following me. So I went online and mobilized them to vote for me and I ended up with something like eighteen hundred votes. Meanwhile, the bigger, more established artists who were signed to real labels and putting out real records, they were only getting four or five hundred votes because they weren't aggressively using their social media presence. They were still doing things the old way, hand to hand, pressing the flesh.

When the nominations came out, a bunch of people said that what I'd done by going on social media was cheating. They got pissed off and they got together and tried to ban me. They kept saying, "These votes are fake," and the people running the awards came back and said, "No, these votes are real. They're just not local. They're fans from all over." So then that became the argument: "The votes don't count because they're not DMV. It has to be people in the DMV voting for the DMV Awards." And the awards people were like, "It doesn't matter where the votes come from. The fact that they're from all over just proves that he's hotter than y'all."

So I got nominated and I bought a suit, my first suit, and I went to this thing and there was champagne and it was a big deal and of course I didn't win anything because there was this backlash and resentment against where my votes came from and then at some point a fight broke out and people were throwing chairs and mother-fuckers started grabbing champagne bottles and somebody hit a waiter and cut his eyeball open and his eyeball was hangin' out of his head and it was the most hood shit ever.

But what was crazy coming out of the DMV Awards wasn't the fight; that shit was normal. What was crazy was that my social media following, even as small as it was, had completely disrupted the nor-mal way of getting votes and getting hype and doing business. CDs and handshakes and business cards, that was the past. Social media was the door to the future, and a few days later that door swung wide open.

I logged on to Facebook one night and saw I had a friend re-quest from this guy named Chris Zarou. I accepted it because back then I accepted everyone's requests because I was trying to generate interest. Then he messaged me to say he'd been up late at night ran-domly scrolling Twitter and he'd seen this video that we'd posted of me walking around freestyling on the University of Maryland cam-pus. This was back when, if you posted a video on Twitter, all it had was a link. It couldn't even embed video. That's how ancient this was. So we started chatting back and forth and Chris said he'd watched the video and realized, "Holy shit, this guy can fuckin' rap," and I was like, "Thanks for listening," and he was like, "So I know you don't know who the fuck I am, but I manage artists and I'd like to talk to you."

I went poking around on his Facebook page and found out he was twenty-one and still in college, some super-handsome guy with blondish-brown hair and these big-ass horse teeth who played Di-vision I soccer. Totally shredded, too, with biceps like Popeye. His profile picture was him wearing a toga.

I was skeptical, but I got on the phone with him anyway and he had this goofy high-ass voice and he's all, "Hey! What's up, man!" and we started talking and I got the rest of his story. He's one of six children from this tight-knit working-class family on Long Island. He was still in college and played college soccer and, realizing he was never going to go pro, he'd decided he wanted to make it in the record business because hip-hop was his next love beyond soccer, so he'd started his own management company. He called it Visionary Music Group, and at the time it was just him and a cell phone and the one artist he'd signed, this guy named Tayyib Ali.

I checked out Tayyib Ali and saw he was getting nearly 150,000 views on his songs on YouTube. That got my attention, because I was posting shit up and getting two, three hundred views max, maybe creeping up over a thousand after a few months. If Chris was getting this guy 150,000 views, he had to be doing something right. The other thing I liked was that he had this sincerity about him. I'd had interest from a few different managers, guys who'd handled a few artists back in the late '90s or whatever, but they all seemed a bit sketchy to me. From the jump with Chris there was no bullshit. At the time I was planning on a trip up to New York to film a music video for "Mind of Logic," one of the tracks I was recording for my next mixtape, *Young Sinatra*. I agreed to hold off on any big decisions until we had a chance to meet and talk.

We all went up to New York to film this video, my first time in Manhattan, me and Lenny and GRVTY and 6ix and DJ BossPlayer. We met up with Chris and we were scouting locations around Times Square and at some point he and I broke off to have lunch. We ended up at a Ruby Tuesday or some shit like that and we were standing outside and Chris was like, "Man, this is a tourist trap. You really want to go here?" In my mind I was expecting him to take care of lunch, so I was like, "Yeah, this is great." We went inside and I got a soda and this bomb-ass burger that cost something like thirty dollars and I was like, "You hungry? You gonna get anything?" and he was like, "No, I'm good," and he just had water. What I didn't realize at the time, and what took me five years to figure out, was the reason he didn't eat was because he didn't have any money—he was that broke.

But I liked him. I started telling him about the video we were shooting and how dope it would be to find a rooftop to film on and he was like, "Oh, I can call somebody to get you a rooftop." And he actually did it. That same day. A few hours later we had a rooftop, and when you're a kid from Maryland, having a rooftop in New York City to shoot a video is like getting the keys to the Universal Studios lot.

It was the first time I'd ever dealt with someone outside of my own crew who did what he said he was going to do. The music industry is full of managers and agents and hustlers who are always telling you what they're going to do for you and they never actually do shit. But this guy said he'd get us a rooftop and he delivered.

A couple of weeks after that, Chris came down to Maryland on a one-dollar megabus and he crashed with me on the floor in Lenny's basement and I was like, "Wow." I had these middle-aged, not-really-that-successful guys offering to manage me and telling me everything they were going to do for me, but I couldn't imagine any of those dudes coming to my house to sleep on the fuckin' floor. Chris was a kid with no more experience than me, but the dude not only did everything he said he would do, he seemed to be from the future when everyone else was still in the past. Plus he was willing to sleep in the dirt with me. Not that the basement was that dirty. Nor was it that clean.

It was a scary thing, but my gut was telling me, "Go with the kid." So I told him, "Look, I'm going to give you a chance. Let's see what you do in six months. We'll do a handshake on everything between now and then, and if you don't blow it, then I'll sign with you." And he was like, "All right, that's fair." And we did it, and that was it.

"Mind of Logic" was the first real music video I ever dropped. Everything before that was homemade shit of me fucking around. And of the few hundred views I was getting on my videos, if I'm being honest, a lot of them were just me clicking over and over again. Now I was putting everything in Chris's hands in terms of promotion, so I'd see what he was able to do.

At the time, music blogs were still huge. Before blogs all you had were mainstream publications like *Billboard* and *Rolling Stone* and they were only going to write up Britney Spears and Justin Timberlake because that's how it was. But the Internet allowed young people to start blogs that set out to find the newest underground shit and put it out there, places like This Song Is Sick and 2DopeBoyz. Social media was about to cannibalize them and wipe them out, but that hadn't happened yet. We were in this brief window of time when social media was amplifying the blogs rather than replacing them, which made them the perfect place to get noticed and discovered.

Zarou might not have had much experience, but one thing he had for sure was connections to the people who ran those blogs. One of the guys I think he knew from college or somewhere, and the rest he'd just made it his business to know. At the time This Song Is Sick was the top music blog on the Internet, and the guy who ran it was this cat named Nick. Zarou had a connect with this guy and he got him to link to the video. Within a day it had twenty-five thousand views. I couldn't believe it. Nobody else could believe it, either. DJ BossPlayer, 6ix, Lenny, everyone was convinced that Chris had to be buying views to juice the numbers and make it look like he was delivering results, because that's what a lot of artists were doing at the time.

We actually called a meeting in Lenny's basement and we all sat with Chris and we started grillin' him: "Are you buying views?" He wasn't mad or angry, but he did get a little offended that we'd questioned him and then he pulled me aside and said, "Look, you just gotta trust me. Yesterday you had two hundred views and today you've got twenty-five thousand views, and before you know it, it's going to be fifty thousand and then a hundred thousand." And I was so happy to hear those numbers I was like, "Dude, whatever you say. I'll make the music, and you do what you do."

Zarou changed everything. When I met him, I was still handing out business cards, and Chris looked at me like, "Business cards?

What the fuck are you doing? Nobody needs that shit anymore. The future's digital, baby." So we ditched the business cards. CDs, too. We started running around with everything on a thumb drive that people could stick into their laptops. Up to that point I had always been like, "We need to use the Internet, guys!" But I had no idea what that actually meant from a business or promotional point of view. I'd built a team and I had a videographer and producer and a DJ and Lenny to drive me around, but I didn't know how to make that go anywhere. Chris did.

The next video we dropped was "All I Do." Chris got that one linked on This Song Is Sick as well, and that song changed my life. It blew the fuck up. It blew past "Mind of Logic" in a matter of minutes. Back then, if you had over a hundred thousand views on a song, you were killing it. You weren't Jay-Z or Kanye, but you were in a new league. You were an "Internet sensation." "All I Do" crossed a hundred thousand views in a week. Then two hundred thousand. Then five hundred thousand, and pretty soon it was a million-plus. Chris had pulled off a miracle. When I saw that I said, "This guy knows what he's doing."

Chris had no idea what he was doing. He just had an instinct about where the record business was going and the confidence to follow that instinct. Honestly, it was a case of being too ignorant to know that you don't know what you don't know but you do know a few things that, by pure luck, happen to be correct.

Looking back, I'm so happy nothing worked out with those other managers or with 368. Raheem DeVaughn is a great guy and he was so good to me and he definitely had more money and was more established at that moment, but 368 was too tied to the past. Same with all the other managers who'd been sniffing around. By 2011, if you were still doing shit the way it had been done six months before, you were already behind the curve. There were so many incredible rappers around D.C. at the time who were way bigger than me, guys like Phil Adé. His shit was amazing, absolutely phenomenal. He was everything I wanted to be and hoped I could be. But he never got to realize his full potential because he had the bad luck to be tied down to established players who couldn't feel the ground shifting below their feet.

The fact that I'd chosen a manager who knew nothing about how the music business was supposed to work actually turned out to be a huge advantage. But that was only part of the equation. What made our partnership fly wasn't just a mutual understanding of digital marketing strategies. It was trust. After *Young, Broke & Infamous,* OB started getting busy with school and he was coming around less and less and I was calling him all the time. "Bro, come over. Let's work. Come over." But he was always giving me excuses. He ended up working on a couple more records, but he produced next to nothing on his own. Meanwhile, 6ix had started showing up and coming through. I think maybe it was because women on campus were like, "Don't you work with that Logic guy?" But whatever the reason, 6ix stepped up right as OB started bailing.

Finally I asked 6ix what was going on, and he was like, "Yo, I'm just trying to keep it real with you. OB came to me and said, 'You're wasting your time. Do you really think Logic's going to make it, bro? It's never going to happen. You need to focus on school.'" OB wasn't being an asshole; he was being realistic. 6ix was skipping class and his grades were all fucked up and pretty soon his parents were going to find out that he was flushing his premed career down the toilet to hang out with some rapper. At the same time, though, it's fucking terrible advice. Because when else are you going to take a shot like this except when you're young and you've got no real obli- gations and nothing to lose? But OB was studying to be an electrical engineer and he felt that was what he needed to focus on.

When 6ix told me what he'd said, I wasn't angry and I didn't get confrontational about it. But I was like, "Okay. This guy doesn't believe in me, so whatever. I'm not going to fuck with him." And OB wasn't the only guy who fell out during the come-up. Things ultimately didn't work out between me and BossPlayer. He was struggling with some of his own issues and one night he threw a phone at GRVTY, and I had to say, "I'm not going to let one of my friends assault another one of my friends." Then GRVTY and I ended up parting ways because of some business disagreements. Castro, too. Some people you outgrow and you have to move on.

At the same time I learned who the truly important people were in my life: They were the people who showed up. Lenny showed up. 6ix showed up. Chris showed up. There was also my boy Slaydro, an immigrant from Costa Rica who was moving pounds of weed across the country when I met him on Facebook. He started hanging around so I brought him on and made him my assistant. There was my man Harrison, this chubby New York Jewish kid I met through a gig who had so much hustle that he ended up taking over from Chris as my tour manager even though he was only nineteen years old.

Those were the people who believed in what I was doing and who put in the time. There was a certain amount of self-interest that brought us together, for sure. We had a common goal of making it in music, and they all looked at me and said, "If this dude blows up, I blow up, so I'm going to give it my all." But it quickly transcended that because we needed each other to get where we wanted to go. I needed a team to support me. Chris couldn't become a talent manager without any talent to manage. Lenny was stuck in a job he didn't want. 6ix was taking a giant risk, breaking with his family's expectations about his career, and he needed us to take that risk with him.

And it wasn't just these guys. It was everyone around them, too. Lenny's mom, Kathy, was the sweetest woman. She was like Mary Jo, motherly and kind. She used to bring me sandwiches because she knew I'd be down there hungry. And she didn't care about the noise at all. We'd be blasting records at four in the morning and she'd be like, "Go ahead. Play your music. Have fun." It was the same with

Chris's family up on Long Island. I was taking the bus up for meetings and I'd crash in his room and he'd sleep in his sister's room. They brought me in and treated me like one of their own.

I was twenty-one years old, and for the first time in my life I was surrounded by people who actually cared about me, who loved me and accepted me and believed in me. Other than the love from Mary Jo, I'd never experienced anything like it. It's not like I consciously thought, "Oh, I'm going to go out and build a surrogate family to make up for the fact that I never had an actual one." It wasn't like that. I didn't even realize it was happening until people started saying, "Yo, the people around you are amazing. You have such an incredible family that you've brought together around you." And I looked around and saw that it was true. I hadn't tried to create it or force it, it had just happened.

I finally had a family, and it felt amazing.

One night back when I was still in Mary Jo's guest room, I was messing around online and Tabi Bonney, who's a huge artist and a real tastemaker for the D.C. go-go scene, was doing a Q&A on Twitter. Part of what was so amazing about social media was seeing artists you loved, like Tabi or Mac Miller and Wiz Khalifa, and feeling you could just reach out and talk to them and they might even hit you back. Of course, they almost never did. I would tweet at them, "Hey, I love your music," and I'd get no response, not because they were assholes but because they had a crazy amount of influx where they couldn't do it. When I discovered Kendrick Lamar he wasn't huge yet. It was before all the Grammys and the platinum albums and the critical accolades, and I found him online and I felt so cool. Not realizing he was already signed to a label and about to blow up, I even messaged him to say, "Hey, man, I like your music. We should work on something together." Which is embarrassing, but it's also the perfect illustration of what that time was like.

So there I was straddling Mary Jo's cat shit and watching Tabi Bonney do this Q&A and I tweeted at him and asked him some questions. Then I went back to whatever else I was doing and a few minutes went by and then: *Ping!*

He'd responded to me.

I can still remember seeing his tweet and thinking, "OH . . . MY . . . GOD." This person I idolized had reached out to me and recognized me. It was the most incredible feeling, and I said to myself right then, "I'm going to respond to every single fan who writes to me. This is what I want to do for people. I want everyone who loves my music to feel what I just felt when Tabi Bonney responded to me."

That first Christmas after *Young, Broke & Infamous* came out, it was me on Twitter all day long, tweeting people, "Merry Christmas, Have a Good Day!" I did it for like twelve hours straight. I look back on it now and I'm like, "Bro, go outside." But I couldn't think about that then. I was too deep in it. I felt like a telemarketer who lived with his headset on. That was me.

The ability of the Internet to connect human beings had fascinated me since I was a seventeen-year-old kid who was scared to leave the house, because it had literally saved my life. That whole year I was utterly alone, in my room, watching the original *Star Wars* on VHS over and over and over. I would see my brother and Christine every now and then, but I was very alone. I didn't have a phone, so I couldn't text anyone. I could only wait until everyone was online to sign in to AOL, and since everyone was in school, I was by myself most of the day. I had Yahoo! chatrooms and Myspace and Spoken vs. Written. Those were my only connections to try to reach out and talk to people. It was all surface-level rap shit; I wasn't talking to anybody about my feelings or my life. But it was still incredible.

The first time the power of the Internet fully dawned on me was when I was chatting with this guy who called himself Well Aware. He lived in London and he made some good hip-hop beats and he would send them to me and I'd rap on them. One day I was talking to him and it hit me: "Holy shit. This dude's in *London*." And that freaked me out, because I realized I could take this crappy used computer my mom had probably gotten from some family at church, put it together with this free month of AOL I got from a giveaway CD-ROM at the drugstore, and reach out and connect with anybody, anytime, anywhere.

The Internet connected me to the people who could change my life, people I otherwise never would have met. At the time I used to go on Twitter and literally type "Mac Miller" in the search engine and then go through and find everyone who was hashtagging #macmiller and then I'd @ them and say, "If you love Mac Miller, you'd love me." Then I'd post a link to some shitty way to hear my songs online. Then this guy Christian from Florida reached out to me to say, "Yo, your music is pretty cool. Are you on YouTube?" I knew what YouTube was, obviously, but I thought you could only do videos; I had no idea there was a way to do just songs. But this guy took it upon himself to go and set me up on YouTube and upload all my music there. We stayed in touch and eventually he became my assistant and then my day-to-day manager and now he's just killing it in Bitcoin and we've been best friends ever since.

Because of the anonymity of the Internet, I was even making connections I didn't know I was making. When I was on Spoken vs. Written as Lord Subliminal there was this cat who was always one of the other top contenders. His name was Unique. I rap-battled with this dude all the time. Fast-forward to five years later and I was talking to Zarou, getting to know him and telling him all about how I got into rap, and I told him, "Yeah, I used to be on this website where you could rap-battle people."

"Really? What was it called?"

"It was called Spoken vs. Written."

"What?"

"Yeah, I went by Lord Subliminal."

"What?! You were Lord Subliminal? Bro, I was Unique!!!"

"WHAT?!"

It was the craziest moment, realizing that all those years I'd been living in hell and loving the Roots and Wu-Tang, he'd been on Long

Island with his great family and loving Eminem and 50 Cent. All the time I'd spent in this chat rap forum thinking I was the shit, he'd been in the same chat rap forum thinking he was the shit. It's insane, but given where we ended up, it makes perfect sense. We were both creatures of this brave new world in a way that the more established people in the music business were not.

Part of the reason Zarou had created his own management company and was hustling unsigned artists on Facebook was because he couldn't get a job at any of the major labels. Not even an internship. He'd applied to all of them and every single one turned him down. It was only after he'd found a little success for himself managing me and Tayyib Ali that he managed to backdoor his way into an internship at Atlantic Records where he worked for John Janick, who was and is one of the most well-respected record executives in the business. One day Janick called Zarou into his office, pulled the "Mind of Logic" video up on his computer, and said, "How did you get all these views?"

"What do you mean?"

"Where did you get the money to do this?"

"It didn't cost anything. We just made it and put it up and people found it and watched it."

And this guy, one of the most powerful men in the music industry, didn't understand a word Chris was saying to him.

From the hood niggas at the DMV Awards all the way up to the biggest executives in the industry, nobody over the age of twenty-five had the slightest idea what was about to happen. But Zarou did. He saw the first steps Mac Miller and Wiz Khalifa and these other guys had taken up to that point, and he saw where it was going to go next: Labels weren't going to create artists anymore, not the way they had before. That power was about to be taken away from them. The artists were going to create themselves. Using social media, we were going to go out and find and build our fanbases on our own, one fan at a time.

From that first Christmas after *Young, Broke & Infamous* dropped, every waking moment that I wasn't recording, I was online, finding new ways to connect with people. I started doing Ustream, which was the first livestreaming service ever, way ahead of its time. I would do that five times a week. Maybe ten people would show up. They'd be watching a video stream of me and I couldn't see them but I could read their comments in the chat. In my mind, even though I was hanging out in my bedroom, it was like I was on a stage. There were ten folding chairs with people sitting around me, and I would talk to them. "What's your name? Where are you from? Nice to meet you." And I still remember every single one of those people to this day. There was Tony and Christian, Nanisha and Mina. There was this kid Silas, who was eleven, and this girl Nicole, who had a twin brother.

We kept dropping videos and tweeting and reaching out, and soon ten people turned into twenty, twenty turned into fifty, fifty turned into a hundred. I was always on Facebook, too, commenting and talking to different people and posting videos. That's all I would do, all fuckin' day. Then 6ix would come over late and we'd record some songs and I'd pass out on Lenny's couch around three in the morning and then wake up around noon and first thing I'd do was check my phone and start all over again. I would have a couple hundred notifications and I'd think, "Okay, cool. Here we go." And I would sit and go through and respond to every single one.

We were tapping into things that people in the industry didn't even know existed. Back then, the idea that people would use the Internet to watch videos of other people playing video games was an alien concept. Before it was a thing, it was a thing, and nobody believed it. But kids were doing it everywhere; these videos were getting millions of views. At the time this group called FaZe Clan was one of the biggest eSports teams in the country. They would make these montages of all their best trick moves from games like *Call of Duty* and they liked my shit and they used one of my songs, "The Spotlight," as the soundtrack for one of these montages. Then the dude who created FaZe Clan, who was like this eighteen-year-old kid, started texting me and he sent me some FaZe Clan hoodies and I wore one in the video I made for "The Spotlight" and it became this thing where we organically blew up together.

You couldn't do now what we did then. The window has closed, and everything's become corporate again. Spotify has a virtual monopoly and if you don't know someone at a label or don't have a powerful manager who can get you on Spotify's playlist, you have zero chance of being successful. Today Facebook and Twitter make you pay to reach your own followers, but back then if you had five thousand followers and you posted a video, five thousand people saw it. Back then these social media companies had built up these massive audiences, but they hadn't figured out what to do with them or how to monetize them. They didn't yet have control over the behemoths they'd built, and they weren't really paying attention to what you were doing there. It was like wide-open, virgin territory waiting to be settled.

Before the Internet, the most you could do independent of a label was use flyers and shows and mixtapes to build up a local following, maybe a regional one. Now you could take that same DIY approach and use it to reach the entire world, and it cost you nothing but your own time and blood and sweat and tears.

And yourself.

Because that's the deal. In the old days the deal was simple: You wanted fame, you sold your soul—to the devil, to a label, what's the difference? They owned you but they made you into a rock god. You were Madonna. You were Michael Jackson. You lived on high and your fans worshipped at your feet and nobody could touch you. The worst that people could do was bitch about you to their friends while you sold another ten million units. Today, on social media, rock stars are like gods come down off the mountain, humanizing themselves and using that to connect directly to their fans, which can be a blessing or a curse.

At the time we only saw it as the former.

Fans and artists have a complicated relationship. The fan doesn't exist without the artist, but the artist is still an artist without the fan; they'll just never reach a certain level of success. So it's symbiotic. Each one depends on the other. When you discover an artist who's starting out, it's like belonging to a secret club only you and a few other people know about. I found Kendrick and Mac Miller and Wiz Khalifa when they were performing in hundred-cap bars and it was just me and a few thousand other people following them online, and that was so cool. I played a show in Pittsburgh not long after Mac Miller dropped his debut album, *Blue Slide Park,* and I was walking around listening to *Blue Slide Park* while visiting the actual Blue Slide Park, because I was obsessed and had seen it in so many of his videos. But in my head I wasn't thinking, "Yeah, Mac did it!" I was thinking, "Yeah, *we* did it!" Because I felt like my buying Mac's music and watching his streams had made me a part of his success.

Because I had that with Mac Miller and those other guys, I was always aware that special feeling was what my first fans had with me. Those ten people hanging out with me on Ustream in Lenny's basement, they had shown up first and foremost because they liked the music. That's what had hooked them, but the reason they stayed and hung around and kept coming back was because they had that feeling of belonging to this secret club.

Until I found hip-hop, I don't think I ever had a place where I felt I belonged. I didn't belong in my own home. When I was hanging out with Robert Naples and Jesse Weidman, who were the two biggest nerds in the world, even then I was like, "These guys are too cool for me." When I was hanging out with Mike and Josh and they were these wannabe gangsters, I wasn't even cool enough or tough enough for that. I was a wannabe of the wannabes.

Then I met Lenny and Castro and 6ix and Zarou and I was like, "Whoa. This is weird. We all belong here." My whole thing since I was sixteen was that I wanted to rap, but saying "I want to rap" is really another way of saying, "I want to be with the people who are rapping. I need a place to belong, and I want to belong over there." What social media changed was that now the fans could be a part of that, too.

The rappers I admired had this thing where they created a name for their fanbases, to create a sense of family and a style and a group identity. Mac Miller had the Most Dope Family and Fun Is 4 Everyone. Wiz Khalifa had the Taylor Gang. So when I first started rapping I decided to do the same thing. I was still going by Psychological, so I was calling my fans Brainiacs. "Yo, I'm Psychological. What up, Brainiacs?" It was so bad.

Then came "Young Sinatra."

"Young Sinatra" was the last song that I made for *Young, Broke & Infamous*. I'd always loved Frank because my mom used to play him around the house all the time. Plus I'd watched him in so many of

Performing in a U Street music club, circa 2011.

her old movies. She'd given me a compilation album of his, *Fly Me to the Moon,* and I used to sit in my room as this seventeen-year-old kid, listening to Sinatra sing, "When I was seventeen . . ." on "It Was a Very Good Year." I just always thought that he was super-cool. He was Sinatra. He was the man.

So I was laying down the vocal on that record and as I was recording I found this effortless flow on the mic. "I'm so fly that I defy the laws of physics / I ain't think it was possible for a check to have this many digits / mathematically exquisite / Am I cocky? Just a smidgen." The words were coming out of me and falling on top of each other. Even as I was recording it, I was feeling myself, like, "Yo, this is like a vibe. This is dope. This is some real swag shit." It wasn't anything bigger than that in that moment. I didn't realize what I'd created; it was more like, "Young Sinatra, cool title."

Then I realized what I'd hit on. Nobody in hip-hop had ever created an image around the elegant throwback style of somebody like Sinatra. So I decided to take that lane for myself, to make this Young Sinatra thing the alter ego of my alter ego, the Slim Shady to my Eminem, the Hova to my Jay-Z. I'd stamp it by making a whole new mixtape around the idea, and I'd call it *Young Sinatra.*

Once the idea of the Young Sinatra alter ego presented itself, I started thinking about how Sinatra always had his crew: Sammy and Dean and Joey Bishop and Peter Lawford. The Rat Pack. It just clicked. I'd call my fans the Rat Pack, only I'd need it to be different to make it unique. I liked that Kanye's label was called G.O.O.D. Music, which stood for Getting Out Our Dreams. So I changed it to the RattPack and made it an acronym like Kanye had: Real All The Time. For a while I was calling my female fans Bobbysoxers, but that didn't work, so I ended up ditching that and everyone was just in the RattPack. Today, only the girls who are really old-school still call themselves Bobbysoxers, which is dope.

Everyone in the RattPack connected with me and, through me, with each other, and the reason it worked is the connection was genuine. Because I was genuinely being myself. Because the Internet had changed that about hip-hip, too. During the 2000s, hip-hop had grown stale in a lot of ways. There were always cool acts doing interesting stuff, but the dominant mode was still mired in the whole gangsta-rap image of the 1990s. It's cool to hear 50 Cent rapping about selling drugs in the projects, but most people can't relate to that because that's not their experience. The young people coming of age online, even if they were from the hood, were being exposed to all different kinds of cultural influences that people from the hood had never had access to before, shit like all the cool Japanese anime and video games and sci-fi that Robert Naples and Jesse Weidman had exposed me to.

When I first started out, nobody was rapping about any of that. Nobody was rapping about the things I cared about. Except maybe Lupe. But I took it to a whole other level. Young Sinatra and Logic were two alter egos, but they were both rooted in who I am. Young Sinatra was the super-cool dude with swag who I aspired to be. Logic was more like the coolest possible version of myself as I actually am: a nerdy guy who loves movies and video games. And when I put that out there, all of these thousands and then millions of people around the world found me online and said, "Holy shit, I found a hip-hop artist who's like me. I like video games. I like anime. I'm kinda nerdy. I can relate to this guy."

They felt close to me because they knew, or at least could tell, that I wasn't on those livestreams with them as some cynical marketing stunt. I was there because I was still the kid alone in my room in my mom's apartment with nowhere to belong. I wanted and needed that feeling of connection as much as they did, so I poured every ounce of myself into it. There was no PR person, no filter between me and the fans. It wasn't even like they were fans and I was the star. It was like we were all family, and people could feel it. They'd be like, "Oh my God, that dude is so real. He's so himself." And I was.

I don't know that anybody's ever connected with their fanbase the way I have, to do it until you literally can't do it anymore. And because I did, and because the music was dope, the RattPack kept growing, like a snowball rolling down a hill. There was no "overnight success" moment when I broke through and got famous and everything was different. We kept hitting small milestones day by day. Every show we'd sell a few more tickets than we did the show before. Every month we'd sell a little more merch than we did the month before.

My first real "oh my God" moment was having my own show at the University of Maryland, at the Nyumburu Cultural Center. It was the same spot where I'd opened for Dead Prez barely a year before. *Young Sinatra* was out and was poppin', and in the same room where hundreds of people had just stood and stared, now I was looking out at five hundred people who had all come to see *me*. I could even look into the crowd and see Nicole and her twin brother and the other die-hard fans from Ustream shouting my lyrics back to me, and I was like, "Whoa."

From the beginning, these people weren't "normal" fans. They'd hung out with me in Mary Jo's guest room. They'd watched, live, as we'd recorded their favorite songs, like they were in the studio with us as it happened. They knew we were no different from them, that we were just some broke-ass kids living in Lenny's mom's basement. There was this one kid, Henry, who'd always turn up at the shows with gifts. One time it was a stack of Chipotle gift cards. He just walked backstage and gave them to Zarou, which was his way of contributing to this ragtag group and being a part of it beyond listening to the music.

And that relationship went both ways because I could see into their lives, too. I could find out who they were and what they were doing. Those fans were devoted to me and were always there for me because I'd been there for them. And not just in the music but actually there for them, like showing up to their house to say hi because I saw they were going through a bad breakup or, later on after

I started making real money, helping them out when they needed it, not because they asked but because I was creeping on their Twitter and seeing that they were having trouble paying rent. There was this other kid, Matt. For a while, everywhere I went he was right there, first in line at every show. I knew him for years. Then he got into a car accident and sliced his face open and broke his neck and almost died and he was in a really low place. I used to FaceTime him to chat and keep his spirits up. It was a new kind of fan-artist relationship that had never existed before, certainly not on this scale.

What's nuts about the Chipotle gift-card story isn't the Chipotle gift card. It's the fact that this kid Henry even knew who Chris Zarou was. Who in the history of music has ever known or cared about who an artist's manager was? But the fans knew everybody from the livestreams and from social media. They knew Lenny and 6ix and Castro and Momberg, the merch guy. What we'd created was a reality show with all these characters you could watch right on your phone. It was me going, "Hey, guys, I'm Logic. I'm from Merlin. I'm trying to be a rapper. I'm also a nerd. Here's my Indian homie, 6ix. Here's my manager, Chris. You'll notice that Chris has horse teeth." And on and on and on. Everybody's making fun of each other and everybody's got a catchphrase and every day there's a new photo or a new video or there's a new running joke about me looking like the stick bug from *A Bug's Life*.

It was more than a reality show, to be honest. It was a virtual-reality show. Because you could participate. You could wake up and spend all day at your shit school or you wack-ass job and then come home and jack into the matrix and be a part of this hip-hip entourage with people you felt you knew and you felt knew you. You'd plop down on your bed and pull out your phone and tweet at your favorite rapper. "Hey, Logic, what's up?" And your favorite rapper would hit you right back. "Shit, just chillin'. What you doin'?" Which made the emotional connection to the music that much deeper. It wasn't just something you listened to because you liked it and the beats were dope. The same way that being Logic and Young Sinatra allowed me to escape from myself for a while, being a part of the RattPack was a way for the fans to escape from their own selves, to live vicariously through someone else for a while.

There's a reason hard-core fandom pops up in adolescence and runs so strong through people's teenage years and into their early twenties. Being a fan of something is a transitional identity. It's an identity you can latch on to while you're still figuring out what your own identity will be. You don't know who you are, but then you discover the Grateful Dead and you can say, "Oh, I'm a Deadhead." You don't know where you belong in the world, but then you stumble on to this guy named Logic and you can say, "Oh, here's where I belong. I belong in the RattPack, and all I have to do to join is click this link."

We succeeded because we weren't actually selling music. We were, but we weren't. Because you can't sell music anymore. In the age of the Internet, music is basically free. Almost nobody buys physical CDs, and if you don't want to pay to download it, it can probably be streamed somewhere. The product we'd created was something else, something people truly needed. The RattPack was an answer to a question. In this vast new unlimited wilderness of the Internet, who are you? Where do you belong? We were offering people an identity and a sense of connection. We were selling a place to be loved and accepted.

And it just sold and sold and sold.

ꌟꌚꌚꌚꌚꌚꌚꌚ

By late 2011, *Young Sinatra* was making all kinds of noise. After the success of "All I Do," a few people from major labels came sniffing around about signing me, but we held off. Given the way music was going, with blogs and social media taking over, being independent was the cool thing. If people knew you were with a major label, you were less real. So we kept doing things on our own because it was still working miracles for us.

After doing a few one-off shows in Brooklyn and some other spots, we decided it was time to go on tour, so Chris arranged for me to do this five-city run across the Midwest opening for Moosh & Twist, a hip-hop duo out of Philly. I asked 6ix to be my DJ and he borrowed his dad's car without telling him what it was for because we knew he'd never say yes if we did, and we took off.

It was the dead of winter and it was me and 6ix and Zarou and we were cold and we were sharing beds in shitty motels and everything was janky and miserable and it was one of the best times of my life. Because even when I only had twenty-five people in front of me, the fact that there were twenty-five people living five hundred miles away from me who cared enough to come out and see me was mind-blowing.

We got to Chicago in the middle of February and it was fuckin' freezing and snowing and 6ix was backing us into a parking spot only he couldn't see out the back window because of the snow and all of a sudden we heard this *SMASH!* and I felt this rain of glass shower over me. We looked back and realized that 6ix had backed up his dad's car right next to this dumpster that had one of those big metal arms sticking out and it had bashed in the fucking window and now there was glass everywhere and snow pouring into the car. We sat there, dead silent, 6ix with this horrified look on his face, like, "How am I going to explain this to my parents?"

I was thinking less about 6ix's parents and more about the fact that we had a show to do plus we still had to drive to Minneapolis that night, so I was like, "Okay. It happened. There's nothing we can do about it right now. Let's fuck this show up." So we did. We rocked it and the whole time 6ix was behind me spinning beats and thinking about the five inches of snow piling up in his dad's car.

After the show we drove back to the hotel, and 6ix was like, "What do we do?" and Zarou was like, "We'll take a bedsheet from the hotel, stretch it across the backseat, and put it in the door and slam the door shut to hold it." So that's what we did. We drove overnight to Minneapolis. 6ix was pissed and me and Zarou were freezing in the back. I was like, "Guys, you know we're going to look back on this in ten years and laugh," and they were like, "Shut the fuck up, Bob."

6ix ended up telling his parents that someone broke into his car at the University of Maryland campus so they wouldn't know he took the car. As far as I know, they still believe that to this day. (At least until they read this shit.) But we finished the tour and it was a pivotal moment because that was when we realized we'd finally come up against the limits of what we could do with a computer from Lenny's basement. The new way of doing things online could only take us so far. Touring exists in the real world and it takes real money. Like, a lot of money.

Everything we'd created up to that point, we'd done with no

money. Zero dollars. Chris was still in college. He still had to graduate. He wasn't going to class at all. On top of that, his family was in
the middle of moving and he and all his brothers and sisters were
staying with his aunt, so he was sleeping on his aunt's couch while I
was sleeping on Lenny's couch and we were talking on the phone late
at night about how we were going to take over the music business
and the world. But realizing we were going to need real money to do
a real tour, we started talking to different labels.

Luckily, Chris had found a good entertainment lawyer, Paul
Rothenberg. He represented a few major clients, and he looked at
me and Chris, these two twenty-one-year-old guys with a big dream
and a lot of heart, and he liked us and said he'd help us out pro bono
while we worked toward the big payoff. Between Paul's contacts and
Chris's contacts we started getting meetings all over New York. We
sat down with damn near everybody, Republic, Sony, Slip-N-Slide,
all of them. Atlantic was the first to make us a legit offer, which was
hilarious because Atlantic was the label that Chris had interned at,
and now, barely nine months later, they were offering to sign Chris's
artist. The deal was for only thirty thousand dollars, so we said no, but
at that point it was just amazing that people were interested.

Then we got a call from Noah Preston, who was a rookie A&R
guy at Def Jam. He'd heard about me and found me on YouTube
and was watching some of my videos when his soon-to-be wife, Nina,
came out of the shower, heard one of the tracks, and said, "Oh my
God, who's that?" And the rest is history. He met with me and we hit
it off and he took me to his boss, No I.D., head of A&R for the label.
I sat down in the meeting with No I.D., this legend who'd produced
Kanye West and Jay-Z and Rihanna, and he told me he wanted to
sign me and produce me. It was a no-brainer.

After the meeting, we were in the car and everything felt good.
Chris was like, "Yo, I think this is the move, and it's not even about
the money, it's about the label you're with." And he was right. The

reason we went with Def Jam was because it was Def Jam. It was a big deal to be signed to the label that started hip-hop with Run-DMC and the Beastie Boys and LL Cool J back in the day. It was about aesthetics. It was about narrative. It was about the story we were telling in our social media reality show.

Over the next couple of days, Chris and Paul ironed out the details. Visionary Music Group would technically still be my label, and Def Jam would cover production and distribution. All in, including the recording budget and everything else, it was a million-dollar offer. My advance was two hundred thousand, which, minus Paul's fees and Zarou's cut, would leave me with a hundred and thirty-five thousand dollars. Which was more money than I'd ever seen in my life.

A couple days later Slaydro was driving me and GRVTY and 6ix back to Maryland in his mom's minivan. That's when I got the call from Chris.

"The money's right," he said. "Paul looked it over. Everything's good. You wanna do it?"

"Yeah," I said.

And as I said it, I broke down crying in the front seat, like hysterical sobbing. This was it. I'd made it.

Sort of.

Because on the one hand it felt like this instantaneous life change that left me sobbing tears of joy, but on the other hand I was still the kid whose dad never came to pick him up when he said he would, so there was this nagging voice in my head going, "You say the deal is done, but it's not really done. It's not going to happen. They could still back out." Then we went back up to New York to Paul's office to do the contracts. Even as I was signing my name on the dotted line I was thinking, "This isn't real. They're going to find out I'm a phony and they're going to take this contract and shred it." They didn't do that, of course, but even then I couldn't feel settled about it. We got back to Lenny's and started recording again and the whole time I was like,

"Well, the money still hasn't hit my account. I'm still fucking broke and living in a basement, so it ain't real yet."

I started checking my bank account every day, calling the 800 number on the back of my card and punching in my four-digit security code to see what my balance was, and every time it was that same automated lady telling me, "You. Have. Twelve. Dollars. In. Your. Checking. Account." Next day, same thing. Next day, same thing. And every time I heard it, my stomach would sink. But then one afternoon I stepped out onto the back porch to smoke a cigarette and I called the bank and I punched in my four-digit code and the automated lady came on and she said, "You. Have. One. Hundred. Thirty. Five. Thousand. And. Twelve. Dollars. In. Your. Checking. Account."

I couldn't fuckin' believe it. It had been a year almost to the day from the time I moved into Lenny's basement and told him, "Just give me a year." And now I was on Lenny's back porch and the deal was done and when you're twenty-one years old and you've been living on food stamps your whole life, a hundred and thirty-five thousand dollars feels like all the money in the world. I was *rich*. At that moment I felt like I could go anywhere and do anything I wanted. So I went to Taco Bell. Because Taco Bell was the shit. Crunchwrap Supreme, baby.

It was the best Taco Bell of my life.

Once we decided to take the deal, Chris was the first to say we shouldn't announce it, so we could keep our independent cred as long as possible. I'd been working toward this thing since I was sixteen years old and now I finally had it and I couldn't tell anybody. Which sucked, but I trusted Chris's judgment and he was right. We kept the signing under wraps, put out my next mixtape, *Young Sinatra: Undeniable,* and started planning our first real tour for that summer.

I say "planning" in the loosest possible sense of the word. Def Jam wasn't involved because we weren't selling or promoting an album for them, so we had to do it ourselves. We had no idea how to

plan or organize a tour or pay for a tour. We had no idea how to an-
alyze audience data and determine where we'd sell the most tickets.
It was just "Well, it looks like we've got lots of Twitter followers in
Chicago. Let's go there!"

Between renting two cars and paying some guy up in Rochester,
New York, to print up a bunch of merch, it cost me thirty-five thousand in start-up capital before we'd even sold a single ticket. I used
my advance to pay for it, which, after taxes and commissions and
expenses, was a massive chunk of what I had left. What had felt like
all the money in the world when it hit my account, in reality wasn't
much money at all.

Since I had no touring history, all Zarou could book were zero-
guarantee deals, meaning if we didn't sell enough tickets we would
lose money on the show. When we showed up to get the rental cars,
unbeknownst to us since we'd never rented cars before, was a clause
that said, "These cars cannot leave New York State." We were about
to take them out to California and up to Canada and back, twenty-
four cities in twenty-nine days, a bunch of twenty-one-year-old kids
in an illegal minivan and a compact car. I don't know how many
speeding tickets we got, and every tollbooth from Boston to Denver
snapped a photo of our license plate and mailed a ticket back to the
rental car agency. We even ended up wrapping one of the cars around
a telephone pole. There were so many things we did that could have
blown up everything. The level of risk we took was insane, and the
only reason we took it was because we were too ignorant to know to
be scared. We didn't understand that if the tour hadn't sold, my career
would have been over before it started. Broke. Out of money. Done.

Out on the road it was feast or famine, which was scary. I was
constantly being gut-checked. I'd sell out Reggies in Chicago with
five hundred screaming fans shouting back every single lyric. Then
I'd hop in our shitty compact car and two days later I'd be down in
Lubbock, Texas, in some bar where the stage was a riser in the corner
and maybe six people had come out.

I remember playing a four-hundred-cap room in British Columbia and I showed up for the VIP meet-and-greet and I was like, "How many people for the meet-and-greet?" and they were like, "Fifteen," and I was like, "Oh, cool. Fifteen people. That's gonna be fun." So I did the meet-and-greet with the fifteen people and then it was showtime and I came out and it was the same fifteen people. That was it. I was like, "Didn't I just see all of you people like twenty minutes ago?" That's when I said, "Fuck it. We're ordering pizza. I'm not even gonna rap. Let's order pizza and talk." So we all ended up sitting on the floor in the middle of this club and talking and having conversations—it was dope.

Luckily we had far more Chicagos than Lubbocks, and the upside of high risk is high reward. By taking zero-guarantee booking, we got a ninety/ten split on the door, which meant if we did sell out we'd make a killing. We sold out damn near every show, and we made a fucking killing.

Other than going to Taco Bell and funding the tour, the first thing I did with my money was take care of the people who'd taken care of

With my crew on the road.

me. I helped Lenny fix his mom's truck, got 6ix a dope-ass production synthesizer. Then, with the money from the tour, I was able to move out of Lenny's basement into an apartment in Rockville near Shady Grove hospital, where I was born. But I was only there for a few months because I was constantly going to L.A. for recording sessions for the album with Def Jam, staying for weeks at a time at the Oakwood apartments, which are these shitty short-term places with leaks in the ceiling where the label puts people when they're living in L.A. but not really. Meanwhile all the cost of the travel and the studio time was adding up and finally my A&R guy, Noah, was like, "You can't live in Maryland, bro. Everything is out here. You have to be here."

Which was scary as shit, because Maryland was all I knew. Even though I'd spent my whole life wanting to get the fuck out of the place, actually having the option to leave was terrifying. "Wait, you're telling me you want me to go away from the only people who know me and love me? Okay!" So I moved out.

In the end it wasn't so bad because Lenny and 6ix and Castro moved with me and we went out there and we stayed in the Oakwood apartments while we looked for a place to live. All through the mixtape days and into the Def Jam days, my circle stayed tight. We were each other's family, and we kept each other close. We'd sleep six to a hotel room, two guys in each bed and two on the floor. It was something we did to save money, but it also kept us close. We didn't have any outside people telling us, "You're the shit," and distracting us from what we were doing, and we were never complacent. We'd huddle up late after shows or in the studio, and we'd work — "All I do is grind." Eighteen-hour days. Smoke breaks at three a.m. Zarou didn't even smoke, but he'd join us for a cigarette just because.

We fed off each other. What I think was amazing was that everyone had come together out of a selfish desire to "make it," but we all saw that the best way to make it was for us to work together. "If you do this for me and I do this for you, we're going to get everything that we want." I think that's why we worked so hard. 6ix was always making crazy beats, so I was like, "I need to make better raps." I was making better raps, so Zarou was like, "I need to market this the best that I can." We were all relying on each other, and nobody wanted to be the one who fucked that up, so we kept it going and kept it going. Any time we dropped a record, we were already working on the next three, never stopping to enjoy and revel in whatever amazing thing we'd just accomplished. That was our life.

Since the day I'd started rapping, I'd dreamed of making it onto *XXL* magazine's annual freshman cover showcasing all the best up-and-coming rappers. That was the sign that you'd made it. Kid Cudi. Wale. Mac Miller. Lupe Fiasco. Big K.R.I.T. Big Sean. Wiz Khalifa. They'd all made the list before me. I was in bed one morning and Zarou called me like five times until I finally picked up and I was like, "What?" and he was like, "What's up, *freshman*?" and I could hear the smile on his face and I was like "WHAT??!" and he was like, "Yeah!" I'd done the thing that, as a kid in Mary Jo's attic, was the biggest thing I had ever aspired to do. Awesome. Keep it going.

I finally moved out of the Oakwood apartments after I found this rental house in this spot called Alta Mesa that was up in the hills and it was crazy. We walked in and our minds were blown, like all those douchebags on *The Bachelor* who get to walk into that huge mansion and are all like, *"Oh my God!!!!"* We had a view overlooking the whole fuckin' city. Awesome. Keep it going.

I announced my Def Jam deal and the mainstream music press and the industry trades all sat up and took notice and acknowledged me for the first time. Awesome. Keep it going.

I went on tour in Europe and stopped in Belgium and had a fire-ass waffle at the train station. Strawberry and Nutella and powdered sugar. Tasty fuckin' waffle. Awesome. Keep it going.

I started meeting all my idols. Met Nas. Met J. Cole. Met Kid Cudi

Playing to a sold-out hometown crowd at the Fillmore.

and he invited me to open for him on tour. Mind blown. Awesome. Keep it going.

I dropped my next mixtape, *Young Sinatra: Welcome to Forever,* from home in bed and watched it blow up and then went and played thirty-two cities in forty-three days, climaxing with a sold-out hometown show playing for two thousand people at the Fillmore Silver Spring. Awesome. Keep it going.

Every week it was more fans, bigger shows. But every day felt the same. From Lenny's basement to sold-out shows in Europe, it all felt the same, and the reason it all felt the same was because every day I woke up with the same feeling of "Damn, I'm still not good enough. I haven't made it yet. I have to keep going."

That feeling had been there, the kernel of it, since the day Josh LaFrance told me, "You're good at rap. You should keep rapping." Even if it was just me listening to Wu-Tang in the dark on my dad's couch and writing rhymes in an old notebook on the bus on the way to work, that feeling was there. "I can't stop. I have to do this." By the time I got to Mary Jo's attic and my sister's basement, it was a kind of mania. I was either writing something or recording something, non-stop. I'd fall asleep every night with my laptop open on top of me and some lyric in midsentence. If I wasn't working, I was lost.

I wasn't doing it for fans or adulation or critical acclaim, because none of that existed yet. I was doing it for myself because it was the only positive feedback I gave myself, the only way I felt good about myself. I would rap over those Wu-Tang beats and I'd feel in my heart of hearts that I rapped as good as they did. It was rewarding. To be able to create something and then sit back and say, "Wow, I did that. There was something I wanted to do, and I did it." It was like a high. It was addictive. Sometimes I'd rap about bullshit and have a good time. Other times I'd go super-deep and look in the mirror and reflect on the pain of my childhood. I was prepared to open any box in my mind. Even when I was scared to open the box, I would open it and reach in and take everything I found and put it into my music. But whether I was having fun or literally bleeding onto the page, whether I was escaping from my shit or dealing with my shit, it all served the same purpose: It made me feel good about myself.

Then came the world I built around me. First it was Lenny and 6ix and Zarou and the surrogate family and common purpose we shared. Then it was the RattPack and all of my fans telling me how much they loved me and how important my music was to them. And since that was all built around work and around rap, I had to keep working and rapping or it might cease to exist. I felt if that was ever taken from me, if there was no more rapping or writing or music or creativity, I would be utterly fucked.

That's how driven and obsessed I'd been when it was me sitting on a box of cat shit putting out mixtapes with my friends. By the time I moved to California to work on my first album with a seven-figure record deal and a crew to take care of and salaries to pay and critics to worry about and hundreds of thousands of fans to keep happy, the pressure had only ratcheted up that much more. All I did was work. Lenny, 6ix, and Zarou were the same. We used to sleep in the studio. On an average day, we were waking up around eight or nine p.m., long after the sun had gone down, then stumbling down to the studio to mix and record for fourteen, fifteen hours straight. Any time we weren't laying something down I was on my phone, checking Twitter and checking Twitter and checking Twitter. The only time I saw the sun was when I'd step outside for cigarette breaks before going back to bed the next day.

I couldn't relax. Not for a minute. The money was all going out as fast as it came in, and not because I was living extravagantly. I'd been spending down my advance to live and to cover the expenses of building something, and refilling the coffers with the income from touring. When I settled in L.A. I had around a hundred thousand in capital to finish my album and pay everybody and fund my first major tour. I even hired a business manager to make sure I didn't fuck anything up and then the business manager ended up being the one who fucked everything up because he didn't handle my taxes properly and I ended up owing a ton of back taxes on some Wesley Snipes shit.

I fired that business manager and then got an awesome one to fix everything and then, in January 2014, after I'd done all the work on the album and prepping the tour and was ready to go out and start earning back everything I'd invested, I couldn't. I got sued. Some dude, this forty-five-year-old guy from back in the day who called himself "DJ Logic," filed a copyright claim against me. This guy didn't even have a record deal, but he'd registered "DJ Logic" as a trademark in 2000, allowed the registration to lapse in 2003, and then reregistered the name in 2013, long after I was all over social media calling myself "Logic" and firmly establishing myself as the best-known musician in the country using that name. But this guy, once my first album was announced, filed suit against me in the Eastern District of Michigan.

Def Jam's first response was to come to me and say, "Can you change your name?" After all the mixtapes and the branding and the tours and what we created, they wanted me to change my name because some dude from Brooklyn was using pro bono lawyers to scare them. I said no fucking way. We decided to offer the guy a settlement, but he wouldn't take it. He was serious. So just as the album was about to drop and the tour was about to start, Def Jam decided they couldn't go ahead. They wouldn't release my album if there was any chance this guy could come after them for a piece of it. They didn't want the liability.

I was fucked. All the money had gone out and there was no way to bring any more in. So we racked our brains and came up with an idea. We milked it. We dropped a few tracks that hadn't made the album, as a teaser. Then we went out on what we decided to call the While You Wait Tour. Thirty-one cities in two months to get the fans all excited about an album that we still didn't know would ever come out. It was fuckin' insane.

So we went back out on the road, and I was in no shape to be on the road. Zarou was always Mr. College Athlete, super-jacked and in shape. When we first went out to L.A. and were staying at the Oakwood, he got an up-close look at how I lived and it horrified him. Growing up on food stamps and powdered milk and day-old donuts for dinner doesn't exactly teach you the healthiest habits. This was the first time in my life when I had enough money to eat whatever I wanted, and I had probably the worst diet of any human who's ever lived. I'd keep Reese's cups on my nightstand and I'd wake up and that's what I'd eat for breakfast. Day after day in the studio and on the tour bus it would be nothing but pizza and McDonald's. It was like I was making up for lost time, eating every Happy Meal I could never afford as a child.

I was still smoking, too. A pack of Newports a day, minimum. I never drank water, either. For weeks at a time, the only liquid I consumed was Coca-Cola. At one point I was pissing out blood clots, which freaked me the fuck out. I went and got Zarou and made him come look in the toilet. I was like, "What do I do?" and he was like, "We need to go the hospital." So we went to the hospital and the doctor stuck his hand up my ass to check out my prostate and he said, "You've got a UTI. You're not drinking enough water."

So I started drinking water but other than that I didn't change too much because when you're that young you think you're invincible. But it was more than the young-and-invincible thing. It was more than the bad habits from growing up in the hood. I was physically deteriorating because I was mentally fucked up from the stress of what I was going through. It wasn't simply that I didn't want to eat properly, I *couldn't* eat properly.

By the time we hit the While You Wait Tour I was running on nothing but cigarettes and adrenaline. I was so stressed out I could barely stomach real food anymore. Even the McDonald's and the pizza were getting to be too much. For a while I was only eating Pop-Tarts and drinking Ensure. The Pop-Tarts were crumbly and mushy and easy to keep down, and with the Ensure I felt like, "Well, this is the most responsible way to get some actual nutrients inside me."

We documented the whole tour in our "Just Another Day" series on YouTube, and there's videos you can see of me where my skin is almost gray. After one show I had to go to an urgent-care clinic because I was hocking up this bloody black-and-dark-green shit because of my smoking and how hard I was going on my voice every night.

For a long stretch of the tour I was running a 102-degee fever. I was puking my guts out before shows, going out onstage, performing, coming backstage and puking after the set, and then going back out and doing an encore. But I kept going. I wasn't asking myself, "Is this healthy? Is this normal? How long can I keep this up?" I didn't think like that. I had my North Star and I was chasing it and running after it by any and every means possible. In my head, all I could think was,

"This is the moment I've always dreamed of and now I'm here, and what? I'm supposed to stop because I'm sick? No way."

The show had to go on. It had to go on because I couldn't give it up. It had to go on because the venue had sold a couple thousand tickets and they had their beer concession and there was merch to sell. More than anything, it had to go on because of the fans. Not because they paid for their ticket but because they'd waited hours in line to get that ticket and they'd spent hours obsessing over the show and getting ready for the show and getting amped for the show. And now I was going to take that away from them?

I love my fans and so many of them have been so wonderful to me over the years and I've tried so hard to give them every piece of me I could. But as my first album drop approached, I was slowly learning what that really means. Having millions of fans is like having a monster you keep in your basement. It's cool and it's dope and it's furry and it loves you and you can go to all your friends and say, "Look, I've got this enormous monster and it loves me and we hang out and it's cool." But you also have to feed it, and you don't ever want to find out what happens if you stop.

One of the nights I had this raging fever, I was outside in the parking lot puking before the show. This kid ran up and was like, "Hey! Logic! Logic! Can I take a picture with you?!" In between puking my brains out, I looked up and was like, "Dude, I'm so sorry. I can't. I don't feel so good right now." And he was like, "Fuckin' *dick*!" Then he turned and stomped off.

I've only ever canceled a few shows in my life. I've performed with a fever, sweating so profusely I felt like I was going to pass out. I've performed when my voice was so shot I was scared I would lose it. I've performed sitting on a stool because I was too weak to stand. Because the alternative is worse. You cancel a show and you're hit with this wave of disappointment and sadness that makes you feel horrible, and then, for some, that disappointment curdles into rage.

Celebrating the release of Under Pressure *with (*from left*)*
DJ Rhetorik, 6ix, Harrison Remler, and Chris Zarou.

I've seen fans go from "We love you! We can't wait to see you!" to "Fuck you! How could you do this to us?!" It happens on a dime, and if you're an artist who believes that you're nothing without your fans, the thought of losing them is not just terrifying. It's existential. It's *I* will cease to exist without *them*. So you puke your guts out and you drink some Gatorade and your security guards help you limp back to the edge of the stage and you get back out there.

Finally, luckily, in the fall of 2014 the dispute over my name got resolved. The case wouldn't actually be over for years. We won in district court because the judge told the guy to get the fuck out of his courtroom with his bullshit, but then he appealed and it went to appeals court and then the appellate court told the guy to fuck off and then he appealed again to the Supreme Court and then those guys told him to fuck off and—three years and $650,000 in legal fees later—it was finally over and done. But the first district court ruling was enough for Def Jam to agree to release the album and on October 21, we dropped my debut, the aptly named *Under Pressure*.

Under Pressure debuted at #2 on the hip-hop charts and at #4 overall. We sold seventy-two thousand copies in the first week and it should have been the greatest day of my life and in some ways it was but in too many ways it was just another day of "Damn, I'm still not good enough. I haven't made it yet. I have to keep going." We'd hoped to sell a hundred thousand copies and debut at #1, because we wanted to make a lot of noise and get people's attention. And we probably would have if not for the fact that Def Jam undershipped me like a motherfucker. T.I., who came out the same day and beat us for the top spot in hip-hop, he had two hundred thousand physical CDs shipped to stores. I had maybe twenty thousand. And Def Jam was so cheap they wouldn't pay for shelf space, let alone the new-release-artist space. My shit was in boxes in the back at Best Buy and at Target. Kids had to go to the salesclerks and ask them to go in the back with a box cutter so they could get their hands on a copy. I felt like a bottom-tier basement worker at Def Jam. I felt like Milton from *Office Space*. I was pissed. Chris was pissed.

Despite watching what Chris and I had been doing, building a fanbase online for close to two years, Def Jam still fundamentally didn't understand what had happened to the music industry and how guys like us were changing it. Their argument was: "But you've never sold an album before." To which we argued, "Yes, but we've sold out hundreds of shows even without an album, so we know the album sales will be there." But they didn't listen. They didn't get it.

Three months later we kicked off the *Under Pressure* tour at the Emerson Theater in Indianapolis. The album was on its way to going platinum, reviews and press were pouring in, fans were blowing it up all over social media, and to the whole world I looked like this big rapper. What nobody in the world knew was that I was still getting sick all the time, still being sued over my name, my label didn't believe in me, and I'd poured nearly every dime I had into doing this tour. I was damn near broke. The day I walked onto the stage in Indianapolis, I had fifteen hundred dollars in my bank account and

I weighed 128 pounds and all I could think was, "This has to work. I have to make this work. I have to make this work."

Because in my mind, if it didn't work I was worthless. I'd never amount to anything. If it didn't work I'd end up right back in Maryland like everybody else in my family, a drug addict or an alcoholic living on welfare and food stamps. This, being Logic, being with the RattPack, was the only place I had ever belonged. So no matter how hard it got, no matter how sick I got, I had to keep going and going and going, because if I stopped I would die.

ᚼᚾᚼᚻᚼᚾᚼᚾᚼᚾᚼᚾ

The last time I ever spoke to my mother was on January 22, 2011, my twenty-first birthday. *Young, Broke & Infamous* had just dropped and it had been almost a year since I'd seen her outside my show at the End Zone. I was at Lenny's house and Amber called me in tears saying, "Mommy is upset with me and calling me names and saying that I'm the reason you don't talk to her." I was like, "What are you talkin' about?" and she was like, "I don't know." So I hung up with her and I called my mom.

"Hello?" she said, kind of terse and flat.

"Mom?"

"Who is this?"

"This is your son."

On a dime, her tone changed and she started playing her sweet side, so excited that I'd called. "My son?! Sir Robert?! This is Bobby?!"

I didn't let her get ten seconds with that shit. I cut her off.

"Mom," I said, staying totally calm and matter-of-fact, "I just talked to Amber and she said you attacked her and told her the reason I don't talk to you is because of her. No, Mom. The reason I don't talk to you is you. Because everything is your way or the highway and I can't even have a conversation with you about anything without you exploding and going berserk and crazy. That's why I don't talk to you. Because you're not a reasonable person. I wish you were, but you're not."

Then, as I was trying to explain myself, she snapped and said, "Okay. That's fine. That's *fine*. That's *FINE*."

Then she hung up on me, and that was the last time I ever spoke to her. I was proud of myself, though, for standing up to her like an adult without losing my temper.

Over the next few years I'd get these cards from her, usually around Christmas. She'd pass them to me through Jesse or my sisters. They were always strange, usually a bunch of Bible quotes mixed in with her trying to show love and affection.

One year it would be: "Dear Sir Robert, Thank you for being born—You ARE loved by me so deeply I cannot explain . . ."

Then the next year it would be: "Sir, You have become a spectacular, wonderful, classy, even more intelligent & gifted man, you are a GIFT to MANKIND! Love Eternal, your mother."

Sometimes I'd pick up the phone and call, but for whatever reason she would never answer. Whatever window of sanity that led her to write the notes had passed, and then she was gone again. Once or

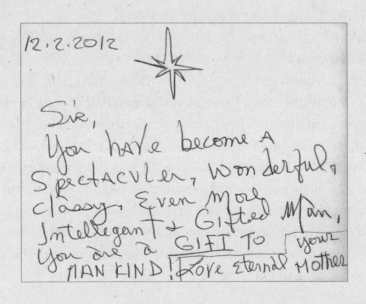

twice a year, I'd ask my siblings, "How's Mom doing?" and they'd say, "She's fuckin' crazy. Don't talk to her. Just don't do it."

So I didn't, and the more my career took off, the farther my mother faded into the rearview. With my dad it was more complicated. The difference between my mom and my dad was that I was able to not have a relationship with my mom because I'd *had* a relationship with her, and it was awful. I knew there was nothing there for me. My dad and I had never had a real relationship at all, so my whole life I've held out this hope, like, "Well, maybe this time it'll be different . . ." And it never is.

Every six months or so, either he'll reach out or I'll reach out or call or text and he immediately ruins it by asking me for money or asking me to bring him into the studio or on tour to play congas. It's always about what I can do to help him after he did nothing to help me. All I want is a relationship where we talk and communicate and share things, a relationship that isn't transactional or him trying to use me for something he needs. But he can't do it. Every time one of us reaches out, it falls apart.

Every time it happens, I try to downgrade my expectations so I won't be disappointed. I'll be like, "Okay, he'll never be my dad, but maybe he'll be like a cool uncle." Then, "Okay, he'll never be my cool uncle, but maybe he'll be like a fun brother." Then, "Okay, he'll never be my fun brother, but maybe he'll be like one of my boys I can hang with." Then, "Okay, he'll never be one of my boys I can hang with, but . . ." And down and down each time, always being disappointed no matter how much I try not to get my hopes up. I can actually remember thinking at one point, "Well, maybe since I'm older now, we'll have more in common." But the funny thing is we had more in common when I was a kid because of how immature he is.

My father didn't even come to a single show of mine until I played the Fillmore Silver Springs in 2013 on the *Young Sinatra: Welcome to Forever* tour. I'd been playing shows around Maryland and D.C. for four years by that point, and he hadn't come to a single one. Still, it was cool that he came, so I brought him up onstage with me, and the minute this narcissistic dude got onstage in front of that crowd, it was all about him and how he was the man, because this was the crowd he'd dreamed of for himself his whole life. He was going, "Yeah!" and talking to the fans. I had to start yelling into the mic, "Dad . . . Dad! . . . DAD! *YO!*" just to get his attention turned on me. I was upset, but it turned out to be funny and I got to introduce him to the crowd and it was actually a pretty great moment, or at least I wanted it to be.

The next time I saw him was when I flew him and my brother Ralph out to L.A. right before *Under Pressure* came out. I wanted to see them. Ralph didn't ask me for shit, but my dad hadn't even been at the house half an hour when he said, "Hey, I need six hundred dollars."

"For what?"

"I caught a case."

"What do you mean, you caught a case?"

"Look, son, I just need you to help me pay for a lawyer."

"What did you do?"

"I didn't do anything, but this girl says I beat her up.'"

I rolled my eyes. "Dad," I said. "The fuck? What do you mean, this girl says you beat her up? Did you beat her up?"

"Well, yeah, but like not really."

"What do you mean, yeah but not really?"

"Well, she was coming at me all crazy. What was I supposed to do, let the bitch beat me up?"

"But you're fucking sixty-five years old. How are you even in a position where some woman is coming after you? What the fuck is wrong with you?"

I wasn't going to give him shit, but then I decided if the case was real I wanted to try to help, so I said, "Give me the lawyer's number. I'll call them and I'll take care of it." So then he tried to bullshit his way around and he never gave me the lawyer's name and I never even found out if there ever really was a case or if he was just trying to get some money on the side.

The next time I saw him was on a promotional tour for my second album, *The Incredible True Story*. It was the day the album came out and I was at the Lakeforest Mall in Gaithersburg at the same FYE where I used to go and buy music in high school and the dude just showed up. First of all, I couldn't believe they let the guy in. All he said was, "I'm Logic's dad," and they just let that nigga backstage when he could have been some deranged psychopath. My shit got super–locked down after that.

But anyway. There he was with this new wife of his I couldn't stand, this woman named T. For years that's all I knew her as, just T. Later I learned it stands for Tiana, which I always thought was a black-girl name, but she's actually white. Debbie was out of the picture at that point. Sometime around *Under Pressure,* Debbie overdosed and went into a coma and while she was in her coma my dad was cheating on her with T. Nobody thought Debbie was going to come out of the coma. Then she did, and pretty much right when she woke up my dad left her for T—which is some real *Jerry Springer*–type shit.

Then this woman, T, who at that point had never met me, started going around Gaithersburg and social media and everywhere else telling people she was "Logic's mom." This bitch even got a tattoo of my name on her body (I don't know where; I don't want to know where). Which, on top of the divorce and the whole cheating-during-the-coma thing, really pissed Debbie off. So Debbie got up in T's face and told her, "You better fucking remove that shit or I'm gonna fuck you up, bitch. That's not your boy. That's *my* boy. You don't know him. You never met him." So then T got it covered up.

So when the dude walked into FYE with this woman, I couldn't even believe it. He wanted me to sign all these CDs for him, and it was weird. Part of me felt like he was there out of some kind of fucked-up fatherly pride, but at the same time it felt like he wasn't there for his son at all. He was there for "Logic." Which is so fucked up. But there was no other way to think about it given that he never really gave a shit about me, but then when I started popping off it was, "He's my baby! He's my favorite! He's my everything!"

I signed a few CDs for him, because I was trying to be the bigger person and that's what you do, and I tried to talk to him, but he was just being extra. I don't even remember what it was. It was him being an asshole or asking for money and I started getting irritated and finally I snapped and said, "Yo, why the fuck did you come here? I don't want to see you."

"Well, I wanted to see you."

"I don't want to see you, Dad. You fucked this up too many times."

"But I'm done. I'm done. I'm done."

"No, Dad, I can't fuck with you."

"Please give me another chance."

Then he started crying, and I was like, "Fuck you, man. What is this? 'And the Oscar goes to . . .' Get the fuck out of here with that shit."

"Give me another chance!"

"Dad, I've given you a million chances."

"Give me a million and one."

"Dad, I love you. But the next time we're in in the same place, you're gonna be in the fuckin' ground, bro."

I can remember saying those exact words to him. I didn't feel bad about it and still don't. In fact, I think I was being too generous. Because I don't think I will be there when they put my dad in the ground. And it's not out of spite. It's that if I go there, the funeral won't be about him and his life and his death, it'll be about Logic. The whole family, they'll act the way my dad did at that signing. It won't be "Bobby is here." It'll be "Logic is here. Can we have money?"

So he left with T and then, later that night, my sister Natalia hit me up on Facebook, saying, "Thank you so much for signing my CD."

I was like, "What the fuck is she talking about?" I looked and she'd posted a pic of one of the albums I signed, and my fuckin' dad had taken a Sharpie and written on top of my autograph, "Love to my baby sister, Natalia." Which is fucked up for two reasons: One, I didn't fuckin' sign that for her, and if I was going to, I would have done it myself. Two, my father is a fuckin' idiot dumbass because *Natalia is older than me*. This fuckin' idiot didn't even know his own kids' birthdays.

Things weren't as difficult with Amber and Geanie, but money became an issue there, too. They asked me to help them out a couple of times and I helped them out and then that turned into a couple more times and that turned into me being like, "All right, I can't do this anymore." Because it was always dumb shit like, "I need three hundred dollars to pay my gas bill." Which, I know what that's about because it was the same shit my mom always did. Being on government assistance is both the hardest and easiest thing in the world. It's hard because you have zero dollars for pleasure, but it's also easy because all of your bills and necessities are paid for, calculated down to the last dime. So if you don't have three hundred dollars for the gas bill, it means you spent the money on bullshit. There were plenty of times I went hungry because my mom did exactly that, and I'm not going to subsidize it. I'm not going to bail them out so they can go buy cigarettes and alcohol.

When you get to the position I have, you want to help people—and I do help a lot of people—but at a certain point you have to say, "This is not my responsibility. You did this. You got pregnant four times with four different men. You went on welfare instead of going to school and becoming a nurse and making ninety-five thousand dollars a year. You fucked that up. I didn't fuck that up. I'm not here to pick up those pieces." The only family member that I want to help and that I've tried to keep a relationship with is Jesse, because he's the only one, the only fuckin' one, who has never asked me for anything. Through all his ups and downs, even when he was on drugs and homeless and sleeping in cars, all he ever wanted was to be my brother.

And it sucks. It hurts. Because I want to have relationships with my family but at the same time I've had to draw boundaries to protect myself from all their fucked-up bullshit. Even though I look to all the world like this famous rapper and rock star, I haven't always been in the most stable place myself. Even after I was getting decent money, I didn't have the money to support two parents and seven siblings who wanted money all the time—especially when money was all they wanted. So it was always this back-and-forth. I'd reach out to them, they wouldn't respect my boundaries and I'd have to cut them off again and every time it hurt and I struggled with it and struggled with it until one night Geanie called me and said, "Mom got hit by a car."

"What?"

"She was riding her bike and she got run over and she's in the hospital."

"Is she gonna die?"

"She's got a big gash on her head, and they say she has bleeding in her brain."

"But is she gonna die?"

"She might. We don't know."

"Okay. Word."

At no moment did I get scared or freaked out. I felt bad. It sucked for her, but at no time was I fretting like, "Oh my God, I'm going to lose my mom." Because you can't be scared of losing something you never had.

Geanie mentioned that my mom's friend Carol Ellen had been there at the hospital with them. I hadn't spoken to Carol Ellen in fifteen years, but I called her and the minute she picked up I was reminded of why I hadn't spoken to her in fifteen years.

There are things I do love about Carol Ellen. She's fat and funny and speaks her mind. Which I respect. But she was on me as soon as we started talking. "You *have* to see her," she said. "It's your *mother*. You *have* to go visit her. You don't know what could happen. It's your *mother*. You *have* to go. It's your *mother*."

I didn't argue with her, but in that moment I decided, "No, I'm not going to go see my mother. I'm not even going to call her."

I understood the gravity of the situation. She didn't end up dying; she just busted her shit open. Still, in that moment we thought she was dying. But that didn't change anything she'd done to me. It didn't change the fact that if I called her, then what? I would sit there and bite my tongue and do my best not to get baited into an argument while she ranted about God and the Illuminati and whatever else, never once stopping to acknowledge or express regret for all the horrible shit she did to me.

I'm not going to say I didn't give a fuck, because I did. But at the same time I had nothing to say to the woman. Even thinking that she was about to die, I had nothing to say to her. It might have been different if she'd been on her deathbed calling out for me: "I want to talk to Bobby. I want to talk to my son." If she'd been asking for that, I probably wouldn't have denied it to her. But that wasn't the case. She thought she was dying and she didn't call out for help from me or from any of us—she didn't give a shit about us.

Society has this weird thing about mothers. If your dad beats you or sexually assaults you then it's "That's terrible" and "He's a monster" and "Of course, yeah, obviously, you should cut him out of your life." But when somebody like my mom spends seventeen years mentally and emotionally destroying her own child, and that child makes the calm and rational decision not to have that woman in his life, then you get all these people like Carol Ellen coming at you. I have cousins who do the same. They all say, "It doesn't matter! She's your *mother*."

I think that a lot of people who believe that are people who've fucked up their own families and want to be given a pass on all their own abusive bullshit. They want to believe that you can yell and shit

The only recent photo I have of my mother.

on your kids and treat them like garbage and they'll always come back because "it's your mother."

Fuck that.

I hung up with Carol Ellen and I called Geanie back, and she had the exact same reaction I did. "Fuck anybody who tells you that bullshit," she said. "You had it worse than all of us. You were trapped with that woman, and I don't care if she is dying, you don't owe nobody shit." And I thought, "Damn, that makes me feel so much better."

The tragedy is not that I didn't call my mother but that I never got to know my mother, the person she was or could have been without all the abuse and mental illness that created the beaten, fucked-up version of her. There were always bits and pieces of a sweet woman underneath it all, but I have no idea who that person is.

It hurts that I can't call her and have a relationship with her, and for a long time I felt like I should or I had to. But then I realized that was me feeling bad because of what people like Carol Ellen were telling me. After my mom's accident, something went off in my head, and I said, "No. I don't need these people. I've never needed these people." I wish I had a relationship with my parents. I wish I had a family. But I don't, and I accept that. I still have moments when I break down and cry, but deep in my heart I'm like, "I don't need a fuck-up drug-addict dad and an alcoholic bipolar mom to make me happy. I don't need their acceptance to make me feel good about myself." And that sucks, but life sucks. I learn from it, and I move on.

The world could end tomorrow. My world as I know it will definitely end when I die. Do I want to spend that time crying about how unfair my childhood was and yearning for some reconciliation that's never going to come? Or do I want to give my time and energy to the people in my life who love me and support me no matter what?

ス卉兔ナ宀‖百

I n December 2015, I was standing in line with my fiancée for the world premiere of *Star Wars: The Force Awakens*. I was so excited because I'd never seen a *Star Wars* movie in a theater because I was too poor when the prequels came out and now here I was at this beautiful theater on Hollywood Boulevard. I was feeling dope because I'd scored tickets to this VIP premiere and I had this beautiful woman by my side. It wouldn't work out with her in the end. We would get married and get divorced, but at the time I was in love and my second studio album, *The Incredible True Story,* had just dropped and I was killing it.

The Incredible True Story was a turning point for me. Prior to that album, most of what I'd done on my mixtapes was all about proving myself, showing how well I could rap, how fast I could rap, telling the story of my come-up. There was a lot of me trying to convey this pose of "I'm a rapper." *Under Pressure* was the end of all that. After that dropped, I was like, "Everyone knows I can rap well, so what else is there? Oh, wait. There's a whole universe of ideas in my head."

The Incredible True Story is the album where I fully embraced myself. It was me accepting all of my nerdiness. It's a futuristic, sci-fi, audio-cinematic experience that follows the journey of two characters, Thomas and Kai, and a sentient computer program named Thalia.

They're the crew of a spaceship called the *Aquarius III*. Earth has been destroyed, the remaining pocket of humanity has escaped to an orbiting base called Babel Station, and the crew of *Aquarius III* are searching the universe for a new planet they call Paradise.

I nerded out so hard making that album. I had Japanese anime films projected on the walls while I was making beats. I went out and found Steve Blum, the voice of Spike Spiegel in *Cowboy Bebop*, to play the part of Thomas. I brought in the illustrator Sam Spratt to design the album and the packaging, creating the visual aspect of this universe, which made the album something people could see and not just hear. It was *dope*.

Ever since I'd discovered sci-fi and anime with Robert Naples and Jesse Wideman back in West Deer Park, telling stories had always been a way for me to build new worlds to escape the one I was in. At first glance, it's easy to see the story of Thomas and Kai as being about my childhood, about not having a family and not being able to go back home anymore and setting out in search of a new

The Incredible True Story *tour bus, with artwork by Sam Spratt.*

home, and that's in there for sure. But for me it was actually about something else.

As with *Under Pressure*, the idea for the album came from what I was experiencing in real life. With *Under Pressure* it was the simple fact that I was under so much pressure to deliver the album, not only to my label but to the world. We were in this time when debut albums meant so much after the success you'd achieved with mixtapes. You had to deliver and you had to kill it. The pressure to overcome that was intense. Plus I was being sued, I had my family begging me for money I didn't have, and I was grinding my body into the dirt. So it was a lot.

The Incredible True Story was a response to a different kind of pressure. When I created the RattPack and the alter ego of Young Sinatra, all these other rappers were going around with this tough-guy posture, putting "Southeast Killa!" in their Twitter bios and shit. From the jump I was like, "Fuck that." I started using the phrase "Peace, Love, and Positivity" instead. I'd call it out at my concerts and post it up on social media. I did it for a simple reason: It was everything my childhood was not. After a lifetime of negativity and pain, I wanted to put the opposite of that out into the world.

Back in the early days of me tweeting that out, there was this one guy, @OGBiscuit. This dude was so weird. Whenever I'd post anything, especially anything positive, @OGBiscuit would come at me. One day I tweeted, "Find what you love in life and go after it!!" And he replied, "no." Which is nothing, but why bother? Another time I tweeted, "Do your best to be a good person! And whatever your dreams are think of them often! The law of attraction is real!" And he wrote back, "fuck you."

One day the dude went and found some picture of me online where I was spilling a drink on my lap at a party and he tweeted it out with: "HA FAG @Logic301 SPILLED YOUR DRINK I WISH IT WAS LAVA." Then he followed that up with: "@Logic301 I wanna slice this man throat," and then a buddy of his chimed in with: "put salt on the cuts," and then @OGBiscuit added, "cut open his chest," and his buddy was like, "lmao omg hahahah lolol i luv u."

And I couldn't, for the life of me, understand why anyone would do that. Why would someone go out of his way to track and follow everything I do online just to shit on me? Luckily social media goes both ways, so one day I started tweeting back at @OGBiscuit, asking him why he felt the need to hunt me down and demean me and my goals and my dreams. He just flamed me more, going on about how everything I rap about is bullshit and I grew up in the suburbs and I wasn't really poor and then, day after day, he just kept going.

"@Logic301 if you can read this, you a bitch" and

"@logic301 lololol, logic a homo ass bitch" and

"@logic301 at least when of he does blow up I can always Say I buttfucked logic. No homo" and

"@Logic301 bruh, you gay as shit" and

"@Logic301 homo ass" and

"@Logic301 I hope you blow up homie. I do, so I can tell people how much of a pussy you were when you use to be a real person" and

"@Logic301 I took the condom off, I'm ready for round 2. Fuck out of here!" and

"@Logic301 noting is rotting my soul you faggatron" and

"@Logic301 I don't even like you on facebook you confused ass kid. Your not black. Your white. Jerkoff" and

"@Logic301 but look. I feel you. You gotta keep this faggot ass bubble gum rap reputation Up. Your faking who you are bro. Stop it" and

"@LOGIC301 WSUP HOMO" and

"@Logic301 WHY ARE YOU LIKE THIS ROBERT? WHY MUST YOU ACT SO VAGINA ???? WHY CAN'T YOU TELL ME TO FUCKIN JUMP OFF A CLIFF?" and

"@Logic301 IF I EVER MEET YOU AGAIN BRO IM

SOOOOOOOOOOOOOOOO GONNA UNTIE YOUR SNEAK-ERS WITHOUT YOU KNOWING <3" and

"fuck @logic301 forever, I don't fuck with logic cuz he's moist vagina" and

"@logic301 fuck logic forever my friend. forever" and

"@Logic301 Robert aka logic raped a little girl" and

"@Logic301 I hate you bruh I hope your varsity 6s split on stage and you fall off the stage and break like 3 of your fingers b" and

"@Logic301 your index finger, middle finger and thumb finger. that will really fuck your life up" and

"everyone coming out the DMV is maaaad dope and has a lot of talent and will make it. except @logic301 you'll burn out in a year pussy hoe" and

"@Logic301: #FaggPack #BitchSoxers" and

"@Logic301 hashtag I pray for your downfall" and

"@logic301 FUCK YOU YOU FUCKING BITCH I HATE YOU" and

"@Logic301 fuck u pussy you weak as fuck yeah I'm hatin so what what ya finna do ya bish" and

"@Logic301 you still suck" and

"@Logic301 is gay as fuck, his bitch ass to famous to entertain my hatred now" and

"@Logic301 I HATE YOU DAWG PLEASE KNOW I FOR-EVER WILL HATE YOU" and

"this guy @Logic301 has ruined more lives but releasing a mix-tape today. forever a faggy bitch ROBERT" and

"I will stop u 1 day @Logic301 mark my words" and

"@Logic301 FAGGY BITCH" and

"@Logic301 fuck your dreams I pray you have nightmares" and

"@Logic301 FUCK YOU. I WILL RUIN YOUR LIFE SOME-HOW. SOMEWAY" and

"@Logic301 given the opportunity, I would break your neck" and

"@Logic301 YOU ARE THE DEVIL, FAM" and

"lowkey wanna rap to make an entire album 18 tracks firing on @Logic301 faggot bitch" and

"I HATE YOU BRA @Logic301 ILL CATCH U SLIPPIN ONE DAY AND FUCK YOUR TIRES UP ON MY CAT YA HURD" and

"@Logic301 u faggot bitch I fuckin hate u" and

"YOUR PARENTS ARE CRACKHEADS AND U GAY AS FUCK @Logic301 U A DISGRACE TO GAITHERSBURG" and

"did @logic301 die yet" and

"I'm finna columbine @Logic301 one of these days just end the evil sin that is his music" and

"YOU FUCKIN SUCK @Logic301 THE WORST RAPPER IN AUDIO HISTORY. IF U DIED TOMORROW I WOULDNT CARE LOL" and

"SETTING AN ENTIRE CITY FULL OF CHILDREN AND BABIES ON FIRE > LISTENING TO @Logic301" and

"I WOULD RATHER SLAP MY OWN MOTHER WITH A CROWBAR THEN TO LISTEN TO @Logic301" and

"THE WORST RAPPER EVER @Logic301 WHOEVER LIKES LOGIC IS AUTISTIC BRU" and

"LOGIC SUCKS. THE WORD LOGIC MAKES ME SAY UGH THE THOUGHT OF @Logic301 PROSPERING KEEPS ME UP AT NIGHT FRUSTRATED AND ANGRY @ THE WORLD" and

"suck my dick @Logic301 u a bitch"

He kept this up for over three and a half years. Sometimes he'd drop out and I wouldn't hear from him for a bit, but then he'd always come back, and I'd think, "Dude, what is wrong with you?"

There have been assholes on the Internet for as long as there's been an Internet, but this was new. Back when I was in Yahoo! music chatrooms and posting on Spoken vs. Written, it was like being at an open-mic night. Everybody at the open mic supports everyone else. Even if you think they suck, you don't attack them because you're at the open mic, too, which means you're doing no better than they are. There were occasionally people who would drag you, writing shit like: "Lord Subliminal, his raps aren't that good." Or: "Oh, this dude is garbage. He's biting somebody's style." But the whole thing was anonymous. They were anonymous, and I was anonymous. So even if you had guys going off about "Your mother's a whore and your face smells like asshole," even then it was like two CGI characters fighting each other; it wasn't real.

The geography of it changed, too. Back in the chatrooms, if you got in an argument with somebody it was because you both happened to be in the chat that night, like you ran into each other out on the corner. You could always choose to go hang out on a different corner. With social media, it was like having dudes hanging around outside your house 24/7, just waiting for you to come outside so they could start some shit.

The whole experience was so mystifying to me that I'd spend hours going down the rabbit hole of @OGBiscuit, going through all this guy's pictures and every tweet he'd ever posted and obsessing over him so I could figure out what his deal was. There were others like him, but never that many. A handful, maybe. Still, they would show up from time to time and trickle into my feed and start shitting on me and I'd always ask them why and I never understood the answer.

As long as I was underground doing mixtapes, everything was cool. Because when you're not famous, other than the random guys like @OGBiscuit, the only people following you are the people who like you, because why else would they be there? Then, once I signed to Def Jam and put out *Under Pressure,* suddenly I was on the radar of every asshole on the planet who'd appointed themselves to have an opinion about shit. Not only about what they liked or didn't like, or what was good or not good, but what was "real" hip-hop and what wasn't.

The music business, in general, sucks. But hip-hop in particular is such a garbage place. In large part that's because, at its inception, it was marginalized in the industry. The people who run the Grammys and award shows, one day they decided to put all the niggas in one category. Look at all the different genres of white popular music: You have rock and roll, pop rock, alt-rock, grunge, experimental. You can even take a genre of music that is much younger than hip-hop, like electronic music, and there are so many subgenres: electro, techno, dubstep, EDM. But with rap, it's rap. And that's it. So they take me and Drake and Travis Scott and whoever put out the most recent version of "I Just Fucked These Bitches with Big-Ass Titties" and they clump us all together in the same category. It's bullshit.

When people lump us together it alters the way we're perceived by the public and it fucks up the way we relate to each other. Everything has to be a fuckin' comparison, which is why all hip-hop people do is shit on each other. You look at other genres of music and it isn't like that. I don't remember Nirvana and the Pixies and R.E.M. ever beefing with each other over who's "really" alternative. You've never seen it because it's never happened. But in hip-hop it does. It's the most hostile, angry, violent genre of music there is.

But IT'S NOT!!! Because it wasn't born of that. It started with the Sugarhill Gang and Grandmaster Flash and the Furious Five, people who had something to say and they had a message and it was positive. The whole idea of hip-hop was that it took everything from every genre of music and broke it all down and mixed it all up and made something completely new the world had never seen before. Yes, it was "black music" to an extent, but really it was music born of a particular culture of a particular time and a particular place: New York in the late 1970s. You didn't have to be black to be a part of that culture. You could be Puerto Rican or Dominican and be a part of that culture. You could even be white and be part of that culture.

Then hip-hop blew up and the major labels came in and this incredible new form of music had to be crammed into the preexisting categories of "white music" and "black music" that the industry had already established. So then it was: "Here's your one radio station in each major market." "Here's your one Grammy category." "Here's your one hour a day on MTV."

Today hip-hop is one of the biggest and most successful and influential and ever-evolving genres of music in the whole fucking world. But certain people in the industry still run that shit like there's only this one little piece to go around. It's all jockeying for status and "Fuck that guy" and "I'm legit and he's not." People feel like they have to police the boundaries of the genre to decide who gets in and who doesn't because heaven forbid we just embrace the fact that the music can be more than it has been in the past.

When I was coming up in the early 2000s, gangsta rap had cast its shadow over everything. You had N.W.A and Ice Cube and Ice-T and Mack 10 and 50 Cent and DMX and all these guys rapping about life in the hood and the guns they carried and the drugs they sold and the niggas they killed and gettin' bitches and having the flyest shit. Which perpetuated the notion that that's all hip-hop is. To be considered a legit rapper, you had to be from a certain hood, look a certain way, dress a certain way, and sound a certain way. But I could never be that because I wasn't that. I was around it. I saw it. I could rap about how my brother Ralph was in that life and what that was like for him, the way I did on a record like "Gang Related." But that was never going to be who I was.

So I said, "Fuck it." That was my attitude from the beginning. I decided I was just going to be myself, which was scary, because being yourself is always scary when you feel like there's nobody else like you. I was this nerd from the suburbs who was into sci-fi and anime and video games and Rubik's Cubes and *Star Wars*. Back then that was nowhere near the spectrum of what was accepted as hip-hop. Nobody was rapping about that stuff, at least nobody was doing it on a level that was widely recognized. But I felt like if I started rapping about what I liked, I would find the people who liked it, too. And I did. Because of the Internet, the gatekeepers at the music labels and the industry magazines couldn't dictate what people heard and liked anymore. So I went around them and found millions of kids all over the world who fucked with me because they related to what I was talking about. They heard me and were like, "Oh, shit, I found a hip-hop artist that's like me. I like anime. I'm kinda nerdy. I'm going through the same things he's going through." I brought kids to hip-hop who didn't even like hip-hop, they just liked what I was about, and then through me they discovered they liked hip-hop.

Because I was expanding the genre of hip-hop beyond what some people were comfortable with, they would say things to me like, "You're rapping about *Star Wars*? You're gay. You're a fuckin' faggot. You fuckin' suck. You're not real hip-hop. You don't belong here." There was an undercurrent of it in the mixtape years, but it really exploded with *Under Pressure*. It was like @OGBiscuit had started multiplying like a fucking Gremlin. You don't get them wet and whatever you do, you sure as fuck don't feed them after midnight. But just by dropping an album that's what I'd done, and now the little fuckers were everywhere.

Which was the genesis of the inspiration that led me to create *The Incredible True Story*. I was tired of being told I didn't belong in hip-hop. I was like, "Okay, you say I can't be on your planet? I'll go make my own universe. You say I'm too nerdy for rap? I'm gonna do a *space album,* nigga. How about that?"

We dropped *The Incredible True Story* in October 2015 and it debuted at #1 on the hip-hop chart and #3 overall, selling a hundred and thirty-five thousand copies in its first week, which in the age of streaming is unheard of; only a handful of artists of any genre are selling that many units. Of course, it didn't silence any of the critics or the Gremlin people online. It was like the more successful I was at being the thing they said I shouldn't be, the madder they became. But whatever. Fuck those people because they were at home in their mom's basement and I was at the *Star Wars* premiere with a beautiful woman and had one of the bestselling albums of the year and everything was good. Until it wasn't.

I was standing in line and all of a sudden, out of nowhere, this feeling of utter panic rushed over my whole body. My chest got super-tight and I heaved and threw up a bit in my mouth and I started freaking the fuck out. I felt like I was out of my own body, like there was glass behind my eyes. Everything about the world around me didn't feel real. Reality didn't feel real, and I didn't feel real, either. It was the worst panic I'd felt since the first panic attack I ever had back when my mother left me alone in West Deer Park after I hurt myself breakdancing, and it was way worse than that even. I had never ex-perienced anything like it before in my life.

Weirdly, I hadn't had any real panic attacks or serious anxiety since leaving my mother's house. It didn't happen at Mary Jo's or my sister's or living in Lenny's basement. Which I think had a lot to do with feeling safe because I was always surrounded by a bunch of people that I love. I would get keyed up and high-strung from time to time. I had anxiety the way a normal person has anxiety, like being anxious about a big performance or a big date or just having too many Reese's cups and cigarettes. But it was never debilitating.

The closest I'd come to anything like an attack was at the Melk-weg in Amsterdam on my first European tour. We'd finished sound-check and all of a sudden it hit me how far I was from home. As a teenager I was scared of leaving my house. Then I went to Florida and that was scary. Then I moved to L.A. and that was scary. Then I toured half the United States and Canada and that was scary, but the whole time I'd been so busy and so focused that I hadn't remembered to be terrified. It was like in the Road Runner cartoons where the Coyote runs off the cliff and he keeps running in midair because he doesn't know he's in midair but then he stops and looks down and realizes he's in midair and that's when he realizes he's fucked.

I don't know why, but after soundcheck at the Melkweg in Am-sterdam, for some reason I looked down and I realized I'd not only left my room but I was on the other side of the world and I was like, "Holy shit!" This wave of panic hit me like a ton of bricks and I was freaking out and I called Lenny and I was like, "Bro, I'm freaking out," and he was like, "Why, what is it?" and I was like, "Yo, there's hostels and shit and it's fuckin' weird and I don't know what's going on." And he was like, "Bro, you're fine. Just have a good time and everything will be all right."

And it was. Until now. Now I was standing in line at *Star Wars* and freaking out and trying to hold it together. They opened the doors and we gave them our tickets and we went in and sat down. The movie started and the fanfare kicked in and my heart was racing and the titles came up and it was "A long time ago in a galaxy far, far away . . ." and after waiting for this moment for my entire life all I could think was "I've got to get the fuck out of here." I turned to my fiancée and I was like, "We have to go," and she was like, "Are you serious?!" and I was like, "I need to go the hospital."

Because I didn't think it was a panic attack. It felt so much deeper than that. We left and we went to our car and she started driving to the hospital and I was still freaking out. At one point I had to have her stop the car in the middle of traffic and I jumped out, full of panic, and I started pacing these tight circles, trying to breathe and get some fresh air.

We got to the hospital and I checked in to the emergency room and the doctor came in and he looked at my chart.

"I think you had a panic attack," he said.

"No, no, no, no, Doctor. No. This wasn't a panic attack. This was physical. This was real."

"Yeah," he said. "That's a panic attack. We're going to give you some Ativan and—"

"Wait—what?!"

I didn't want to hear about drugs because I don't like drugs because I'd seen what all those psych meds did to my mom.

"Look, man," he said in a funny kind of way where you could tell he'd been through this a million times before. "The Ativan's gonna help. It seems like what you're going through is anxiety."

"This isn't anxiety. This is a physical feeling; it's *physical*."

"I know. That's what anxiety is. Talk to a therapist."

So they gave me some Ativan in my drip and I started to calm down and I went and talked to a therapist and she was like, "It's anxiety," and I was like, "No, it's not." Then Zarou flew out and we talked and he was like, "Bro, it's anxiety," and I was like, "No! It's not!" And meanwhile I kept having these episodes that were like mini-flashes of what I'd felt outside the *Star Wars* premiere, feeling disassociated from my own body. It was like in *Men in Black* when there's that alien inside in that dude's head controlling him. I felt like I was the alien inside my own head, telling my body what to do and not feeling like I was the one actually doing it. I'd pick up a glass of water and drink it and think, "Did I just pick up that glass of water?" Everything was out of whack.

So I started googling and reading and I came across this thing called derealization, a condition brought on by extreme stress that makes you feel like the world isn't real and you aren't a real person in it. Things that are totally familiar feel alien and bizarre. The sensation of having a pane of glass behind my eyes, like there's a barrier or a membrane between you and reality, that's a common symptom, too. I read about it and I was like, "Holy shit. Derealization. That's what this is." And I'd brought it on myself. This was my mind and my body catching up with me after six years of overwork and exhaustion and a terrible diet and no exercise. The life of a rapper, in other words, constantly moving and working and grinding, and now, despite what I'd just been through, I still had to go back on the road.

The tour for *The Incredible True Story* was a monster, the biggest thing I'd done up to that point. We'd gone from playing five-hundred-cap bars to four-thousand-cap theaters. It was forty-one shows in eight weeks starting in Vancouver and going from there to Albuquerque to Fort Lauderdale and every place in between, followed by a twenty-day stretch of fourteen shows across Europe.

One thing that helped was the fact that I was becoming so famous

I had to have security with me. I'd been looking over my shoulder in public ever since getting assaulted at sixteen. I'd get jittery any time I thought somebody looked at me wrong, and that was when I was nobody. Once you become a public person, people look at you, stare at you, all the time. The good thing was that, unlike Bobby the scared kid at eighteen, Logic at twenty-six could hire two big-ass security guards, Jordan and my boy Big John from Houston. They came on board with us for the tour and followed me everywhere I went and handled me like fine china. That did a lot to calm me down.

Even with security, my problem was that I was stuck in mixtape mode. It was still in my mind that "Logic is the guy on his come-up who connects with his fans. That's who I am. That's what they expect, and if I stop doing it, all this will go away and I'll be a failure and that's it." Only now it wasn't ten people on Ustream, it was thousands, every single night.

I had dozens of people paying VIP prices to come backstage, all of them wanting their five minutes to tell me their story about what my music meant to them or a memory they had about a particular song. I loved that they wanted to do that, but giving that time and attention to so many people was draining me and I didn't have anything left in me to drain. I would do the shows and come offstage wired and stay up all night. Then I'd collapse on the bus and wake up the next day at five p.m. and drink an Ensure because I couldn't eat. Then I'd go back out and do it all over again, night after night after night.

Halfway through the tour we were playing the State Theatre in Portland, Maine. I was getting ready for the show and I remember being onstage and nobody else was there and all of a sudden I felt like I was on the verge of having a complete psychotic break. It was like everything going back to the *Star Wars* premiere and everything from my whole life had been snowballing up to this moment, and I was going to crack. I felt like I was not a free person. The way we talk about people who are pushed to their limit and they snap and go berserk, I think I was *right there,* at the brink of insanity. I was on that precipice. I was scared I was going to die. I didn't want to kill myself; it wasn't that. It was more being terrified and thinking, "I'm so fucked up, what if I snap and kill myself?"

I've gotten over it now, but back then and for my whole life up to that point, I used to freak out at the thought of turning into my mother. The idea that I might lose my sanity had always freaked me out, in the same way that my fear of becoming an addict kept me away from drugs and alcohol. You hear addicts say things like, "I want to drink until I don't even exist anymore. I want to get so high I can't even see myself in the mirror anymore." That's how I felt in that moment, but fortunately I'd been too afraid of drugs to do it.

I don't remember all that much of the episode, to be honest. I remember crying hysterically and calling Zarou and screaming and yelling at him, going, "I DON'T WANNA BE ON TOUR! I DON'T WANNA BE HERE!" At some point my tour manager, Harrison, put me on the phone with his godfather, who happened to be a psychologist who dealt with inmates in prison and shit. He was an amazing guy and he talked me down.

"You need to understand," he said, "you're on the right path already."

"What do you mean?"

"You don't drink or do drugs," he said. "Why do you think so many people who do what you do are dead by your age? They drug themselves. Hard-core drugs, pills, heroin, alcohol, that's what they use to cope."

The immediate terror subsided but the deeper problems remained. We ended up having to cancel the European shows because I just couldn't do it, physically or mentally. But I stuck it out for the rest of the U.S. tour because I didn't have any choice. Every night I was pacing back and forth with Jordan on the bus. I couldn't sit still with my own thoughts. I was scared to sit still. I was so fucked up that I always felt like I was going to pass out. I had to constantly be walking because it made me feel better. And Jordan would stay up and hold my hand and pace back and forth with me, and there was a peace of mind that came from knowing he was there. As someone who was always skinny and who saw myself as weak, I'd never had that feeling in my whole life. Even in my own home, I never felt safe and protected. I was scared of the world for years. But once I got security I reached a point where, for the most part, I could relax, and that feeling is priceless.

I mean, it's not priceless. It's six figures in salary and benefits annually. But you know what I mean.

Slowly, as we wrapped up the tour, I started getting my mind right. Since I had always escaped the world by building a new one, that's what I did. I'd always loved storytelling and stories, but at that point in my life "stories" invariably meant movies or TV or comic books or rap. It was almost never books. My experience at school had been so dismal that it turned me off of serious reading. The big novels that everyone reads in high school, I'd never even cracked them. I decided to fix that. I picked up a bunch of novels and started plowing through them. I think I read nine of them in a week, and as I was reading, I was like, "I'd like to do this." My day-to-day manager, Christian, was like, "Yeah, right. You can't write a novel." I was like, "Why not?" and he was like, "Dude, just because you read nine novels in a week doesn't mean you can sit down and write your own." Because I don't like anybody telling me what I can't do, I was like, "Yes, I can." And I did.

I sat down and started writing and what came out was this semi-autobiographical story of a guy named Flynn who works at a supermarket (like I had) and who suffers from crippling mental health issues (like I did). For the rest of that tour and the months that followed, it was just book, book, book, book, book. I'd be at music festivals writing the book. I'd be backstage writing the book. Everything was the book. I was taking all these things that I'd felt and experienced and I was putting them down on the page. It was form of self-reflection and self-excavation, a kind of letting go. Everything that I wrote about started to dissipate in my life because I was dealing with it. It was like therapy. I didn't intend for it to be that; it just seemed like a fun, creative challenge. But it ended up being this incredible catharsis, which I didn't even realize until I was deep into it. As I was writing, things started getting way better, a million times better. I was eating better and feeling better. I stopped smoking. I could sleep and sit still again. It changed everything.

I hit a wall about halfway through. I wasn't sure where to take the story or how to finish it, but I was feeling good enough that I was ready to step back from it a bit. So I set it aside, figuring I'd come back to it at some point. Which I did, when the anxiety and depression came back and clobbered me again.

ナよんふⅡナⅡ否

When I released *Under Pressure* with Def Jam, it was everything I'd ever wanted. I was on the OG label of hip-hop. I was being produced by a legend like No I.D. It was like every aspiring rapper's dream come true. But looking back on it now, the closest thing I can compare it to is being assaulted in Bohrer Park when I was sixteen. I was just going along, minding my own business, and then *BAM!* I got cold-cocked from behind and life was never the same. It was just as abrupt, just as violent, and just as traumatizing. And just like in Bohrer Park, I was assaulted for wearing the wrong color.

Growing up in West Deer Park, I was just Bobby. I was a little mixed kid and that was me and everybody knew it no matter how I looked. By the time I got to high school, race was more of a thing. You'd see more groups breaking off by color and sitting in different parts of the cafeteria, but even then a lot of motherfuckers were hanging out together. Ultimately it was more about culture and class than race. The cheerleaders were mostly white with the one Hispanic chick and a couple of black girls mixed in. But culturally they were all the same. They all came from well-off families and they dressed nice and they all said Valley Girl shit like, "Omigod! Really?!" It just so happened that some of them had darker skin.

It was the same with one black kid named Ambrose who was African and super-dark-skinned but also super-emo. He'd hang with the white emo kids and he'd take his hair and perm it to the side and wear red flannel and a wallet chain and say shit like, "'Sup?" Because he was African, Ambrose was probably the blackest kid in school by his skin color, but nobody looked at him as black because he never rolled with the black kids and didn't like hip-hop or sports. Everyone treated him like a white boy. The color of his skin had no bearing on the culture he chose to adopt, and everybody loved him anyway. Like me, he was just himself and he didn't fit into any boxes and it was whatever. Which is not to say we lived in a world with no racism. Everybody knew about the cops fucking with black kids and shit like that, but as far as how we related to each other, it just wasn't that deep.

That was true even in underground hip-hop, going to open mics and playing in shitty bars around the DMV. I didn't go around introducing myself like, "Yo, I'm Logic, biracial hip-hop artist from Merlin." It was never that. That scene was predominately black for sure, but you'd see all colors, black, white, brown, whatever. I remember playing shows in Gaithersburg with Knowledge, the heavyset white guy with a patchy beard and the bomb-ass girlfriend who was fine as shit. He was a sweet guy and he was super-dope and everybody loved him. Nobody questioned his right to be there or my right to be there. That's how it was. I was mixed and 6ix was Indian and Knowledge was this fat-ass white nigga, but the only thing that mattered was "Can you rap?"

My race only sort of started becoming a thing when I went on the air at WMUC, but not even in a bad way. I'd be in the studio with a bunch of brothers and sisters and they'd be like, "Damn, you're good, and you're white?" And I'd have to be like, "No, well, you see . . ." And then I'd tell them my story, white mom, black dad, and nobody cared. Nobody was like, "Whoa! Wait! *What?!* You're *what?!* What do you mean black *and* white?" They were like, "Okay, cool." People didn't give a shit; it was just about the music.

Then I put out *Under Pressure*. Now *everything* was about race. Everywhere I went, it was race, race, race, all the time. It was the first thing people would ask in interviews. It was all over social media. It was you're black or you're white or you're this or you're that or you're not really black or you're not black enough or you're just not black, period.

And the worst of it, I hate to say, was from black people. White interviewers might be naively curious about my blackness or ask ignorant questions about my blackness, but none of them ever tried to fight me about my answers or accused me of lying about who I was. In those spaces there was never a question of where I come from or who I am, and if I'm being candid, I always felt commercially accepted by people who weren't black—always.

And it's weird. I love it, and I hate it. I love it because I get to go on *Good Morning America* and they say, "Oh, this is going to be an interesting guest, so let's have an interesting conversation about interesting things." It's the same when I sit down with someone like Trevor Noah at *The Daily Show*; he doesn't give a fuck about the American standard of what is and isn't black because he's African and he's mixed, too. So the two of us can get together and it's just two people having a conversation. And that's how I've felt in any interview I've done outside the world of hip-hop.

But at the same time I hate it because it makes me sick that hip-hop doesn't think that way. I hate that the biggest media in rap is always driven by angry clickbait. The anger was what I didn't understand at first. When I blew up, so many black people, when it came to how my appearance impacted their idea of what blackness is or what it means to be black, they were *angry*. They came out swinging, and for a long time I didn't even understand why. Why me? J. Cole is biracial, fair-skinned, white mom, raised with white family members. But he looks black so he's black, no questions. Same with Drake. Same with Obama. Obama's not biracial in hip-hop. That's a *black* president, 100 percent. But then I come along with blue eyes and fair skin and all of a sudden it's: "Well, how black are you, though? Let's go do a 23andMe." Somehow we'd gone from the One-Drop Rule to the "Okay, You've Got 50 Percent Black Drops but We Don't Like How the Drops Showed Up on Your Face" Rule.

Which is insane because I'm literally the epitome of the underdog fuckin' rapper. I came from nothing, had nothing, cooked crack, fuckin' shot guns, my parents ain't shit. Only I came up on peace, love, and positivity and I treat others with respect, and yeah, I rap about sci-fi and nerd shit because I'm me and I'm always going to be me but then people shit on me for it because the only thing that matters is my skin ain't dark enough and my hair ain't braided enough, and that's just the realest shit.

And it was all because I was successful in hip-hop: in a black space. If I'd been a biracial guy blowing up in a white space like network TV, like Jesse Williams on *Grey's Anatomy* on ABC, or Wentworth Miller on *Prison Break* on FOX, black people would have been falling all over themselves to claim me. "Oh, he ain't white! He's black! He's one of ours!" But here I come, fucking up the game in hip-hop, looking the way I do but having the father I have, rapping about what I rap about, finding the success that I have with the skin that I do, and that fucked people up.

From day one there were people who were out to tear me to shreds, and it had nothing to do with liking or not liking my music. It was all about exposing me as a liar and a fraud, making me feel like my life was a lie. It was "He's not black" and "He's from the suburbs" and "He's from *Potomac*" and "His mommy and daddy paid for his albums" and all this shit. It was constant. It made me feel like my life was a lie.

People used to say to me, all the time, "You're only as big as you are in hip-hop because you're white." They used it as an excuse to write off my success: "He's only that successful because of the way he looks." As if it's easy to be a white guy in rap. Mac Miller got shat on just as hard as I did. Mac Miller had a love of hip-hop as deep as anyone I've ever known. He was a student of hip-hop. He knew more about the history and the culture than probably anybody I've ever met, and that came out of a sincere and genuine devotion to the music, which is something that ought to be celebrated. But people clowned him. They called him "white boy" and a frat rapper and a culture vulture and they straight-up told him he didn't belong.

Still, as hard as it is to be a white guy in rap, I think my life would have been simpler if I had been white. If I had said, "Yep. I'm just a white guy who hung around all the brothers!" it would have been different. Because there's a lane for that in hip-hop. It's not easy, but it exists. Some people may not like Eminem because he's white, but at the end of the day, that's a cold white boy, so people have to accept him. "Yeah, you trailer trash, white boy. But you've got some bars, so you cool." Same with MC Serch and the Beastie Boys. You can put those guys in a box and understand them. But you couldn't put me in that box. They tried, but it didn't work, because I wouldn't go in the white box because I'm not white.

And here's where it gets fucked: If I push back and refuse to go in the white box, then I'm the one being defensive and combative and insecure. But if I *don't* push back, if I let it go and let people assume I'm white, then it becomes, "Oh, what, he's ashamed to be black?" Then it's a no-win situation. I'm left sitting there defending myself, my heritage, and my identity. Meanwhile, I have millions of people trying to tell me who I am and how I should be. And it's fucked up to force me to choose because, regardless of my complexion, I'm both.

If you put a gun to my head and made me pick one identity over the other, I'd lean black because everyone in my family's black and most of my friends are black and everything I know about life is more from black culture. But if I say, "No, I'm black," then it becomes, "Man, why you pressin' being black so much?" Or "Fuck you, because you don't know what it's like to walk down the street as a black man." To which I say, "Of course I don't know what it's like to walk down the street as a black man. But you don't know what it's like to walk down the street as a black man in a white man's body who won't be accepted by his own culture. It's not a contest about who's got it the worst, and the difference is: I'm not angry at you for having your experience, so why are you angry at me for having mine?"

And that's why blowing up in hip-hop after *Under Pressure* felt like being assaulted in the park. It completely fucked me up because my whole life I was looking for a place to belong and then I found hip-hop and I found the RattPack and I finally had it. Then I blew up and all of Twitter and Facebook and Instagram clapped back in unison to say, "Fuck off, white boy. Fuck off, faggot. You don't belong here."

The crazy thing is that, among real OG rappers, my blackness was never questioned. Never. Not once. Because at the end of the day, real recognize real. At the same time I was dealing with all this "You ain't black" shit online, No I.D. was introducing me around the industry. I met and was instantly accepted by dudes like Black Thought, Killer Mike, Chuck D, the entire Wu-Tang Clan. I'd meet those guys, shake their hand, and we weren't even talking about race. We were talking about rap and life and whatever. If it even came up, it was just, "Your dad's black? Oh, shit. All right, my nigga." Then we'd never talk about it again, and that's because those guys are confident and secure in who they are and their place in the industry. They're past all the bullshit. There's no way I could ever take their spot, so it's not even a conversation. Ultimately, after years of being made to question myself and to feel like a fraud, my relationships with those guys helped me to feel secure again in who I am, because they taught me an important thing: that the way people respond to the color of my skin says nothing about me and everything about them.

The Breakfast Club on Power 105.1 was and still is one of my favorite radio shows. It's where I found out everything there is to know about all my favorite rappers. Landing an interview on that show, with DJ Envy and Angela Yee and Charlamagne Tha God, is a rite of passage in rap; you haven't made it until you've sat in that chair. For years I couldn't wait to get on. I think we asked to do it a few times and they said no because I wasn't big enough. Then I got big enough and they had me on and I remember walking in and being excited, and from the jump the whole thing turned into a fight over why I belong in hip-hop. Charlamagne told me I don't look black and my dad can't be black and there's no way I'm black.

Then he ended the interview with "What are you doing for the Black Lives Matter movement?" Now, I'm the only biracial person he has ever put that question to. He didn't ask Drake or J. Cole of any of those other light-skinned motherfuckers on that show. He asked Post Malone. He asked Mac Miller. That's two white boys and me. Now, how does that make me feel? That this self-appointed gatekeeper of my community is treating me like a white person who doesn't even belong? I was like, "Damn, that's fucked up."

And Charlamagne was only the most prominent example. As the Black Lives Matter movement took off, it only got worse. Because now there was this war with the cops and you had to declare your loyalty and prove yourself and whose side are you on? Twitter was 24/7 with people upset and hashtagging #blacklivesmatter, and me, I don't hashtag politics. I fuck around on social media and say, "What's up, RattPack? Check out this new dope track I dropped." But when I have something meaningful to say I don't put that shit on Twitter. I don't try to say it in 140 characters. I put it in my music. So everyone was shitting on me for not hashtagging #blacklivesmatter and not being black enough and not doing enough for black people. They were blowing me up with thousands and thousands and thousands of tweets per day. "Why aren't you hashtagging? Why aren't you hashtagging? You don't think black lives matter? You say you're black but you don't believe in black rights? Why aren't you hashtagging?"

All this was coming on the heels of three years of every fucking interview pushing me: "So, being white . . . So, being white . . ." It was like all the years of poking and poking that my mom did to me before I exploded on her. I called up Killer Mike because I wanted someone

I could be real with, and I was like, "Man, I wanna make a difference on this, but I don't wanna fall in line with these fuckin' goobs on social media, all these stupid-ass, pretend-to-be-woke seventeen-year-old white kids talkin' about Black Lives Matter and having no idea what it fuckin' is. I don't want to hashtag it for a month, I want this shit to live forever. I want to do an album about it." And he was like, "That's what you should do."

So I decided to set the record straight. Because it is true that I came by my success, in part, because of the way I look. Because I look like a lot of people, especially a lot of young people who don't look anything like what this country used to be. Back in the '90s you had young black kids like LeBron James looking up to Michael Jordan and seeing this amazing, successful black man and saying, "I want to be like Mike." And there are other kids today—white kids, black kids, Asian kids, Hispanic kids, and mixed-up kids of everything in between—and those kids are like, "If Logic, who looks different from all these other rappers, can make it, shit, then maybe I can, too. I don't have to be discouraged because I don't look like I fit in."

Because that's the difference between America then and America now. We still have millions of young black kids who need strong black role models and we still need to address the racism that affects them. But we've also got this melting pot of multiple races. All of these people are fusing and mixing together, sometimes in the same body. Those kids don't identify as one thing unless society forces them to, and through me and through all the other people they met in the RattPack, they found a place where they weren't forced to be anything. Just like I've gotten people mad because they can't put me in a box, I've gotten even more people who think it's dope that I can't be put in a box because they can't be put in a box, either—and I decided to make an album for them, an album that dealt with everything people were demanding that I address about race and Black Lives Matter, but that also went further into these complicated issues of identity.

So I went to work and, honestly, it was an incredible time. It was dope. I dropped my first *Bobby Tarantino* mixtape, which was nothing but bangers and trap music, just something I wanted to do for fun and to let people know I could do something different. I co-headlined the Endless Summer Tour with G-Eazy, which was like one big party without all the pressure of carrying every show by myself. I'd gotten married and my wife and I had moved into a new home in Tarzana, the first home I ever owned, and I had a nice nest egg from touring and a good merch deal I'd done and I'd built out my home studio and I was working my ass off, still working on my novel, *Supermarket*, a bit and writing a screenplay and making records and loving what I was doing.

I went into that album like I was Kanye working on *Graduation*. This was going to be my masterpiece. The concept I came up with was based on a short story by Andy Weir called "The Egg." It's about a guy who dies and wakes up in what he believes to be heaven and God tells him that he cannot cross over into the next plane of existence until he's lived in the shoes of every man, woman, and child regardless of race, religion, or sexual orientation, from the beginning of time until the last human being dies on our planet or in our universe, depending on where we go with advancements in our future. Only then can the man enter heaven.

It's an idea that basically says, "Treat other people the way you want to fuckin' be treated. Have empathy. Be kind." It wasn't like every single track was about race, but I was definitely confronting the issue head-on. I brought in Chuck D and Black Thought to rap with me on "America," which was my big "Fuck Trump" song. I brought in Killer Mike on "Confess," about a man at his wits' end praying to God and repenting his sins and wishing he could be someone else. I wrote "Black SpiderMan," which is a song about accepting change and evolution and transformation, because a world that can't accept transformation is a world that can't accept people like me. I wrote "AfricAryaN," which is a provocative term but also just honest. You take my DNA, my ancestry, and I come from both the slave and the master. It's a song about how people had branded me my whole life because of my complexion, saying that I shouldn't exist, that my crackhead dad never should have never fucked my cracker mom.

My attitude was I wanted to provoke shit and start conversations, which is why my original idea was to call the album *AfricAryaN*. I told that to Zarou, and he was like, "Uh . . . yeah. We cannot do that." And he was right, not just because of the potential controversy but because the album had evolved from being a response to people who said I wasn't black to being about something more universal. It was about everybody's struggles with prejudice and identity and having empathy. So we called it *Everybody* instead.

The album dropped on May 5, 2017. It debuted at #1 on the Billboard 200 and sold nearly a quarter-million units the first week. It was my first #1 album, the biggest achievement of my career, and it started a conversation for sure, a conversation about how fast the Internet could shit all over it. All these white people were coming at me online about "So why does this album demonize white people?" and at the same time all the black kids who were on me about hashtagging were like, "This is some All Lives Matter shit." That's what they called it: the "All Lives Matter" album.

Meanwhile, the whole "biracial" thing got turned into a meme and I got clowned and it became a joke. There was no credit given to what I was trying to say, and I know that was all based on my skin color. From Kendrick Lamar all the way back to Run-DMC, rappers have been out there on damn near every song going, "I'm proud to be black and I'm black and I'm black! I'm blacker than black! My dick is black! I'm black! Black! Black! Black! Black!" and everybody's like, "Ooh, wow! That's amazing!" Then I put out one album that says, "I'm two things at the same time!" and niggas is like, "Stop talking about that shit." But the only reason I was even talking about race in the first place was because everybody was giving me shit and demanding that I speak up and say something.

My friends kept telling me all the time, "It doesn't matter. Hundreds of thousands of people are buying the album. You're selling out arenas. What all these people say does not matter." And I know that's true. And I know it's not actually about me because the Internet shits on everyone from Eminem to Drake to Jay-Z. And I know it's not actually about Jay-Z or Drake or Eminem or me; it's about these people having anger and insecurity that they need to unleash on somebody. I know all that.

But I'm not going to lie: It hurt.

ꯑꯣꯏꯅꯥ

Since the day I started rapping professionally, at least once a year I thought about quitting. The nonstop hate and abuse were too much. All the haters abusing me would be like, "Bro, you have to learn to take criticism." And I know criticism comes with being a public person. But real criticism is: "Oh, I don't like what he did with the high hat on that song" or "Those lyrics feel clumsy" or "His message doesn't resonate with me." I can take that criticism; I welcome it, because it challenges me. But there's a difference between critiquing someone's music or their message and saying, "Fuck you, faggot. Why don't you fuck off and kill yourself." You read that about yourself a hundred times a day and you can't help it: It makes you depressed and you think about giving it all up.

But I never did, because I loved so many other elements of it, and even though I'd accomplished so much, there were so many things I still wanted to do. Top of that list was to have a hit single. I'd had videos with a million views, #1 albums, but what I always wanted more than anything was a big, fat crossover radio hit, one of those can't-escape-it, song-of-summer, hear-it-everywhere-you-go hits. Zarou always used to piss me off because he'd say, "We're building something. It's a slow burn. It'll come. Be patient."

I wasn't patient. Every mixtape and every album, I was trying every angle I could think of to craft that hit, especially on *Bobby Tarantino,* a trap album that was wall-to-wall with bangers. But no matter what I did, it never worked. The albums sold well, but none of my singles ever took off. By the time I got to *Everybody* I'd given up. If you listen to that album, it doesn't have any hits on it. Because I didn't make the album to have a hit. I made the album to say something. I wasn't in a place where I wanted to quit entirely, but I was done with the rat race of trying to score a hit single. I was like, "Man, fuck it. I'm done with it."

Then Zarou called me up one day out of the blue while I was in the middle of the *Everybody* tour and said, "Yo, MTV wants you to perform at the Video Music Awards."

My immediate response was to say no. I was exhausted. I would have to cancel a show in Toronto, fly out to L.A., then fly back to the tour, then make up the Toronto show later on—it was too much. Plus awards shows were already becoming a joke. Even the Grammys now, people don't watch. Nobody cares anymore. But Zarou insisted.

"You gotta do this, bro. VMAs, bro. This is huge."

"Dude, I don't care."

"I'm telling you."

"No."

"Bro, I'm telling you."

I finally relented and agreed to do it and Chris flew out to meet me on tour and we went to dinner to go over the details. The song I wanted to do was "America," because that was my song with Chuck D that was all "Fuck Trump," and with everything that was going on in the country I had this chip on my shoulder like, "Now I'm gonna stand up for the people!"

Chris said, "Fuck that noise. It's '1-800.' I'm telling you."

"Aww, man. I don't know."

"Bro, I'm telling you."

"I don't know."

"Dude, I'm *telling* you," he said. *"Trust me."*

When he said that, I had to pause, because me and him and 6ix and Lenny, we'd all had "Trust me" moments over the years, about tours and songs and samples for albums, and those are the moments when you're really putting your balls on the table because you're asking everyone to put their lives in your hands based on nothing more than your gut intuition.

"1-800-273-8255" was the first track I came up with for *Everybody*, and it was the last track I recorded for *Everybody*. The inspiration for the song had come from fans coming up to me on the road and telling me how inspirational my music was to them, how it had carried them through dark times in their lives, how much my message of peace, love, and positivity had resonated with them. The thing about it, though, is that I never made my music to inspire anyone but myself. I made my music to pull *myself* out of a dark place. Every lyric I ever wrote, I was always talking to an audience of one. If I was going through something difficult or hard, I could say, "Yo, Bobby, it's going to be okay. Don't worry, if you're going through hard times, you can make it." I didn't give a fuck who was listening, and for a long time nobody else was listening. It was just me rapping into my dinosaur computer monitor in my bedroom. I was the only one there.

As a result, organically and from the heart, other people like me heard my message and were like, "Fuck yeah! I feel that way, too." So I was always helping people indirectly by helping myself, and the deepest it ever got was when people would say to me that they were thinking of killing themselves but my music had helped them hold on and stay alive. When I heard that, I started to think, "Shit, I'm helping all these people and I'm not even trying. So what would happen if I did? What kind of positive impact could I make if I really set out to do it?" And the idea for "1-800-273-8255" was born, a track titled with the number for the National Suicide Prevention Lifeline to help people struggling with mental health.

So I wrote it, but I couldn't record it. I kept putting it off and putting it off. Because when I sing from another person's point of view, it's like acting. I'm not reeling off those lyrics as myself. If I'm rapping from my brother's point of view as a gangster being scared of getting shot in the streets, or from my sister's point of view as woman who's been raped, I'm feeling that. I'm becoming that person the same way Daniel Day-Lewis does. It's emotionally taxing. As dark as my life had been at times, I'd never seriously considered or tried to commit suicide; the closest I'd ever gotten was being terrified that I'd snap and be in some deranged mental state where I might try to kill myself. But to sing that song and sing it well, I had to put myself in the same dark place as someone who did want to kill himself. Even though the song ultimately comes to a hopeful place of redemption and joy, it is dark and depressing and draining. Every day I showed up to the studio like, "Ugh, I don't wanna do this shit." So I made all the other records and procrastinated until I couldn't put it off any longer. Then I finally did it. I reached out to Alessia Cara and Khalid, who came in and laid down the guest vocals and fucking killed it. Then we had an orchestra come in to do the strings and I got to conduct them, which was super-cool. But the process of laying it down was so depressing, I was like, *"FUCK!"*

When we dropped "1-800" as a single that spring, it didn't feel like it was going to be anything different from any single we'd put out before. It wasn't popping off in terms of sales or anything like that. Nobody was jumping on a record about suicide to be the song of summer that year. So it was out there and I was proud of it and it was doing okay, but to me it was just another song in the catalog.

Zarou was always bullish on it, though. He had a hunch about it. I hadn't written a song about suicide to be a massive crossover hit; I'd have to have been crazy to think that it would be. But Chris had seen what happened when we played "1-800" at the Barclays Center, how it resonated, how the entire arena had their phones out and lights up as they sang along. He saw that something had been simmering in the culture that year. There was the trauma and the aftermath

of Trump's election. There was *13 Reasons Why* debuting on Net-
flix and driving a big conversation about teens and suicide. Chester
Bennington from Linkin Park took his own life that summer. So did
Chris Cornell from Soundgarden. There was something about mental health and pain and suffering in that moment that demanded to
be recognized, and when Zarou lobbied for me to do it at the VMAs
I wanted to argue the point, but ultimately I had to concede that it
was the right play. He didn't always see every angle better than me,
but that time he did.

He laid out his whole idea of how it would work with all these everyday people onstage, survivors and people struggling with mental
health and people who'd lost family members to suicide, all of them
wearing matching shirts and creating this beautiful moment driving
home the song's message. Which was an insane thing to try to pull off
given that we only had a few days and we were talking about wran-
gling dozens of nonprofessional everyday people and working them
seamlessly into an awards show performance. It was a lot of moving

Backstage with Zarou at the VMAs.

parts and a lot that could go wrong on live national television. But I said, "Okay. Let's do it."

Zarou flew off to L.A. to get with Harrison and plan the performance while I played my next couple shows and got ready, which was when I realized that if I was going to do the show I couldn't just perform the song. I needed to say something. Because any asshole could get up on TV and use survivors to look good and not mean it. I knew that if I could speak, everyone would know that I meant every word I was saying, that who I am and what I stand for is built upon honesty and respect and kindness and empathy. It was important to me. I had to say it.

So forty-eight hours before the broadcast, I called Zarou and I was like, "Bro, I need you to get me another minute. I need to say something." I read him what I wanted to say and he loved it and said he'd see what he could do. I knew I was asking for a lot. In TV time, a minute is like an hour. But I knew if anybody could get the producers of the show to give it up, it was Zarou, and he fought and fought and fought and he got the minute.

The day of the performance I was the most nervous I'd ever been in my life. I'd never performed at an awards show. I'd never performed for a TV audience this big. Plus I wasn't going to be rapping. I'd mostly be singing, and I wasn't that good at singing yet. Then there was the speech. I'd spent the past two days obsessively going over the speech in my head, in the car, in the shower, memorizing every word, because I knew I wouldn't have it in my ear or on a teleprompter to read and I had to hit it perfectly because I wouldn't have a spare second to make a mistake.

I was backstage and everyone was running around. Chance the Rapper was there. Cardi B was there. Ellen DeGeneres was there with her wife, Portia de Rossi, and I was talking to them and I was like, "This is crazy as fuck. How did I get here?" Then it was time for me to go on and I took my position at the rear of the stage inside this house of mirrors thing they'd built and everywhere I looked there were dozens of reflections of me looking back at me, reflecting all of the different emotions I was having at that moment. I looked over here and I was smiling and grinning ear to ear like, "You've fuckin' made it." Then I looked over there and I was pissing my pants, terrified. Then another where I was having a panic attack, another where I was just in the moment, and another where I was contemplating and reflecting and saying to myself, "This is karma. This is everything you've ever worked for. Every time you were on Spoken vs. Written, every time you were writing raps in Mary Jo's attic. It wasn't about the songs. It was about becoming the person who could do this, here, delivering this message and bringing people together and helping them heal." Then I heard the opening chords, *"Dum . . . dum-dum . . ."* and I stepped out onstage in front of twenty thousand people and I killed it.

It was the craziest thing I've ever done but also the easiest. Once I went out there, everything flowed and I didn't miss a step and Alessia came out and sang her part beautifully and then Khalid came out and nailed his part and then it was time for the speech and I just did it. One word came out after another after another and I don't know how but I did it.

"I just want to take a moment to thank you for giving me a platform to talk about something that mainstream media doesn't want to talk about: mental health, anxiety, suicide, depression, and so much more that I talk about on this album. From racism, discrimination, sexism, domestic violence, sexual assault, and so much more; I don't give a damn if you are black, white, or any color in between. I don't care if you're Christian, you're Muslim, you're gay, you're straight, I am here to fight for your equality because I believe that we are all born equal, but we are not treated equally and that is why we must fight. We must fight for the equality of every man, woman, and child regardless of race, religion, color, creed, and sexual orientation. So I say here and now if you believe in this message of peace, love, positivity, and equality for all, then I demand that

The VMA performance.

you rise to your feet and applaud not only for yourselves but for the foundation we are laying for our children."

The moment I finished, the whole arena erupted, and that doesn't happen at awards shows. People were crying and cheering. It was like something broke open, and I became a rock star *in that moment*. I could feel it. I could feel my life changing, and I was like, "Oh, shit, nigga. We made it. I'm about to be really famous."

The song and I were both trending on Twitter the entire night and the entire next day. Within hours the video was getting millions of views on YouTube. Everyone was talking about it on every entertainment show, every celebrity gossip blog, everywhere. It was a life-changing moment. Ellen even invited me on *Ellen,* and I'd wanted to go on fucking *Ellen* for years. I got all the press I'd ever dreamed of. I got a hit song bigger than any hit song I'd ever even imagined I would have. I can remember visiting record companies before I signed a record deal and being at Britney Spears's label and seeing a diamond plaque for ". . . Baby One More Time" and thinking, "I will never do that. There is no fuckin' way I will ever do that."

But I essentially have. "1-800" hit #3 on the Billboard Hot 100, and since then it's passed a billion streams and it's seven times platinum and it's on its way to going diamond for sure.

But more than the sales or the money was the feeling that I'd had an impact on the culture. Calls to the National Suicide Prevention Lifeline spiked by something like 50 percent. I wanted to bring these issues of mental health and suicide to the forefront of people's minds and make them stop and look and pay attention, and I did. Which is almost impossible to do nowadays, but I did it, and if it sounds like I'm bragging a bit and patting myself on the back when I say it, I am, because in that moment I needed to pat myself on the back. I was like, "Good job, bro. You had millions of people clowning you for talking about anxiety and depression. You had millions of people shitting on you and telling you that your music's not good enough and that you're not good enough, but you proved tonight that your music is good enough and, more importantly, you are good enough."

It felt good to feel good enough. It lasted at least a good twenty-four hours or so, and that's when I got hit with a wave of hate unlike anything I'd ever experienced in my life.

The blowback and abuse I'd experienced in the wake of the VMAs was like nothing I'd ever experienced. Everything I'd seen up to that point was mild in comparison. It was all the same @OGBiscuit "Fuck off, faggot" shit as before, only it was like someone grabbed the volume knob and cranked it all the way to eleven. It was a tsunami of hate, and I couldn't turn it off.

Or, more accurately, I couldn't not turn it on. Nobody was making me check my phone except me, but I couldn't put it down. It was like the fucking thing was glued in my hand. I'd wake up and check it first thing. I'd eat my morning cereal looking at it. I'd take my morning shit looking at it. Lenny would drive me to the studio and I'd be looking at it. I'd go in to record, come out for a smoke break, and look at it. It was every day, because this thing in my hand was like my home. It was where I lived, in this world of the RattPack and all my friends online. I didn't know how not to be there. Only my home had gone from the place where I was loved to the place where I was hated. The love was all still there, of course, but I was so accustomed to it that for the most part it faded into the background. All I could see was the hate.

That was also the moment some of my own fans started turning against me, because I didn't belong to them anymore. The same fans who had heard "1-800" and been like, "This is amazing. This is so special. This is needed," now they were the ones going, "This sucks" and "He's too mainstream." The most popular thing I'd ever done, the song that was going seven times platinum, suddenly became "the worst song Logic ever made."

And I thought I was a strong guy, given everything that I've come through, but at the end of the day, I'm a human being and if your mindset going into public life is "I need people's love. I need people's acceptance," then you're going to be fucked. Which is exactly where I was. All I'd ever wanted since the day I stepped in front of a microphone was to blow up and get famous and sell records and have the whole world know my name and then it happened and all I wanted to do was crawl in a hole and do nothing and not be around anybody. I was riddled with anxiety, more than ever. I headed back out on tour, and the tour was amazing and arenas were packed and the fans were incredible—in-fucking-credible—but I couldn't appreciate it. I wasn't happy, and I wasn't prepared for what came next. Because then, on top of the abuse, came the pain.

I'd put off recording "1-800" for months because I had to go to such a dark place in order to do it. Now I was singing it every single night, night after night after night, with twenty thousand people singing it back to me. I was singing about suicide every night and talking about suicide every day, all day, every interview, every radio show, every television show. I'd become the Suicide Guy. I'd been the FaZe Clan Guy and the Space Nerd Guy and the Biracial Guy, and now I was the Suicide Guy. At every backstage meet-and-greet everyone was coming to me with their saddest and most gruesome stories, family members who'd committed suicide, family members who'd been institutionalized with depression. It wasn't just the fans, either. It was everyone I'd meet in a day. It was the hotel people at check-in and the arena staff at the show and the producer in the greenroom. Everybody who had a traumatic or depressing story wanted a minute to share it with me and thank me for the song. And I couldn't say no, because it wasn't like someone asking for a selfie. How can you be rude to someone when they're sharing the story of their best friend's suicide with you?

And what I encountered in person was the tip of the iceberg compared to what was incoming online. Social media was a constant stream of anguish and trauma and grief and "my mother killed herself" and "my father killed himself" and "my brother killed himself" and "my sister killed herself" and "I tried to kill myself once" and "I've tried to kill myself twice" and "I've tried to kill myself three times" and "I cut myself because I'm too scared to kill myself" and "I wish my son had had a chance to hear your song before he killed himself last year." As if I could have saved all those people somehow.

It was thousands of incoming messages a day. It was all these people with all this pain bottled up and they needed somewhere to let it out so they gave it to me. How was I supposed to even begin to process that or take that on? Even the healthiest, most stable person on earth would buckle under that kind of emotional weight, and I was not the healthiest or most stable person on earth. I was working and working and doing this and traveling here and going there and doing four shows in a row with one day off but the one day off was eighteen hours in a tour bus to the next location to go sit in greenrooms with radio personalities who didn't give a shit about me, they just wanted me in and out of their shit because I was a hot topic. Everywhere I went it was suicide, suicide, suicide, suicide and killing yourself, killing yourself, killing yourself and "Do the suicide song, man!" and at the same time as all this my marriage was coming apart so I had that to deal with, too, and any time I wanted to rest I had people telling me, "Yo, you have obligations. People have paid money. The fans are expecting you. You can't take a break."

Now, after all the years of my mom's abuse and my dad's addiction and never once thinking about suicide, I finally *was* thinking about suicide. It was almost like *Inception*, like the idea had been planted so deeply in my mind that I couldn't escape it. Not that I was actually going to kill myself, but I found myself thinking, "Well, if I killed myself, at least I'd get to take a break from all this, forever." But then just as quickly I'd think, "Oh, fuck. If I kill myself, it'll just become a meme about how the Suicide Guy killed himself. Shit. Now I have to stay alive so I don't turn into another meme."

A month after the VMAs I was headlining a music festival outside Pittsburgh, and I don't remember too much about it but I do know that it was the worst moment of my life. Going all the way back to and including everything my mother had ever done, Pittsburgh was the lowest I've ever been, because that was the moment when it felt like it could all come apart. I was headlining a music festival for tens of thousands of people, and I just didn't care. I didn't give a fuck. Which is sad. I was finally the rap star I'd always dreamed of becoming and I was too depressed to enjoy it.

I was puking backstage that night before I went out to perform. Then I went out and the venue was terrible because it was one of those shows where the spotlight is coming from out in the crowd instead of up over the stage, so I couldn't see anything because I was being blinded by a giant laser beam in my face. I was supposed to do an hour and a half and I made it about forty minutes in and I turned and told DJ Rhetorik to do something to fill time so I could run off and puke some more. Then I went back out and I tried to perform and I couldn't. I felt like I was going to faint. Up to that point in my life, I'd never not finished a show. Even performing with a 102-degree fever, I'd never not finished a show. But that night I just couldn't do it. So I stopped the music. I was sweating and pacing back and forth, and everybody got their iPhones out to capture whatever was about to happen next so they could post it online. I didn't know what to say, so I spoke the truth.

"This is all I ever wanted," I said, "and as I'm here it's everything I ever thought it would be. I just thought I'd get a little more me time to rest. I'm tired. I'm sick. I feel like shit and I've been pushing myself too hard. And I was just about to leave because I feel like I'm going to faint. I feel like if I continue to perform I'm going to have to go to the hospital. I just need you to understand that if I'm not jumping in the crowd and not going crazy it's because I'm literally doing my best not to pass out. And I'm going to do my best to continue to perform anyway. I love you all so much. And I appreciate you and I'm tired but I'm going to keep going and I'm going to continue to persevere. Even in this hard time. So I hope that you continue to persevere as well. Because you deserve everything this world has to offer. In my weakest state I've ever been in as an artist on this stage speaking to you, it's to tell you that you're special and you're amazing and that I will give every last ounce of myself to tell you how incredible you are."

As I said it, I kept fighting back the tears and fighting back the tears. Then finally the tears came. I broke down onstage and started crying.

And people on the Internet made fun of me.

THIRTEEN

When I walked offstage in Pittsburgh, I was like, "I'm done. It's all over. Everything has to change. Cancel it all. Cancel everything." It was the first time in my life when I began to understand the word "no," and when I finally found and sat down with a therapist, she helped me understand why I had such a hard time saying it.

She helped me understand that I had always been driven so hard and worked so hard out of fear. I used to say yes to everything and then freak out, especially about money. Everything with money, it was "I have to do it. I have to do it," no matter what it was. People would push me, "Bob, we gotta do this show. We gotta do this gig. We gotta go here," and what was implied, or at least what I heard, was "This isn't going to last forever. We gotta get it while we can get it," and I always felt like I had no other choice.

My therapist taught me the importance of value over fear—how to make decisions based on what you value and not what you fear. It's okay to value money because we live in a world where you need money to live. But far more important than money is time, especially after you've reached a certain level of comfort. Because you can always make more money, but you can never make more time. So if what you value is spending time with your family or even just time to do nothing, choose that. Say no and spend less so you can be comfortable making less. I started to learn when to say no, not apologize for it, turn my phone off, and go away.

I started getting in shape, too. Jordan had to take some time from running my security, so my man Pepé came on in his place and he said he would train me. I started eating real food. We worked out five days a week for two hours a day. I would cordon off that time from everything else, no business calls, no Internet, no phones, no social media, none of it. Just doing that helped a lot.

For the first time, I didn't feel weak; I felt strong. I was walking around straight and not hunched over like Bobby Hall. I looked like I could fuck somebody up. I was like, "What up?" I got my sports car and I was driving around. I was that nigga. Life was good and I was on top of the world. I'd scored two Grammy nominations for "1-800," for Song of the Year and Best Music Video. I didn't win even though I think I should have, but I was the star of the night anyway because I gave a dope-ass speech telling Trump to fuck off, live on TV, and then I was at the after-party and if you're at the after-party it doesn't matter who won a Grammy because you're at the after-party. Erykah Badu was spinning records and I met Trevor Noah and Dave Chappelle and literally every other person you'd ever want to meet and it was the craziest shit ever.

I re-signed with Def Jam and landed another dope business deal and had $24 million in cash, a free man at twenty-eight. I sold the house my wife and I had shared in Tarzana and bought another place in Calabasas and started the renovations to make it my dream home, full recording studio, dope-ass home theater. I picked my novel *Supermarket* back up and started writing it again and it was helping me work through so much of my shit and it pulled me out of the darkness of being the "1-800" guy and for the first time in my life I made a conscious decision to say, "Yo, I'm going to start enjoying myself." Because I never had. I'd only worked, because any moment spent not working was a moment spent in fear that all my success was going to disappear. Most of 2018 was spent enjoying the college years I'd never had, and by "college years" I mean I started drinking.

Because of my parents, I had always been terrified of alcohol, terrified of addiction. I'd first started letting myself have a drink or two here or there the night of my bachelor party, when all my friends decided they wanted to see me shitfaced because they'd never seen it before. But up to that summer it was still rare that I'd let myself have a beer or a Scotch or even a glass of wine. Then I decided, "Fuck it." I moved into my new house and I started inviting all my friends over for what I started calling Scotch Wednesdays. Every Wednesday we'd get together and play pool and drink and just relax and have fun.

I started smoking weed again, too, which I hadn't done since I was a kid for the same reasons I hadn't let myself drink. I started vaping with a pen, and that shit chilled me out. The THC chilled me out just like the alcohol chilled me out. Sometimes I'd get too high and I'd get paranoid and have a panic attack, but usually it was cool, and an amazing thing happened: The alcohol and the weed changed my relationship with anxiety.

Growing up in a family of addicts, I'd always thought that the only way to be responsible and deal with anything was to be stone-cold sober. Since I never used mind-altering substances, the only mind I knew was the fucked-up, overanxious monkey mind that I had, always amped up and worried about everything and gaming out worst-case scenarios around every corner and generally just running at a thousand rpm standing still. I'd just accepted that was how my mind had to work and would always work without ever really questioning why it worked that way, not to mention how I could change it. But as I started letting myself experiment with weed and alcohol, I started to see my mind as a thing I could exert some measure of control over, because that's what mind-altering substances do, they speed it up or slow it down, tune it in or tune it out. What I noticed was that when I drank or vaped, all the thoughts in my head that were going and going and going and going and going and going and going just kind of slowwwwed dowwwwwnnn and went, "Heeeey, mannnn . . ." Like taking a record down to thirty-three rpm from forty-five. And as I learned how to see my mind moving through these different states, I started to recognize how my mind was working whether I was drinking or smoking something or not. If I started to feel anxious or depressed, I could step back and analyze my own feelings as they were happening to me and I could play detective and go, "Okay, I'm feeling weird. What's causing it? Is it because I've been on my phone all day? Have I taken any time for myself today? Did I eat anything strange?" And so on.

My anxiety didn't go away. But for the first time I was in control of it instead of it controlling me. Then I dropped *Bobby Tarantino II*. The album came out at the perfect time. You couldn't have made it any better. It was a surprise drop and still landed at #1 on the charts and did over a hundred and nineteen thousand the first week. It was just riding off of "1-800," and at that moment I was the biggest rapper in the world for sure. Yeah, everyone knows Drake's killin' it. But as far as who's poppin' right now? Logic is poppin' right now. Logic could do no wrong. Logic's got bangers. Logic's on the fucking radio getting spins. Logic's online getting millions of streams. Logic's killin' it. Go Logic.

Then I went out on tour. The Bobby Tarantino vs. Everybody Tour. The biggest tour I've ever done. That shit was amazing. I was eating well, drinking green juice and eating premade meals. I was ripped and swole and I didn't get sick. Every other tour I've ever done, I usually got sick four or five times. This time I didn't get sick at all and I was killin' it every night onstage and already laying down the next Young Sinatra album, *YSIV*, even calling up RZA and asking him if we could reunite the entire Wu-Tang Clan for a song. He said, "Let's do it," and by the end of the tour I had every Wu-Tang member's verse, which was something no one else in hip-hop had ever done.

I was just letting myself have fun. I was doing things I'd never let myself do before. During the tour, one afternoon we had a day

*Flying high with Jordan (*front, left).

off between shows up in Oregon and we decided, "Fuck it," and we went tubing on some river somewhere. It was a totally spontaneous decision. To get there we had to ride with all these guys I didn't know and I was drunk and rattling around in the back of their pickup truck doing fifty miles an hour up this country back road on this hot summer day and then the water was fucking freezing and I lost my shoes and it was a level of freedom I never could have imagined having back in Gaithersburg as a seventeen-year-old kid who was scared to leave his bedroom and all I could think to myself was "You're on top of the world, dawg."

And then on top of all of that, I fell in love.

I'd wanted to start a family pretty much from the moment I became an adult. You don't have to be a psychologist to figure out why. After growing up in such a fucked-up family, I wanted to have a real home, to change the course of things, put things right. I would have proposed to Christine at twenty years old if things had worked out differently. In my first marriage, if it had been up to me, I would have

On top of the world.

put a baby in my wife before we'd even tied the knot. I was young and I had this sort of overdetermined vision of how I wanted that part of my life to go and it didn't happen and ultimately that turned out to be the right thing because one day I randomly decided to walk into a smoothie shop for a smoothie. Which is something I never do because normally I would have gone to get a slice of pizza or a milkshake but on this one random day something was telling me to go into SunLife Organics in downtown Calabasas and I went in and saw this beautiful girl. I ordered my smoothie, went home, and wrote six songs about her in the two weeks that I kept going back to see if she was there.

Finally she was. We met and her name was Brittney and we hit it off and the crazy thing was the songs I'd written were all about who I thought she could be or hoped she would be, and it turned out that's exactly the person she was. She was everything that I could

have hoped for. Our first date was skydiving and then we were en-
gaged and she was down to start trying to have a family the moment
I popped the question, so much so that it surprised me. We were lying
in bed and I was like, "You're really down for this?" and she was like,
"Yeah. Because you're my person." So we kind of looked at each
other like, "Oh, shit. Fuck it. YOLO. Let's do it," and we threw out
her birth control pills and got to it and three months later we were in
Japan and we made this little person and three weeks later she was
late and she took the test and I was like, "Shit. I'm gonna be a dad."

ᎪᎥᏅᏎ

Right as I was putting Little Bobby in the oven I was also dropping my other baby: I published my first novel, *Supermarket*. I dropped a soundtrack to go with it. That was fucking annoying because I had a bunch of rappers and rapheads going, "Yo, this shit sucks!" because they were judging it like it's a hip-hop album, which it isn't at all. But I didn't give a shit because the book was a #1 *New York Times* bestseller and I think I did a great fuckin' job for somebody who never had written anything in his life. To this day I see a lot of people and they're like, "Yo, this is my favorite book. I fuck with this, and I didn't even know this dude was a rapper."

Even that didn't matter so much because I wrote that book for one person: me. Writing about my experiences is what allowed me to heal. When the protagonist in the book has a psychotic break, that's me having a psychotic break outside of *Star Wars*. When the protagonist wakes up and sees reality, that's me waking up and seeing reality. It was also amazing to go out and promote it because I crossed over from the hip-hop and music worlds to the book world and I went on *The Daily Show with Trevor Noah* and *Good Morning America* and it was the most astonishing, eye-opening experience. Unlike with hip-hop "journalism," which is a bunch of gossipy bullshit about who's beefing with who and who's legit and who's not, people actually just talked about the work. Whether they loved the book or were critical of the book, they were respectful of the fact that I'm a creative person who put my heart into something. Someone at *The New York Times Book Review* might critique your story or say they don't think your characters are believable, but nobody at *The New York Times* is writing, "This nigga suck ass." Which was a refreshing change of pace.

Right on the heels of *Supermarket,* I was getting ready to drop *Confessions of a Dangerous Mind.* Having climbed out from the depths of Pittsburgh and coming off the success of *Bobby Tarantino II* and a RattPack throwback like *YSIV,* I was beyond confident. I was like, "I can do no wrong. I'm the fuckin' Jedi Master of this shit." All the white-hot hate that came at me after "1-800," I thought I had that shit handled. I'd learned how to manage it and process it. It was like my whole career was one long game of *Call of Duty* and I'd leveled

On the press tour for Supermarket.

up and leveled up and I'd faced the boss level and I'd kicked its ass and now I knew how to keep playing the game.

A few months before *Confessions* came out, I dropped the first single from the album, "Keanu Reeves," one of the biggest singles I've ever had, and nobody was hating on it. Then I dropped the single for the title track, one of the realest songs I've ever written, and nobody was hating on it. Then I released the single for "Homicide" with Eminem and it blew the fuck up. It was the biggest rap song in the world, and nobody was hating on it. So on the eve of dropping the album I was like, "*Damn,* this album has so many bangers. This is going to be amazing." *Confessions* was going to be the album that finally silenced my critics. I just knew it.

I have never been more wrong about anything in my life.

It was panned, universally. Everything I thought was going to work on that album didn't. People didn't dislike the album. People were *angry* about the album. It was everyone and their mom and they were like, "Kill yourself. This isn't what we want. This is terrible. This is garbage. Your career is over."

Of course, the album debuted at #1 in hip-hop and #1 overall. It had platinum singles. Once I went out on tour, I was playing to sold-out arenas across the country. On Spotify it's the #1 most popular release of my entire career to this day. But I couldn't see any of that at the time, because that's what this world does. That's what social media does. It forces you to judge your own happiness relative to what everyone else has and what everyone else thinks, never mind the reality. All I could see was the hate, and this high I'd been riding through my college years and *Bobby Tarantino II* and meeting my wife, it all came crashing down and I plunged into a depression worse than anything I'd ever experienced.

I tell people that *Confessions* was the darkest period in my life, and they don't believe me. People don't understand how you can be on a stage in front of twenty thousand people cheering your name and still feel like a worthless piece of shit. But it's true. The anxiety and depression I felt that year were the darkest things I've ever experienced. They hit me worse than anything I experienced as a child. Hands down. Which is something that almost nobody understands. As bad as my childhood was, I had the benefit of being born into a life of ignorance. Most of the people I grew up with were ignorant. And that's not a slight; it's just a fact. Most people living in those conditions are ignorant of pretty much everything that's not a part of the immediate physical reality that's in front of them. If you don't have the awareness to understand what life is doing to you and the ways it's traumatizing you, then your day-to-day actually isn't too bad. You just self-harm and self-medicate and self-harm and self-medicate and it's a self-destructive loop and it kills you in the end, but the ride itself isn't necessarily so unpleasant because you just don't know any different.

I talk to my therapist about it a lot, that sometimes I feel like I was happier when I was more ignorant. Then, slowly, through Mary Jo and Zarou and 6ix and my fans and my wife, I got to see the whole big, amazing, beautiful world. But to see and understand what's beautiful about the world is also to see what's terrifying and horrible about the world. It's like being an AI that's suddenly aware of its own sentience. You eat from the tree of wisdom, and with wisdom comes suffering. I'm glad that it happened, for sure. I would rather have everything that I have now than go back to being ignorant, but that doesn't mean it wasn't simpler back then.

The blowback from *Confessions* was also different from what had happened in Pittsburgh. Pittsburgh was a moment. It was like getting hit by a wave of unbearable anguish and pain that no human could possibly endure, but then the wave passed. Slowly I was able to pick myself back up and move on. This was something else. This was chronic, grinding, unrelenting.

The thing that gave me all the joy in my life had stopped giving me joy. I had lost all joy in my art. Ever since the nights I spent rapping over Wu-Tang beats on my dad's shitty, cold leather couch, rap had carried me, buoyed me. When I was just a kid who was too dumb to pass ninth grade, rap told me I was good at something, worth something. It meant so much to me that I walked away from my high school sweetheart, naively thinking that I should put everything into my craft because, unlike with people, I would always get it back—and now I wasn't getting it back.

Rap was my therapy. It was a place where I could go and pour out all of my pain and my problems and thoughts through a pen and a microphone and deal with them. But once you create something that holds enough weight to make you successful, you're not allowed to complain about anything anymore, because then you're whining. With *Confessions*, I tried to talk about everything that was going on with social media and mental health on songs like "Clickbait," and nobody wanted to hear it. Everybody loved hearing about the struggles of a young man on the come-up, but nobody wants to hear about a millionaire rapper who's unhappy, because it's champagne problems and who cares. Which is why so many famous people OD and kill themselves, because they get to a level of fame or success and then they're not allowed to be human anymore. You can call it a champagne problem but a problem's still a fuckin' problem, and I was losing the ability to deal with my problems the way I always had: through my art.

I was losing the connection I had with my audience as well. My favorite part of making music has never been making it, it's been watching people react to it. Whenever I play a track to a friend or my wife, I try to find a spot in their peripheral where they can't really see me, and I just watch them to see if they catch a lyric and go, "Whoa." It's fuckin' amazing. It's the best high in the world. In the early days of the Internet, and on social media in particular, I got that feeling a thousandfold. It's why I created the RattPack, and I had so much fun with them through the years. Then one day I realized, "I can't be here anymore."

The RattPack changed after *Confessions*. It had been happening for a while, but that's when it really flipped. For years, whenever a fan did something cool, like making a tribute video, I'd recognize them. I'd retweet them and say, "Thanks." I'd invite them to a meet-and-greet or to come hang out backstage and we'd post pictures together online. The biggest and most devoted fans, I would follow them back. I did that with hundreds of Logic fan accounts, and anytime I did, *BAM!* overnight, they'd go from 175 followers to 175,000 followers. It would be, "Oh, Logic follows this person. Logic has pictures with this person. Logic brought this person backstage for being such a devout RattPack member. Let's follow them, too."

Once that happened, these fans became famous inside this little world I'd built. Most of them stayed the same warm, kind, loyal fans they'd always been. Others didn't. Once they had hundreds of thousands of followers, they began to realize what I'd given them. They'd be on their phone watching me and Lenny and 6ix in the Logic reality show and they'd go, "Hey, wait a minute . . . maybe somebody wants to see what *I'm* doing?" That's when they'd flip the camera back around on themselves. Now they had a starring role to play in the Logic reality show, too.

Because that's where social media ultimately takes you: "Why watch the Kardashians when I can be a Kardashian?" And that road doesn't lead anywhere good. Maybe these fans fell in love with my music because they were nerdy high school kids who never fit in. Now they've got hundreds of thousands of people liking them and quoting them and cheering them and now they're fucked. Because social media has taken them and turned them into something else. They're not just fans alone in their room anymore. Now that person's online going, "Look at me! Look at me!" and then another person's going, "Look at me! Look at me!" and then the first person's going, "Don't look at them. Fuck them! Look at me!" And then another person does that and another person does that and then this whole thing that started out as a family of me and ten people in a chatroom a decade before becomes this roiling 24/7 cauldron of backbiting and narcissism and bitching, because everybody wants to be the person at the center of the storm and it's the negativity and the yelling that get the clicks.

I've literally seen fan accounts go from posting, "Hey, What's Your Top Ten Favorite Logic Songs" to posting, "What's the Top Ten Shittiest Ass Logic Verses That Suck?" I've seen other fans posting, "I've known Logic personally for seven years and I know him and I know his heart wasn't in the right place when he recorded this album, and therefore it's a piece of shit and that song was ass," followed by a bunch of crying and poop emojis. That person doesn't know me. That person met me once backstage for five minutes. But it was like me and my music had become irrelevant to whatever was going on, because now it was just about all this internal drama of beefing and chest-puffing to decide who gets to be the Most Important Person in the RattPack that day.

It wasn't even that many people. A few dozen, maybe. But that's all it takes: a little drop of poison. It rippled through the fan community, and this place of love and acceptance we'd built wasn't the same anymore. And it was my fault. I'd given those people too much power by giving them too much of myself because ten years ago giving too much of yourself to the Internet felt like good idea. But the Internet isn't that anymore.

So I had to end it. I unfollowed all the negative fan pages, marginalized them, pushed them to the periphery of the conversation. It was one of the hardest things I've ever had to do in my life. These were some of the most loyal and devoted fans I've ever had, and I had to cut them off. When I did it, I was so scared. I thought I would lose everything. I thought all my fans might leave me. But I also knew I didn't have a choice.

I couldn't have articulated it at the time, but the day *Confessions* came out, I knew it was over. I didn't yet have the courage to say, "I'm going to retire." But I knew. I started working on the album that would become *No Pressure* right then because I had this chip on my shoulder to write. I'd had the idea for years. I knew it was the album fans wanted, but I'd been putting it off. I needed to go back and re-create the young, hungry, skinny Logic, the guy who was on his come-up. But it's hard to be a multimillionaire, platinum-selling artist and make people feel like I'm struggling just as hard as they are. I was and am still struggling with many aspects of my life, but it's hard to find a way to make that work creatively.

I went off on the *Confessions* tour and I wrote and wrote and wrote and I was exhausted and I was trying to get the album finished before Little Bobby came and at the same time I was mapping out and planning all the albums I'd needed to get done to fulfill my contract with Def Jam. How I had to do this album and then I'd have to do another album to get out of my deal and I needed to do this *Lightyear* album I wanted to do that was going to be alternative and dope and the *Ultra 85* album that was going to tie together the events that started in *The Incredible True Story*. I started thinking I might make the *Ultra 85* one the last one and then I was like, "Wait, why not just do it now? Why not make this one the last one?"

As that thought came over me, what I realized was that I didn't feel like Logic anymore. Rappers adopt alter egos because they need to be superheroes. Bruce Wayne becomes Batman because part of him needs to be Batman. But then Gotham is saved and, more importantly, *he* is saved. He's dealt with his demons, so he takes off the mask and fucks off to Italy with Anne Hathaway and My Cocaine.* Because he's a fucking billionaire and why the fuck not?

Logic was who I needed to be when I was living in Mary Jo's guest room rapping with a litter box under my legs. But Logic was and would always be a kid on his come-up, the guy who had to prove why he should be loved. Logic was who seventeen-year-old Bobby aspired to be, but thirty-year-old Bobby had outgrown him. I wasn't

---

* The actor.

a kid anymore. I didn't have shit to prove to anybody. And the more I thought on it, the more I was like, "Yeah. Fuck this. I'm just gonna do whatever I wanna do."

I'd made noises about quitting before, for sure, but it was always me being manic and upset and pissed off and lashing out. But this wasn't from an angry place. It was a real, premeditated thing. My whole career, any time I'd wanted to quit, walk away, or just take back time for myself, I'd heard nothing but agents and promoters telling me, "This is in the contract. We agreed to this. You have to do this." And in my fear of losing everything I'd always relented and kept grinding.

Then, after what I'd been through with "1-800," I'd started to think, "But if I were dead, then what? If I'm so depressed and exhausted that I kill myself, then what?" Which wasn't me wanting to kill myself. It was me coming to the realization that if I didn't exist, the show would be over. There's only one me, which means I'm the one in charge. I was one of the top-selling music acts in the world. I was a lion, but I still thought of myself as a cub. I'd been beholden to the ringmaster in the circus because I hadn't realized I was bigger than he was now. But in that moment, I did. I realized I can walk away from rap. I don't have to live my life trying to get something from toxic people who have no interest in giving me anything in return. Even my fans, who I love, I don't owe them my life. I don't owe them my *self*. I can create music and tell stories and share them, and I don't owe anybody anything else beyond that. The only thing I owe is to take care of myself and take care of the people I love and who love me. That's all I *have* to do. Value over fear. It took me thirty years to understand it, but I finally did. I decided to take control of my life. I decided to leave rap on my own terms so I wouldn't end up leaving it the way others had left it.

The inspiration for the title track on *Confessions* came to me in a hotel room in Paris on September 8, 2018. Brittney and I were just chilling and having a good day and she was on her phone and she blurted out, "Oh my God! Mac Miller *died*?!"

"Fuck! No! Was it drugs?"

"Yeah. He OD'd."

Right then I knew I was going write something about it. Mac Miller died young. He was two years younger than me. He was a kid who went out into the world with his music looking for acceptance and wanting to be loved and everybody on the Internet clowned him and abused him and shat on him nonstop—and now he was dead. Mac had other things going on his life, for sure. Addiction is no joke. But it was the abuse that kept spiraling him back into the addiction.

That's what the title track for *Confessions of a Dangerous Mind* needed to be about. It was one of the scariest things I ever had to write. I knew it had to be executed in a way where nobody would look at it as being insensitive, because then the abuse would just pile up on me more. I was terrified to stand up with that song in front of everyone on YouTube and Twitter and Facebook and Instagram and say, "Y'all killed Mac Miller. The man is dead because of you." But I did it, and Mac's manager, who'd been best friends with Mac since they were teenagers and who knew him better than anyone, called Zarou to say, "Please thank Bobby for what he said. Because everything he said is the truth."

I've seen people literally just post an image of me and say, "Like this if this nigga look ugly," and then it will get thousands and thousands of likes. I don't even know what to make of that. All I know is that I was born into a magical time. Back at Mary Jo's, when I discovered Mac Miller and J. Cole and all the other rappers making their own way online, it was mind-blowing. For a kid too scared to leave the house and too poor and too uneducated to do anything with his life, it was a gift beyond anything you could imagine. I reached out into the universe with my janky AOL CD-ROMs and I found my people. I found my place.

As social media took off, that became my universe and I had so much fun there, just making stupid shit with my friends and posting it online and laughing back and forth with thousands of people around the world. I loved it so much. It was like living in a science-fiction movie. We had our hands on the greatest technological innovation since the cavemen discovered fucking fire. We were walking around with God in our pockets. But then something happened and we took this magical thing that gave us so much joy and love and happiness and literally gave us the power to save and uplift and unite all of humanity and we turned it into something else. Now it's just a bully telling you to spit in a retarded kid's Gatorade, and I've been there and I've done that, and I'm just fuckin' done.

刀召米氐

In the end, my decision to retire wasn't just about what I had decided to leave behind. It wasn't about what I was retiring from. It was about what I was retiring to. Part of what had kept me stuck in such a dark place for so long was not believing I had any other place where I could go. Now I did. By the fall of 2019 the *Confessions* tour was winding down and all I could think about was getting home to Brittney and Little Bobby growing in her tummy and settling in to get our home ready for the day he arrived. I was blowing out as many arenas as I could so I could take the next year off and just be with my family, but before I could head home I had to make one stop. I wanted to meet my little brother.

At some point while I was living in L.A. and making albums and not talking to my dad, he was hanging with this woman he knew from A.A. She was dying, and before she died she asked my dad to look after her daughter, who was twenty-three and a hard-core heroin addict. My dad said, "Of course I'll take care of her," and he did. He took so much care of her that he put a baby in her, despite the fact that he'd had a vasectomy thirty years earlier, right after he'd had me.

Nine months later this kid, Ashton, my little half brother, was born. And this new mom, the twenty-three-year-old, was so fucked up on drugs that the court took one look at her and then turned to my father—a sixty-five-year-old recovered crack addict and deadbeat dad on welfare who'd abandoned every other child he'd ever had—and they awarded custody to him. Which would have happened eventually anyway because not too long after that the mother died from an overdose.

I didn't even hear about any of this until maybe a year after everything had happened. At first I didn't believe any of it. I honestly thought it was just some scam to get an extra social security check. But no. It was real. So in November 2019, on my way to play a show for *Confessions* at the EagleBank Arena in Virginia, I decided to stop by my dad's place in Gaithersburg to meet this kid, who by now was almost two years old.

When I knocked on the door to my dad's apartment, my brother John opened the door. He just stared at me. It was eyes wide open, jaws on the floor, like he'd seen a ghost. But he hadn't seen a ghost. He'd just seen Logic. Because all he sees now is Logic and not Bobby, which I understand and it is what it is. The vibe wasn't, "Hey, how are you? Let's catch up." It was, "Yo! Let's take some pictures for the Gram!" So we hung out for a minute and eventually I was like, "Where's Dad?"

John took me to the back bedroom and knocked on the door and my dad opened it and he was all excited and I was like, "Yeah, you guys are cool, but I just want to meet this Ashton kid." My dad pointed over at the bed, and I saw this little dude, curly hair, wearing these orange-and-blue-striped pajamas. He was so beautiful and adorable, just lying there on the bed, sleeping and breathing his little breaths in and out. Then I realized what he was breathing. This tiny nine-by-twelve room with one little closed window was choked with cigarette smoke because my dad had been sitting in there puffing away with a fucking toddler sleeping right next to him. This little guy was breathing it all in and the room was piled up with boxes and hoarder shit, and that's when it hit me: "Holy shit. This kid is me. This kid is going to have my life all over again. This kid is *fucked*."

My heart sank, and this wonderful moment turned so bitter-sweet, seeing this beautiful, innocent kid and knowing all the shit that he was going to have to endure. A few minutes later he woke up and I played with him and held him. I've held a lot of babies over the years, friends' babies or whatever, and this was the only baby I ever held where I didn't feel like he belonged to a stranger. I didn't even know him, but he felt easy and familiar.

As chill as the kid was, I got the fuck out of there pretty quick. All my dad did was talk about music and when was I bringing him out to be on the next album and I just couldn't deal with it. So I split. On my way out I pulled my dad aside and told him I wanted him to come to my show the next day and that he was on the list. Then I gave him five hundred bucks, just in the hope that it might help the kid a little. I was going to do the same for John, but then he said, "Hey, nigga, let's take another picture!" and I realized he had the new iPhone 11 and I was like, "Wait, even I don't have the new iPhone 11. I ain't giving this guy shit."

The next day at the concert I was up onstage, rapping to a hometown audience of some ten thousand people. In the middle of the show I looked down and there in the front row was my dad and T and John—and little Ashton. They'd brought a two-year-old to an arena show. And my shows are bumpin'. My shit is *loud*. And this kid was right in the middle of it, with no ear protection. I couldn't believe it. I was furious. Who brings a fucking two-year-old to the front row of a concert and puts their tiny little delicate ears right in front of a thirty-foot-high wall of speakers and subwoofers? I mean, who fucking does that? The kid was crying, and my dad was just holding him, bopping along to the music, like it was nothing.

In that moment my brain immediately split and started running on two separate tracks. One track just went on autopilot. I had to keep words coming out of my mouth to entertain the crowd. Meanwhile, in the other half of my brain, I was just staring down at my father, screaming inside my head, *"What the fuck is wrong with you?*

You're going to fuck up this kid's life the same way you fucked up mine, you fucking asshole!"

At all of my shows I have a talkback mic, so I can switch over to a separate channel and say things to the crew that the audience can't hear. I was so panicked for this kid that in between verses I kept switching over and barking at the crew, "Yo, my dad's a fuckin' idiot! Somebody get the baby out of the front row! Somebody get him some ear protection! Now! Hurry!" Then, before the concert was over, John got into a fight with somebody in the middle of the crowd and the cops had to kick him out of the arena.

The rest of the night and all the next day, I just couldn't get the image of little Ashton breathing in cigarette smoke out of my head. Part of me felt like I feel about the rest of my siblings: "This isn't my problem. This isn't my burden. I didn't create this fucked-up situation. I have my own family to think about. Little Bobby is on the way." But that was in my head. Deep in my heart, I knew that I had to at least try to do something. And then this thought popped into my head: "I have to adopt him." I almost couldn't believe that I'd thought it. "Wait, *do* I want to adopt this kid?" I sat and turned it over and finally was like, "Yeah! Do it! Do everything you can and fight for this kid, because this kid is you."

And that's what it was: I wanted to adopt myself. Plucking that kid out of that stale, smoky bedroom would be like getting in a time machine and going back and slipping into my mom's apartment in Farmingdale, tiptoeing past all the overflowing ashtrays and the piles of empty Coors cans, grabbing little two-year-old me, and taking myself away from all the abuse and the poverty and the screaming. It would be like giving myself the childhood I never had.

The difference between Ashton and me was that this time around my dad is actually present. I know there's a part of him that thinks, "I never did anything for my kids before, so I'm going to love this kid and do it right this time." And in his own living-in-the-hood, smoking-around-the-kid, taking-the-kid-to-arena-shows kind of way, he means it. The same thing is true of T. She loves Ashton. But you can love a kid and still not have a clue how to parent a kid, and my dad doesn't. He's an old man who's never thought about anyone but himself his whole life.

I sat on it for a couple of days. The biggest obstacle was knowing that bringing Ashton into my life would mean bringing my dad back into my life in a big way, which I was hesitant to do. But in the end I decided, "No, I need to do this." I called Brittney and I explained everything about the situation and asked her what she thought and she didn't even flinch. She was like, "Yeah, I'm down. If it's what you want, I'm with you." She's ride-or-die, which is why I love her so much.

So I called my dad, and he wouldn't even hear it.

"No," he said. "That's my son."

"But Dad," I said, "you're sixty-five years old. And let's be honest, you've done a lot of drugs. I can help. I can give him a better life."

"You can give him a good life now," he said. "Just give me money."

"Dad, you know I can't do that."

Realizing I wasn't getting anywhere, I retreated to my fallback position.

"Why don't you at least name me legal guardian in your will," I said. "That way, if anything happens to you, I can take care of him."

"No, he's going with his mother."

"His mother? I thought she OD'd?"

"No. He's going to T."

"T? But T's not his mother. They're not even related."

"It's already done."

So I had to let it go. There was nothing I could do for the kid but pray. I knocked out my last two weeks of shows and then I flew back to L.A. and we celebrated Thanksgiving and we celebrated Christmas and we celebrated New Year's and Brittney's belly was getting bigger and we were assembling bassinets and shit and then, on February 5, the contractions started. It was around one-thirty in the afternoon.

We waited a couple of hours until they got closer together and then we drove to the hospital in Beverly Hills and went to the place where they check to see if you're ready to be admitted and we were in that room for about two and a half hours and then they finally admitted us.

We moved into the birthing room and the contractions started getting more intense and then it was six o'clock and then it was seven o'clock and then it was eight o'clock and *Shazam!* was on so we watched *Shazam!* Then *Crazy Rich Asians* came on so we watched *Crazy Rich Asians.* Then it was midnight and Brittney was really feeling it and the pain was intense and crazy and she decided to get the epidural. They took this thick fuckin' needle that was like six inches long and they slid it into her spine and she was in so much pain she didn't even give two shits about the giant needle in her back and then ten minutes later the pain was gone.

A little after three a.m. the nurses came in and checked on her and they were like, "Oh yeah. You're fully dilated. The wall is broken, and we can feel the baby's head." They started having her push and they called the doctor in and I was like, "Holy shit! This is happening!" and I was holding Brittney's left leg while her mom was holding her right leg and the nurse was checking out the goods and making sure everything was cool. Brittney was killing it and pushing as hard as she could but like every woman who's doing an incredible job she apologized for not doing an even better job and in between pushes I was pacing and my knees were shaking because I was filled with adrenaline because I was so excited. Then the ob-gyn walked in there like the Terminator, saying, "Oh, we're having this baby!" and she put on these latex gloves that went all the way up her arms like socks and the nurses were putting rubber mats down on the floor and I was thinking, "Damn, this shit's gonna be *crazy*."

Brittney kept pushing and pushing and Little Bobby started coming out and I could see his head and I was like, "HOLY SHIT!" I couldn't believe it. I was crying and I couldn't stop and Brittney was in another dimension with the pushing and as the doctor pulled him out and began to lift him up I did one of those old-lady-throw-your-forearm-over-your-eyes moves, bending backward like Neo dodging bullets in *The Matrix,* and I ended up hunched over and crying and so ecstatic and happy. Brittney reached forward and pulled Bobby out with the doctor and brought him up and rested him on her tummy and there was a ten-second vibe when he wasn't crying but I wasn't freaking out yet because they told us it takes a second and then he cried that insane first baby cry and I was like, "Cool." We just laid there with him for a minute and they put that little hat on him from out of nowhere and it was so cute and next thing I knew someone was putting scissors in my hands and saying, "Do you want to cut the cord?" and I was like, "Fuck yeah, I wanna cut this cord!"

The best way I can describe an umbilical cord is that it's like ten pieces of raw bacon folded longways like a pencil. It's also gray; I wasn't expecting it to be gray. So I cut through that and it was disgusting but it was awesome and then they were like, "Okay, we're going to weigh him now." Then the nurses took him over and these women were amazing and even though I'd never met them before that afternoon I just trusted everything they told me implicitly and they weighed him on the machine and his balls looked huge like a Tootsie Pop and then they put the gel in his eyes and clamped and cut off the rest of the umbilical cord and they wrapped him up in a little blanket. They asked me if I wanted to carry him back over to Brittney. I said yes. So they laid him gently into my arms, and I held my son for the first time. I looked down at him and stared into his face. He was so tiny and cooing and wriggling. I was so excited I started crying again. I smiled and said, "Hey, buddy. How are you?"

He squinted back up at me with a look that said, "What's this all about? Who are you people? What's going on here?"

He was the most beautiful thing I'd ever seen in my life.

EPILOGUE
PARADISE

When Brittney and I got home from the hospital, I was carrying Little Bobby in his car seat and we walked in the front door, and our friends had hung up a beautiful banner that said, "WELCOME HOME, BOBBY AND HIS MOMMY," and we took some pictures and it was cool. I set the car seat down on the carpet and we just stared at him while he slept and then we stared at each other like, "Holy shit. We have a human that they gave us. What the fuck?"

Five weeks later the COVID pandemic hit and the whole world shut down and I felt weirdly blessed because I'd planned to take the year off and do nothing but be home with Little Bobby and Brittney anyway. So it was like the whole world changed, except our lives didn't really change at all, at least not right away. We were already sequestered at home, and every day the kid was growing and changing and just a few weeks before he'd been inside another person and now he was his own person and the whole thing is just weird and amazing.

I know I'm not going to be a perfect parent. I'm going to have to learn. I might raise my voice here and there by accident. I might have to be firm and grab him and say, "Chill," if he's being a real brat in the middle of the supermarket. But I know I'm never going to abandon him. I know I'm never going to get drunk and ignore him or leave him at home for two weeks by himself. Now that I have my own kid and I'm so consumed with love for him every minute of every day, it's even more insane to me how my parents treated their kids. It's made me understand even more just how broken they truly are, because only a broken person could have done what they did.

The hardest part of writing this book has been knowing that, once it comes out, my parents will likely deny a lot of what I've said. My father will say some things never happened. My mother will say she just doesn't remember, which, to be fair, there's a good chance that she doesn't. In some ways, having them deny things is more painful than having gone through them. But I'm good. Because I love my parents. I love my sisters. I love my brothers. I haven't written any of this from a place of anger or hatred. All has truly been forgiven on my end. I made it. I did it. I am financially and emotionally secure. I have the family I always wished I had—not just my wife and son, but all the people who've been there for me in so many different and important ways.

None of what I've said in this book was to try to hurt anybody, but sometimes the truth hurts. I chose to reflect on those experiences so that I can heal, first and foremost, and so I can help others who've been through hard times by letting them know they're not alone. But I also chose to write the book because reckoning with the truth is an essential step for forgiveness.

The hardest part of my entire life has been feeling the constant need to explain myself and prove myself to get the love and acceptance I need from the people I want to love and accept me. Before it was social media and hip-hop, it was my mom and dad, and that's a love and acceptance I still don't have to this day. However, even though they may not be able to understand it, I hope you, the reader, will understand that this whole book is about my coming to terms with my love and acceptance of who they've always been and always will be.

The fear I have for Little Bobby is that I know he'll have pain in his life, too. He's going to make mistakes, too. He's going to have his little heart broken by some girl, he's going to bust his lip open or break an arm. These things are going to happen to him, and I know they're going to happen because of what happened to me. All I want to do is protect him from all of it because it's scary, but going through those hard times is also how you become a human being. Those are the experiences and the memories that make you who you are, and as much as I want to protect him, I know all I can do is make him know that he's loved so he'll grow up to be a good person.

I still have anxiety. I still get panic attacks. I still feel derealization at times, and it's nothing. I've just learned that if I'm feeling out of it, I can't pay attention to it. It's a pink balloon or a pink elephant—the more you feed into it, the more the monster grows. Now, whenever I feel a bout of anxiety coming on, I go, "Huh, I feel a little out of it." And I have to talk myself down or just sit and work my way through it. But I've already dealt with the worst part of anxiety. The worst thing about anxiety is feeling like you're alone and trapped inside this bubble of fear all by yourself, which is how I felt for most of my life, and that's the biggest difference between then and now: I know I'm not alone anymore.

I have my wife and my son. My in-laws are cool as fuck and they live around the corner and come over all the time. Jordan and Pepé are still with me and we've become family and they have my back any time I need them. Same with 6ix and Zarou and Harrison and everyone I came up with. Lenny's still with me, too. He lives with us because now it's my turn to give him a home and get his career off the ground; as I write this, I'm producing his first album and it's going to be dope as fuck.

I'm still in touch with Mary Jo and Bernie all the time. I always make sure to ask about Josh, who's out of prison and back living with them again. I don't talk to Amber and Geanie too often, but Jesse's been back in my life more. Ralph, too. And I'm grateful for that. My dad and I, I can't even say where we'll be by the time you're reading this. Sometimes we don't talk at all. Other times he calls and he wants help with promoting his music and I try to get him to open up and talk about himself and our relationship and sometimes it works but usually it doesn't. But at least with my dad he can call and we can have a conversation about something. As for my mom, nothing's changed, and at this point it is what it is.

And I still have my art. The irony is that I'm doing more in retirement than I ever did while I was working. I told everyone that I was putting my foot down to go away and do nothing, but everyone who knows me knows I can't ever do nothing. I wrote this book you're reading right now. I'm writing screenplays and another novel. I've literally never been so happy. I feel like I'm fifteen again, just learning and conquering new horizons every day. I can spend a whole day strumming the guitar or a whole day watching movies, or I can drop it all at a moment's notice to go and be with my wife and my son. I'm a workaholic who gets paid to play, a workaholic who's addicted to joy and discovery instead of fear and the need for recognition.

I'm still recording music, too. I know when I drop any new music some people will be like, "Hey, I thought that guy said he was retired," and how it was all a stunt and all that. But it wasn't. I am retired, because I'm doing it all for fun. I don't have a job. I don't "work." I'm a creator who creates.

What's funny is that I feel more financially secure even though I have less money, because my fear was always that I would never have enough to retire, but by retiring I've proved to myself that I do have enough to retire, so I can finally just relax. I'm secure. I've made it. You can't make it any more than I've made it. I get such a kick because I look back now at all the professional haters, the vloggers and the morning DJs and the gatekeepers who thrive on creating backlash to get clicks and get money, and those motherfuckers *can't* retire. They have to keep hating and churning up the phony outrage and the negativity and drama every day, because that's their whole livelihood. And that's been fun, sitting back and seeing those guys still having to hustle every day. They still have to hate, but I don't have to be hated. I can just chill.

On July 24, 2020, at the height of the pandemic, we dropped *No Pressure*. It sold two hundred and twenty thousand copies in the first week, which is unheard of, especially on some rap shit. It went to #1 on the hip-hop charts and #2 overall and it would have been #1 overall if Taylor Swift hadn't made a surprise drop that same week.

After *Confessions* dropped, I was fuckin' Rick Dalton from *Once Upon a Time . . . in Hollywood*. "It's official, buddy, I'm a fuckin' has-been." That's how I felt. Now, with *No Pressure,* I felt like I'd just walked up Sharon Tate's driveway, like I'd ridden off into the sunset, which is kind of cool. The reception has been low-key undeniable. Everyone loves the album and I couldn't be happier. Professionally speaking, it's been the best moment of my life. People were really sad and happy for me at the same time. Even a lot of the people who used to shit on me were sad. It was like the series finale of their favorite reality show was ending, which meant their role in the reality show as the people who loved to hate on the reality show was ending, too. They were like, "Shit, this dude's leaving? Like, he's *gone*? Whoa." I saw a lot of the hate and criticism turn into "We'll miss you."

It made me feel old, but in a good way. Hip-hop is a young man's game. I was a teenager when I started, and as long as you're on your come-up, every album is not as good as the album before. Your new shit ain't as good as your old shit until your new shit is your old shit. But by retiring from the game, I put a stop to all that. Now people can just look back on and enjoy the work that I've done, and I'm starting to feel that appreciation from the general populace of rap, which is pretty cool.

Part of saying "Fuck y'all, I'm out" was to see what would happen. Because I wanted to know: "Did I ever actually have a place in hip-hop? Was it ever really real?" But then my leaving created an absence, and it was only by seeing the me-shaped hole I left behind that I knew I'd ever really belonged for sure.

Then, right around the time we dropped *No Pressure,* it was time for another kind of departure. I was never an L.A. guy. The only reason I'd ever moved there was because my label told me I had to. Once COVID happened and everything moved online, it made me realize I didn't need to be there anymore, either, and with Little Bobby in the world, it was time for a new chapter.

I'd always thought about moving to the country and Brittney was down, so one day we pulled out a map of the world and laid it out and that was when it dawned on us, like, "We could literally go *anywhere*. Oregon? Washington? Northern California? New York? Maine? London? Hawaii? Japan?" We started looking and found this beautiful house in the mountains. It was gigantic, amazing, and it had everything we could want or need, way more, which I liked because my family is a village. It's not just me and Brittney and Little Bobby. It's Lenny and his sister, Chrissy, and Pepé and Jordan. It's all these people who've become a part of my life, and I wanted a place where all of us could come together and be together.

So we did it. We bought the house and called the movers and started packing up and a few weeks later, the movers arrived to take the bulk of the furniture and everything else. They loaded it all up and took off, and Brittney, Little Bobby, and I were alone left in this big house that was utterly empty, no sofas, no beds, no nothing. At five-thirty the next morning, an RV would be pulling up to take us away, and we had one last night to spend in the house. Bedtime came and we rolled out sleeping bags in the middle of the living room. It reminded me of the last time I'd slept on the floor in an empty house, with my mother when we were squatting in a vacant unit in Farmingdale because we had no place to go, which gave me an idea.

"Hey," I said to Little Bobby. "I want to show you something."

I pulled out a flashlight we'd kept with us and I pointed it up and I made shadow puppets for him, little dogs and horses dancing around on the ceiling. Of course he'll never remember it because he was only six months old. But Brittney and I will remember it and it'll be one of those memories we hold on to and cherish for the rest of our lives.

ACKNOWLEDGMENTS

This book would not have come into this world without the hard work and dedication and support of a lifetime's worth of incredible people. For helping me bring my story to the world, I owe a debt of gratitude to them all. First, to my literary agent, Sarah Passick, the sweetest, most kindhearted, snapping-necks-to-get-my-vision-through woman I've ever met in my life. To Tanner Colby, without whom this book wouldn't be, the man who helped me organize and relive my life in a way I never thought possible; the entire experience of working on this book together has truly been a highlight of my life. To Daniel Hoffheins, who sat through countless hours of stories, even the ones that didn't make it into the book, hanging onto every word so I wouldn't have to. To Stuart Roberts, who believed in me, was willing to give me a deal before anyone else, and who had the vision to show the world my vision.

To Chris Zarou, my brother, who I love and who didn't know a damn thing about music or the business but who did the one thing no other managers do: you didn't leave me in the dark as your knowledge and music-business IQ expanded. You tutored me and taught me every last detail while you were learning it, so I would always truly understand, down to the last decimal, what was going on in my career. To Harrison Remler, for being the rock of the entire Visionary Music Group company; without you everything would crumble.

To Paul Rothenberg, who literally took a couple of kids off the New York City streets; you welcomed us not only into your firm, but your life, and forever changed ours. To Mike Holland, my friend, my producer, my partner; from the time you were eighteen to now, you've always stood by me and helped me in all my creative endeavors. To 6ix, thanks for dropping out of med school. To Bobby Campbell, the man without whom none of my music would be as great as it is. Thank you for all of your years of collaboration, dedication, hard work, sleepless nights, deadlines, and amazing conversations. I love you with all my heart.

To Chris Castro, the friend and brother I needed when I had no one else; thank you for getting me a job at Joe's Crab Shack. To Raheem DeVaughn and everyone at 368, you showed me just how real and possible things are and can be. To DJ Boss Player, one of the most kindhearted humans I've ever met; your generosity is a large part of why I am here today. To GRVTY, for the videos we did together on my come-up, which are still my favorite videos that I've ever done; you're incredibly talented and I think of you often and I thank you for the time you spent with me. To OB, thank you for being there through the first few mixtapes; you were always a great friend and incredibly wise.

To Christian Martin, thanks for just always being my friend no matter what. To Sam Spratt, without whom I never would have never been able to build such an amazing world for my fans; you've shown me that anything is possible, any idea, any dream, no matter how big or small, can be executed with not only the right people around you, but the people to push you to do better, and you've always pushed me, so thank you.

To John Momberg, I love you, and without you my live shows would have been nothing; I also love that you are obsessed with pugs. To DJ Rhetorik, the only guy on the planet who has made me believe that telepathy exists; onstage, it's like we're one performer—I love you. To Josh Aguilar (Rookie), though our time working together was short, our time as friends and brothers will last forever; you made my life easy when the work was hard—thank you, I love you.

To Jordan Harris: When I was at my weakest, you were always there to keep me strong; you have an amazing voice, too—I love you. To Pepé Araujo, the man who's seen me at my lowest and helped me become the man at my highest, the Cliff Booth to my Rick Dalton. I'll love you forever.

To No I.D.; I could thank you for starting my career, but I would rather thank you for helping me become the man that I am today. To Noah Preston and his wife, Nina, without whom I would certainly not be here today; thank you for doing what the record business no longer does: being patient with me and developing me and being my friend. Thank you for being a hardass. Thank you for the shouting matches and all the hugs. Thank you for being a brother in arms. You mean the world to me. Much love to everyone that believed in me at Def Jam, and the real homies: Justin Duran, Leesa Brunson, Nicki Farag, and Noah Sheer—you guys are amazing. Lawrence Lam, you've been an amazing addition to the company at VMG. We're all indebted to your hard work.

To the RattPack, I love you and I've cherished all the memories that we've had so far, and I'm excited for all the memories that we'll have in the future.

To Troy Johnson, my cousin who was always there to motivate me and pat me on the back. To Lenny; words cannot describe what you mean to me and how you've affected my life, so I won't even try—I love you. To the entire Ressalam family, with a special shout-out to Kathy, the mother who is no longer with us but will forever be with us; thank you for supporting me when I was blasting music in your basement at four a.m. To the Zarou family, thank you for taking me in and letting at me sleep in your house for days on end while me and your son were chasing a dream that, statistically speaking, should have never worked out.

To Mary Jo and Bernie, the parents I should have had, and now, as a man, do. I love you; all the cigarettes and beautiful conversations shared on the front porch, all the stern ass-kickings and talking-tos from Bernie, they all sunk in and stayed with me and made an impression forever, which has gone on to make an impression on the world. I love you, and thank you for changing my life. To Josh, I truly love you and can't thank you enough for crushing my dreams of skateboarding and showing me a world bigger and better than any dream I may have had before music. I'm sorry your life has been hard, but know that my heart is always with you.

To Mike and Rashad and all the homies from the neighborhood, you guys gave me a life outside my apartment and memories that have obviously lasted a lifetime; wherever you may be in the world, I hope that you are happy, healthy, and smiling, because when I think of you, I know I am.

To Robert Naples, thank you for showing me that a black man doesn't have to fit into a certain category. Thank you for showing me what art is. Thank you for introducing me to the world of creativity. I love you and I hope to track you down one day and be friends again. To Jesse Weidman, thank you for the days of skipping school, listening to the Gorillaz, and smoking cigarettes in your mom's basement. You were there when I just needed to be a teenager, and you wanted nothing from me but my friendship—thank you.

To Tony Bransford, a man taken from us too soon. I wish you had been my dad. Thank you for showing me that men can be kind and sweet, no matter how big and strong, and for showing me that men can cry, and thank for all the rides on your Harley Davidson. To Carol Ellen, thank you for being the family that we never had. Thank you for every Christmas and every child that you brought into the world that left an impression on me, and thank you for always being there for my mom no matter what.

To my mom, thank you for the memories that we did have that were nice. To my dad, thank you for showing me the man I didn't want to become. To Debbie, thank you for being so sweet to me; I'm sorry you're gone. I send my love to you, your children, and the rest of your family. I could never forget you.

To Jesse, my brother, thank you for all the amazing times we've shared together, both in the past and here in the present day; no matter whatever was going on in our family, we always had a bond, and we would always laugh, and I think that's the most beautiful and important part of our relationship. To Geanie, I love you, you're a good woman and you've always been there for me. To Amber, I love you with all my heart. To Ralph, thanks for showing me what a big brother was and still is to this day. You're a good man with a kind heart.

To Kurt and Susan Noell, I hit the lottery marrying into your family. I'm so excited for all the years that we will have together watching Little Bobby grow up. To Brittney, my wife, my rock, my love, my best friend, my homie, you made me want to be a better man, and make me want to be the best man I can be every day I wake up next to you. The love I have for you is immeasurable, thank you for making every single day of my life the greatest day. You are the woman I can confide in, cry with, and laugh with. You ease my anxiety and I can't believe you're all mine—I love you.

And finally to Little Bobby, my son, the whole reason this book exists. I went through everything in my life, the hard times and the good times, not for success or money or fame or awards, but for you. The knowledge that I have gained up until this point has all been to teach you to be better than I could ever be. I love you. I will always be here for you. I will never leave you, and I give you my word that I will give you the life that I never had.

ABOUT THE AUTHOR

BOBBY HALL, aka Logic, is a Grammy-nominated, platinum-selling recording artist, author, actor, streamer, and film producer. In addition to his three number one albums, ten platinum singles, and billions of streams, Hall's debut book, *Supermarket*, made him the first hip-hop artist to have a #1 *New York Times* bestselling novel.